INDEX TO THE WILLS OF MARYLAND

THE AMERICAN INDEX LIBRARY

MARYLAND

INDEX TO THE WILLS OF:

GARRETT COUNTY, 1872–1960
HARFORD COUNTY, 1774-1960

Edited by Joan Hume

Magna Carta Book Company
Baltimore, Md. 21215
U.S.A.
1970

Copyright 1970
Magna Carta Book Company

Library of Congress catalog number: 75-114227

IBSN: 0-910946-13-2

FOREWORD

The earliest records of Maryland were the land records. It was extremely important for new title holders of land to have their ownership recorded; and for the Lord Proprietor, it was quite as important because the quit-rents on land were his most important gain for his proprietorship. There was also a need for recording probate records because, however fruitful the land and salubrious the climate, men died, and left estates governed by wills. At first the Secretary of the Province made the probate records and kept them safe. This arrangement continued until about 1671 when an officer was especially appointed to assume these tasks. This officer was known as the Commissary General, who, with the help of the Judges of the Prerogative Court - from one to four - handled all the probate affairs of the Province.

In the 1690's, the country having been settled to the westward, it became more and more difficult for persons, principally executors and administrators, to come all the way to St. Mary's City and shortly thereafter, to Annapolis, to carry on their businesses with the Commissary General and the Prerogative Court. When it became obvious to the Lord Proprietor that this travel imposed an unusual hardship on the colonists, he established county officers known as Deputy Commissaries to be local administrators of probate business. Only unusual estates and confusing wills were thereafter referred to the Prerogative Court.

This system continued satisfactorily until 1776 when the constitution of that year and the laws of 1777 abolished the Court and the Commissary and decentralized probate work altogether by the creation of a Register of Wills for each county and an Orphans' Court. This system has been affirmed by the three constitutions since that time and is still functioning.

All of the records of the Colonial period were preserved in the central probate office - by whatever name it was called. After the Revolution the papers in the Annapolis office were sent to the Register of Wills of each county to be recorded there. As a result, we have two sets of will records preserved for all but two of the counties, Calvert and Dorchester, where later courthouse fires destroyed the local records. The central records, after more peregrination, are now at the Hall of Records.

All but three years (1770-1772) of the colonial wills have been calendared by Jane Baldwin Cotton, Annie Walker Burns and James M. Magruder, Jr. An all-name index was prepared for the Calendar by Magruder, processed and now available in offset.

The county sets have been indexed by the local Registers of Wills offices and microfilmed by the Hall of Records Commission. These indexes are useful because in the transfer to and from the counties after the Revolution, some papers were lost and do not appear in the central records. The wills of the post-colonial period have not been worked on at all, with the exception of those for St. Mary's County, which have been printed in alphabetical order in the St. Mary's Chronicle.

This is the importance of the present printing of the county indexes to the wills of Maryland, which will make them available to interested persons everywhere.

Morris L. Radoff
Archivist of the State of Maryland

EDITOR'S NOTE ON THE INDEX TO THE WILLS OF HARFORD COUNTY

Harford County was formed in 1773 from part of Baltimore County. Its County Seat is Bel Air, and the searcher should write to the Register of Wills at Harford County courthouse in Bel Air regarding the wills referred to here, or to the Hall of Records in Annapolis, where there are microfilm copies.

The names in this index of wills are arranged under the first and second letters of the surnames. Thus, all names beginning with the letter B are further subdivided into those beginning with BA, BE, BI, BL, BO, BR, BU and BY. Some letters have more but some others have fewer subdivisions, so that this type of index is even less satisfactory than the Campbell index, such as that for Allegany County, which has a potential twenty-six subdivisions under each letter. For a very large number of names it would be inadequate but in the present instance there are rarely more than three or four pages, and usually fewer, to be searched through. The names are not in reliable chronological order.

The most that can be said of this index is that it is considerably better than nothing. A strictly alphabetical index might be preferred but it must be remembered that the time and expense involved in card-indexing would have rendered the present printing impossible.

The Hall of Records has microfilmed a handwritten index compiled by the office of the Register of Wills for the county, and this printed index has been copied from the microfilm. The editor cannot vouch for the correctness of the original index, which must have been copied from other handwriting, but where legibility was poor, or accuracy in doubt, it has been checked against another index at Bel Air.

The Magna Carta Book Company is indebted to Dr. Morris L. Radoff, Mr. Gust Skordas and other members of the staff of the Hall of Records in Annapolis, and to the Registers of Wills for Harford and Garrett Counties, for their help in the preparation of this work.

INDEX TO THE WILLS OF HARFORD COUNTY,
1774 - 1960

Aaronson, Harry E.	1925	AJG 19 278
Aarnes, Sadie Taylor	1956	RLW 23 421
Aaronson, Henrietta	1953	TLA 24 475
Abels, Andrew		JA 16 237
Abbott, William F.	1924	CSW 17 113
Abbott, Catherine	1933	AJG 19 73
Ady, William	1804	AJ C 205
Adams, John	1853	TSB 6 346
Ady, Elizabeth	1844	TSB 6 35
Adams, William	1856	CWB 7 120
Adams, Mary	1864	CWB 7 337
Adams, Samuel P.	1872	BHH 8 290
Adams, John W.	1882	WSR 9 375
Adams, John	1884	WSR 10 72
Ady, William	1889	JMM 11 41
Ady, Henry	1893	JMM 11 368
Adams, Sarah A.	1906	HTB 13 321
Adkins, Margaret Kenny	1928	CHR 18 141
Ady, Samuel J.	1927	CHR 18 152
Adams, William N.	1924	AJG 19 31
Ady, Isabel	1887	AJG 19 175
Adams, George Bristow	1936	AJG 21 372
Ady, Elizabeth B.	1943	RLW 22 9
Adams, Beulah Baker	1946	RLW 23 125
Adams, J. Victor	1953	RLW 23 362
Adkinson, Lilly M.	1955	WFNP 14 032
Addicks, Lawrence	1954	TLA 26 548
Addicks, May Maulsby	1954	TLA 26 553

Airey, Wm. F.	1918	JA 16 285
Akins, William	1824	SR 1 314
Allender, John	1784	AJ 2 4
Allender, Lucien	1788	AJ 2 5
Allein, William	1791	AJ 2 8
Allen, John	1810	AJ C 493
Allen, Rebecca	1814	AJ C 771
Allen, Aaron	1822	SR 1 268
Allender Nicholas	1827	SR 1 438
Alexander, John	1825	SR 1 337
Alderson, Abel	1841	TSB 5 520
Alexander, Robert	1837	TSB 5 287
Allen, Eben N.	1840	TSB 5 495
Almony, John	1833	TSB 5 66
Allen, Matthew I.	1857	CWB 7 132
Allen, Martha D.	1851	CWB 7 187
Allen, William	1860	CWB 7 230
Alexander, William	1865	CWB 7 389
Allen, Israel	1873	BHH 8 332
Allibone, Thomas	1876	WSR 9 118
Allen, William	1883	WSR 10 9
Almoney, Benjamin	1874	WSR 10 51
Alexander, John T.	1884	WSR 10 55
Alexander, Matilda	1883	WSR 10 239
Almoney, John S.	1889	JMM 11 51
Alden, Mary A.	1893	JMM 11 422
Alexander, Mary	1892	JMM 11 438
Almony, James R.	1898	GSN 12 186
Almony, Sarah J.	1904	HTB 13 237
Allender, Mary	1908	JA 15 204
Allen, Annie	1915	JA 16 52
Allibone, Mary L. M.	1913	CHR 18 3
Allen, Martha	1915	JA 16 218
Almoney, Atho S.	1913	JA 16 391
Allibone, Thomas M.	1919	CHR 18 10
Almoney, Caroline	1926	CHR 18 62
Almony, James T.	1917	AJG 19 160
Almony, Mary Sophronia	1930	AJG 19 212
Allen, J. A. Graeme	1921	AJG 19 251
Albright, Maggie L.	1934	AJG 19 430

Almony, Juliet Elizabeth	1906	AJG 20 352
Altvater, Eva	1939	AJG 21 254
Allen, Mary O.	1938	AJG 21 297
Almony, Charles L.	1929	AJG 21 498
Almony, Mary R. M.	1952	RLW 22 447
Alder, Christian	1955	RLW 23 393
Allison, George E.	1958	TLA 25 431
Amos, Benjamin	1775	AJ 2 1
Amos, William	1783	AJ 2 2
Amos, James of Joshuah	1802	AJ C 110
Amos, James Sr.	1805	AJ C 268
Amos, James	1811	AJ C 550
Amos, William	1814	AJ C 753
Amos, Benjamin	1815	SR 1 9
Amos, Thomas	1816	SR 1 88
Amos, William of James	1816	SR 1 90
Amos, Robert, St.	1818	SR 1 148
Amos, Sarah	1821	SR 1 233
Amos, Benjamin of Benj.	1821	SR 1 244
Amos, Hannah	1828	SR 1 434
Amoss, William	1833	TSB 5 69
Amoss, Martha	1833	TSB 5 72
Amoss, Elizabeth	1841	TSB 5 544
Amoss James B.	1844	TSB 6 44
Amoss, Ann	1845	TSB 6 61
Amoss, James	1845	TSB 6 90
Amoss, Abraham	1846	TSB 6 111
Amoss, William Sr. of W.	1852	TSB 6 326
Amoss, William of Wm. S.	1852	TSB 6 333
Amos, George	1854	CWB 7 20
Amos, William of Thomas	1859	CWB 7 190
Amos, John M.	1859	CWB 7 193
Amos, Joshua	1859	CWB 7 214
Amos, Jushua M.	1860	CWB 7 219
Amos, Ruth	1861	CWB 7 268
Amos, John T.	1862	CWB 7 282
Amos, Martha	1863	CWB 7 316
Amos, Oliver H.	1864	CWB 7 351
Amos, Benjamin S.	1865	CWB 7 369
Amos, James	1868	BHH 8 48
Amos, James (noncupative)	1868	BHH 8 72
Amos, Susannah	1868	BHH 8 83

3

Amos, Wm. Lee	1870	BHH 8 182
Amos, Temperance	1871	BHH 8 211
Amoss, William	1872	BHH 8 314
Amoss, George K.	1878	WSR 9 191
Amos, Martha	1882	WSR 9 341
Amos, James A.	1882	WSR 9 346
Amoss, Lemuel H., Sr.	1883	WSR 9 428
Amoss, Elizabeth A.	1884	WSR 10 80
Amoss, Abigail J.	1887	JMM 11 146
Amoss, Thomas A.	1899	GSN 12 252
Amoss, Garrett	1903	HTB 3 186
Amos, Martha Eugenia	1905	HTB 13 217
Amos, Angeline V.	1903	HTB 13 400
Amos, Sr., James	1912	JA 15 218
Amos, Hugh T.	1922	JA 16 387
Amos, Mary E.	1924	CSW 17 94
Amoss, Carville E.	1925	CSW 17 202
Amos, Susannah	1931	AJG 19 92
Amoss, Wm. Lee	1928	AJG 19 159
Amos, Mary A.	1929	AJG 19 221
Ambrose, Eda B.	1935	AJG 19 420
Amos, Nathan T.	1930	AJG 20 40
Amrein, Charles H.	1936	AJG 20 290
Ambrose, Herbert Louis	1941	AJG 21 240
Amos, Annie A.	1935	AJG 21 334
Amos, Austin D.	1944	AJG 21 341
Amoss, Benjamin W.	1957	TLA 26 264
		TLA 24 145
Amoss, Dora B.	1959	WFNP
Annan, William	1791	AJ 2 9
Anderson, Catharine	1798	AJ 2 10
Anderson, James	1809	AJ C 572
Anderson, Hugh	1813	AJ C 704
Anderson, Sarah	1816	SR 1 75
Anderson, James	1815	SR 1 79
Anderson, Cassandra	1817	SR 1 116
Anderson, Elizabeth	1853	CWB 7 16
Anderson, Ann	1856	CWB 7 105
Andrews, Margaret	1857	CWB 7 130
Andrews, Mary A.	1870	BHH 8 176

Andrew, John	1875	WSR 9 70
Anderson, Elizabeth	1881	WSR 10 20
Anderson, Columbus	1886	WSR 10 309
Andrews, Isaac	1888	JMM 11 112
Anderson, William H.	1896	GSN 12 25
Anderson, Marion	1899	GSN 12 230
Andrew, John R.	1902	GSN 12 395
Anderson, George	1902	GSN 12 433
Andrew, John W.	1886	HTB 13 92
Anderson, Edward T.	1904	HTB 13 100
Andrew, W. Holland	1904	HTB 13 105
Anknin, S.J.	1892	HTB 13 206
Andrews, William H.	1902	HTB 23 487
Andrew, Margaret T.	1902	HTB 14 256
Anderson, Susan Rebecca	1919	JA 16 424
Andrew, Albert E.	1924	CSW 17 168
Anderson, John W.	1925	CSW 17 208
Anderson, John Thomas	1928	CHR 18 53
Anderson, John C.	1928	CHR 18 127
Andrew, Charles A.	1914	CHR 18 493
Anderson, Clara P.	1929	AJG 19 70
Anderson, C. August	1932	AJG 19 274
Ancocella, Augustine	1936	AJG 20 320
Anderson, Bettie Nelson	1930	AJG 21 354
Anderson, Andrew L.	1922	AJG 21 467
Anderson, Luella J.	1949	RLW 23 21
Antone, Sofi	1956	TLA 24 357
Anderson, A. Roy	1943	TLA 24 426

Armstrong, James	1790	AJ 2 7
Archer, John	1811	AJ C 536
Archer, James	1815	SR 1 86
Archer, Thomas	1822	SR 1 248
Arnold, William	1825	SR 1 356
Archer, John	1830	SR 1 511
Archer, Elizabeth P.	1836	TSB 5 238
Arnold, Ephraim	1846	TSB 6 92
Archer, Stevenson	1848	TSB 6 183
Archer, Mary	1864	CWB 7 362
Archer, Ann	1867	BHH 8 25
Same (Codicil)		BHH 8 262
Archer, Thomas	1870	BHH 8 152

5

Archer, Robert H.	1877	WSR 9 142
Archer, Caleb G.	1881	WSR 9 331
Same		WSR 9 333
Archer, Amelia	1883	WSR 9 448
Archer, Henry W.	1883	WSR 10 293
Archer, Henry W.	1887	WSR 10 365
Same	1888	WSR 10 366
Archer, John	1888	WSA 10 403
Archer, Susanna P.	1887	JMM 11 46
Archer, Henry Wilson	1898	GSN 12 121
Arnsfield, Martha		HTB 13 82
Archer, Roberta H.	1897	HTB 13 133
Arthur, John T.	1905	HTB 13 271
Archer, Mary E.	1895	HTB 13 476
Archer, Henry W.	1909	HTB 14 151
Archer, Jane C. or Blanche F.	1895	JA 16 72
Arthur, Henry L.	1912	JA 16 395
Arnold, Laura J.	1905	JA 16 421
Archer, Robert	1924	CSW 17 147
Arthur, Thomas F.	1925	CSW 17 268
Armstrong, Charles H.	1925	CSW 17 348
Archer, Blanche F.	1920	CSW 17 481
Archer, William S.	1921	CHR 18 320
Archer, John Potter	1932	CHR 18 467
Armstrong, Lewis	1931	AJG 19 25
Archer, Mary Angela	1926	AJG 19 332
Archer, Hannah L.	1928	AJG 20 318
Archer, C. Graham	1926	AJG 20 487
Armstrong, Winfield S.	1918	AJG 21 22
Arthur, Dr. Wm. E.	1907	AJG 21 67
Archer, Alice Poullain	1941	AJG 21 232
Archer, Lewis H.	1943	AJG 21 247
Armstrong, Ambrose	1945	RLW 22 63
Archer, Robert H.	1946	RLW 22 106
Archer, George	1916	RLW 22 482
Archer, Elizabeth R.	1952	TLA 26 7
Ashbridge, William	1865	CWB 7 386
Ashton, Richard	1854	CWB 7 49
Ashton, Joseph	1855	CWB 7 83
Ashton, Edward	1856	CWB 7 122
Ashton, John	1860	CWB 7 215

Ashton, Harry	1923	CSW 17 13
Ashton, St. Clair B.	1924	AJG 20 424
Ash, John Ann	1914	AJG 21 56
Asher, Arthur G.	1919	AJG 21 102
Ashton, Elizabeth A.	1942	AJG 21 195
Ashcroft, Jacob H.	1928	RLW 22 318

Atkinson, Mark	1847	TSB 6 139
Atkinson, David	1875	WSR 9 50
Atkin, Benjamin	1876	WSR 9 94
Atkin, Mary	1882	WSR 9 354
Atkinson, Isaac	1882	WSR 9 357
Atwell, Pauline H.	1943	RLW 23 206
Atkins, Robert P.	1956	WFNP

Ayres, Thomas	1836	TSB 5 242
Ayres, John	1852	TSB 6 302
Ayres, Mary S.	1856	CWB 7 116
Ayres, Elizabeth	1858	CWB 7 178
Ayres, John	1865	CWB 7 398
Ayres, Charles	1870	BHH 8 168
Ayres, Thomas J.	1881	WSR 10 229
Ayres, Benjamin T.	1892	GSN 12 50
Ayres, Benjamin A.	1893	HTB 14 272
Ayres, Julia	1918	JA 16 88
Ayres, Mattie E. P.	1920	JA 16 384
Ayres, John T.	1925	CSW 17 273
Ayres, Thomas J.	1928	CHR 18 411
Ayres, J. Upton	1943	AJG 21 395
Ayton, Alfred A.	1951	RLW 22 379

B

Baker, Maurice	1774	AJ 2 24
Barton, John	1777	AJ 2 37
Baker, Christian	1793	AJ 2 59
Barnes, Amos	1797	AJ 2 67
Barclay, John	1800	AJ C 4
Barnes, Mary	1801	AJ C 9
Barnes, James	1804	AJ C 219
Bayless, Samuel	1808	AJ C 434
Bay, Hugh	1808	AJ C 441
Barnes, Foard	1809	AJ C 477
Barnet, James	1813	AJ C 686
Bankhead, William	1815	SR 1 27
Barnes, Mary	1815	SR 1 31
Barnes, John of Amos	1816	SR 1 32
Bay, Hugh	1818	SR 1 154
Baldwin, William	1826	SR 1 367
Bay, John	1827	SR 1 403
Bay, Hugh	1829	SR 1 469
Baxter, Jacob	1830	SR 1 486
Balderston, Jacob	1830	SR 1 514
Barnes, Richard	1830	SR 1 522
Bagely, Susanna O.	1831	SR 1 535
Bankhead, Hugh	1832	SR 1 549
Barclay, John	1833	TSB 5 90
Barnes, John	1843	TSB 6 7
Barnes, Bennett	1845	TSB 6 57
Baldwin, Silas	1845	TSB 6 79
Bartol, George	1848	TSB 6 180
Barnes, Elenor	1849	TSB 6 214
Bagley, Samuel H.	1851	TSB 6 272
Bayless, Zephaniah	1851	TSB 6 274
Barney, Charles	1853	CWB 7 1
Bayard, John R.	1853	CWB 7 4
Bankhead, John	1858	CWB 7 164
Barley, Aquila	1861	CWB 7 269
Barnard, Margaret	1864	CWB 7 349
Baldwin, Timothy	1865	CWB 7 367
Baldwin, Franklin C.	1870	BHH 8 147
Bay, James M.	1870	BHH 8 169

Bayless, William F.	1873	BHH 8 327
Bayless, Samuel M.	1873	BHH 8 333
Barton, John	1873	BHH 8 366
Bay, Thomas	1876	WSR 9 124
Barber, William	1877	WSR 9 146
Barrow, John	1878	WSR 9 173
Barnard, Parker	1873	WSR 9 195
Bailey, Jas. Hervey	1883	WSR 9 450
Baker, Conrad	1881	WSR 10 178
Bartleson, Mark	1881	WSR 10 264
Bailey, Aquilla	1882	WSR 10 419
Baker, George W.	1888	WSA 10 432
Base, Andrew	1887	WSR 10 434
Ball, James H.	1884	WSR 10 455
Barnes, John	1890	JMM 11 78
Barton, Lewis	1890	JMM 11 85
Barton, Mary A.	1888	JMM 11 131
Ball, Hiram	1890	JMM 11 229
Bavington, Christian S.	1892	JMM 11 273
Baker, George	1892	JMM 11 293
Baer, Henry J.	1890	JMM 11 398
Ball, Sarah C.	1890	JMM 11 436
Baxter, William	1893	JMM 11 448
Bailey, Chas. Lewis	1883	JMM 11 456
Baldwin, Silas	1885	JMM 11 469
Baker, Nicholas	1893	GSN 12 57
Bahr, Witoria	1880	GSN 12 63
Bailey, Mary	1900	GSN 12 278
Barnard, William H.	1900	GSN 12 324
Ball, Mary Smith	1901	GSN 12 328
Barnes, George W.	1903	GSN 12 470
Baldwin, Jarrett T.	1901	HTB 13 21
Bay, William	1899	HTB 13 53
Barker, Georgie H.	1900	HTB 13 231
Bailey, Howard Justin	1905	HTB 13 254
Barnes, Frances Cordelia	1902	HTB 13 338
Bartleson, William D.	1910	HTB 14 164
Baker, William B.	1897	HTB 14 228
Baptist, Willim	1911	HTB 14 291
Bailey, John B.	1912	HTB 14 303
Baker, James B.	1911	HTB 14 330
Bavington, James C.	1910	HTB 14 365
Barnard, Frances W.	1907	HTB 14 441
Barton, Annie E.	1906	HTB 14 458

Baldwin, Edward A.	1939	AJG 20 326
Bachmann, Florence A.	1939	AJG 20 329
Bavington, William C.	1909	AJG 20 435
Bay, Dr. James H.	1940	AJG 21 6
Bay, John W.	1891	AJG 21 32
Bay, Emily Williams	1936	AJG 21 35
Babka, Margaret	1934	AJG 21 141
Baker, Pendleton T.	1942	AJG 21 150
Bavington, Mary E.	1917	AJG 21 166
Bartol, J. Howard	1938, 1945	AJG 21 181
Bailey, Harold M.	1943	AJG 21 221
Baker, Winfield L.	1914	AJG 21 302
Baird, Edward	1919	AJG 21 384
Baldwin, W. Littleton	1945	AJG 21 435
Barnes, Wilmer L.	1934	RLW 22 126
Bayless, Nina I.	1946	RLW 22 143
Baker, (now Bishop), Mary A.	1943	RLW 22 201
Bay, Robert P.	1924	RLW 22 362
Bartlett, Edward L.	1905	RLW 22 426
Bawroski, Michael	1950	RLW 22 445
Barnes, Ellen R.	1953	RLW 23 50
Barnes, Leila	1945	RLW 23 121
Barnard, Leona	1938	RLW 23 171
Barron, Elizabeth J.	1938	RLW 23 215
Baldwin, Jefferson Warner	1954	RLW 23 218
Barnes, Sadie K.	1944	RLW 23 249
Baumgart, Alice M.	1942	RLW 23 252
Barron, Preston M.	1937	RLW 23 354
Baker, G. Harold	1949	TLA 24 41
Bailey, W. Sanner	1955	TLA 24 154
Bay, Mary Cochran	1948	TLA 24 290
Baxter, Belle	1952	TLA 24 388
Barnes, Robert S.	1957	TLA 24 391
Bauer, William C.	1957	TLA 24 423
Bagley, Charles, Jr.	1957	TLA 24 445
Bauer, Frank	1952	TLA 25 103
Baugess, Blaine M.	1959	TLA 25 199
Barber, Francis Munroe	1961	WFNP 13 789
Baker, Ethel Lee	1959	TLA 25 407
Baker, Jesse S.	1959	TLA 26 280
Barbour, John V.	1951	TLA 26 369
Bahel, Frank	1957	WFNP 14 191
Barnes, Dorothy R.	1946	TLA 26 447
Banks, Edward	1952	WFNP 14 268

Banks, Mabel	1952	TLA 26 578
Battle, Alfred	1953	WFNP 14 316
Bell, Robert	1779	AJ 2 35
Benfield, David	1779	Aj 2 31
Bell, Jane Hambleton	1804	AJ C 211
Bell, Mary P.	1804	AJ C 217
Beaty, William	1811	AJ C 570
Bever, Charles	1812	AJ C 681
Benson, Benjamin	1812	AJ C 662
Bell, David	1813	AJ C 696
Beaty, Archibald	1815	SR 1 17
Bevard, Charles	1818	SR 1 136
Bell, John	1824	SR 1 304
Bell, John	1826	SR 1 372
Beaty, Frances	1826	SR 1 379
Bennett, James	1831	SR 1 532
Bell, David	1846	TSB 6 123
Beaty, John	1852	TSB 6 335
Bell, Nelly	1854	CWB 7 50
Beaty, Samuel	1860	CWB 7 229
Berry, Thomas	1865	CWB 7 391
Benson, Amos	1866	CWB 7 403
Bevard, George	1869	BHH 8 110
Bennington, Sarah A.	1877	WSR 9 139
Benson, Benjamin	1878	WSR 9 202
Beatty, William	1882	WSR 9 340
Bell, Margarett	1882	WSR 10 76
Beaumont, Mifflin	1882	WSR 10 78
Beatty, Maggie R.	1886	WSR 10 173
Berry, Eli	1885	WSR 10 204
Benson, Joshua P.	1885	WSR 10 244
Beeman, Joseph J.	1880	WSR 10 453
Beeman, Mary L.	1874	JMM 11 60
Beattie, John	1892	JMM 11 298
Becker, Nicholas	1883	JMM 11 303
Benson, Margaret Ann	1899	GSN 12 251
Bell, James C.	1900	GSN 12 302
Beattie, Agnes G.	1901	GSN 12 386
Benson, Elizabeth E.	1902	GSN 12 446
Beaumont, Thomas L.	1903	GSN 12 484
Berry, Ellen	1893	HTB 13 84

Beaumont, Elias	1899	HTB 13 104
Bell, Ellen	1905	HTB 13 317
Beard, George W.	1908	HTB 14 75
Benson, Melchior	1910	HTB 14 195
Besler, Christina	1904	HTB 14 329
Bell, Nelson	1913	HTB 14 416
Bennett, John E.	1897	HTB 14 477
Benson, Sarah A.	1914	JA 15 30
Bell, John Cohel	1901	JA 15 37
Bennington, Amelia Proctor	1909	JA 15 242
Benson, Charles A.	1916	JA 15 383
Benson, Ella Grace	1919	JA 16 125
Bennett, John E.	1897	JA 16 225
Beall, Daniel E.	1902	JA 16 236
Berrill, Jas. Francis	1906	JA 16 317
Berrill, Iola G.	1922	JA 16 367
Bell, Alexander S.	1923	CSW 17 18
Berry, Henry	1897	CSW 17 238
Beatty, Millard Fillmore	1925	CSW 17 354
Berriker, Tillie	1928	CHR 18 174
Bennington, Galena D.	1923	CHR 18 239
Bevard, Geo T.	1928	CHR 18 284
Bennett, Isaac M.	1926	CHR 18 288
Bennett, Elmer E.	1929	CHR 18 421
Bevard, Liston B.	1933	AJG 19 84
Bechtold, Veronica	1922	AJG 19 102
Beatty, Sara A.	1932	AJG 19 152
Bell, Wm. Boyd	1895	AJG 19 168
Bennett, Fletcher M.	1933	AJG 19 172
Benson, David T.	1926	AJG 19 205
Beatty, Lizzie A.	1914	AJG 19 297
Benson, Anna R.	1934	AJG 19 300
Beatty, James E.	1935	AJG 19 338
Bechtold, William	1933	AJG 20 474
Becker, William J.	1940	RLW 22 13
Beall, Charles W.	1948	RLW 22 309
Bechtold, Anna	1942	RLW 23 233
Bell, Margaret A.	1954	TLA 24 12
Bentley, Alex, Jr.	1955	TLA 24 13
Bennington, Hugh Edward	1957	TLA 24 137
Berry, Thomas H.	1929	TLA 21 120
Beamer, Ralph	1958	TLA 24 250
Benzio, Albert Charles	1958	TLA 24 251
Bentley, Hannah J.	1951	TLA 24 418

Black, John	1803	AJ C 139
Black, Agnes	1809	AJ C 457
Blackburn, Jehu	1834	TSB 5 118
Blackwell, Samuel	1858	CWB 7 183
Blair, James	1877	WSR 9 159
Black, Jeremiah S.	1883	WSR 9 460
Blackburn, John	1887	WSR 10 333
Blair, William E.	1892	JMM 11 428
Blake, John M.	1898	GSN 12 216
Blackwell, William R.	1901	HTB 13 294
Blair, Thaddeus C.	1907	HTB 14 123
Blair, Margaret	1910	JA 15 114
Black, Mary C.	1918	JA 16 64
Black, Josephine V.	1921	JA 16 351
Blevins, Rush F.	1933	AJG 19 107
Black, Barnet H.	1912	AJG 20 421
Blackwell, Elizabeth H.	1935	AJG 21 27
Blackburn, Earle W.	1951	TLA 24 210
Blake, James H.	1951	TLA 24 275
Blevins, Walter T.	1947	TLA 24 352
Blake, Alexander	1951	TLA 26 639
Bond, Daniel	1780	AJ 2 14
Boardeman, William	1778	AJ 2 18
Bond, John	1791	AJ 2 21
Bond, Elizabeth	1783	AJ 2 38
Bond, Jacob	1780	AJ 2 40
Bond, Nathan	1782	AJ 2 44
Bond, Thomas	1788	AJ 2 53
Bond, William	1788	AJ 2 73
Bond, Ann	1784	AJ 2 74
Boyce, John	1786	AJ 2 27
Bond, Thomas	1800	AJ C 21
Bond, Ralph	1801	AJ C 30
Botts, John	1802	AJ C 107
Bond, James	1803	AJ C 165
Boyce, Ann	1803	AJ C 189
Bond, Jacob	1804	AJ C 225
Bond, John	1805	AJ C 276
Botts, Elizabeth	1807	AJ C 356
Bond, Dennis	1809	AJ C 459
Bond, Ann	1815	SR 1 96

Bond, Buckler	1823	SR 1 288
Boarman, Robert	1825	SR 1 342
Botts, Isaac	1825	SR 1 352
Bosley, James	1832	SR 1 547
Bowman, Henry	1834	TSB 5 139
Bond, Freeborn	1837	TSB 5 277
Bond, Jane	1838	TSB 5 359
Boyd, Elizabeth	1840	TSB 5 490
Bond, Benjamin R.	1843	TSB 6 21
Bond, Mary	1844	TSB 6 36
Bodden, Irvin W.	1844	TSB 6 45
Botts, James	1845	TSB 6 91
Boyd, Rachel	1848	TSB 6 182
Bosley, Joseph	1848	TSB 6 206
Boyd, Cooper S.	1850	TSB 6 253
Boyd, Stephen	1854	CWB 7 28
Bowen, Deborah	1855	CWB 7 87
Bond, Rev. Thomas E.	1856	CWB 7 109
Bond, Grace	1860	CWB 7 217
Bond, Benjamin	1861	CWB 7 251
Bond, Caroline G.	1866	CWB 7 406
Bond, Nicholas M.	1866	BHH 8 1
Boarman, Benjamin W.	1869	BHH 8 129
Bowman, Henry	1871	BHH 8 213
same		BHH 8 387
Bond, Thomas E.	1872	BHH 8 309
Bond, Mary Ann	1876	WSR 9 105
Bond, Annie M.	1878	WSR 9 178
Bosley, Willimina	1880	WSR 9 269
Bond, Elijah I.	1881	WSR 9 301
Bond, Stephen	1865	WSR 9 339
Boarman, Frank	1882	WSR 9 351
Bolton, Mary A.	1880	WSR 10 3
Boarman, Charity M.	1889	WSR 10 457
Boyd, Chas. Andrew	1887	JMM 11 3
Boyd, Eliza C.	1877	JMM 11 16
Bolton, Robert	1887	JMM 11 66
Bosley, Joseph C.	1890	JMM 11 150
Bowman, James L.	1890	JMM 11 159
Boyd, Patrick	1891	JMM 11 339
Botts, John	1895	JMM 11 485
Bond, Lennox B.	1901	GSN 12 345
Bond, Sarah Jane	1901	GSN 12 374
Boyd, Francis J.	1902	GSN 12 421

Bodt, Fredericka	1900	HTB 13 75
Bogart, Maria Louisa	1894	HTB 13 409
Bosley, Milton	1904	HTB 13 429
Bogert, Corns R.	1876	HTB 14 47
Bogert, Maria Louisa	1894	HTB 14 51
Boarman, Fannie E.	1899	HTB 14 186
Boughter, Thomas	1899	HTB 14 309
Bowman, Ella C.	1911	JA 15 16
Bodt, Edward A.	1912	JA 15 25
Bowne, Sarah L.	1912	JA 15 82
Boyer, Mary J.	1915	JA 15 426
Bowser, Robt. J.	1916	JA 16 79
Boone, Sarah	1918	JA 16 228
Bornaman, Mary	1914	JA 16 242
Bond, Alexander T.	1918	JA 16 271
Botts, Margaret A.	1909	JA 16 426
Boyce, Obed B.	1908	JA 16 440
Bonn, Charles F.	1922	JA 16 482
Boarman, F. Bond	1919	JA 16 496
Boyd, Margaret A.	1922	CSW 17 244
Boswell, William C.	1922	CHR 18 117
Boyce, Louisa A.	1923	CHR 18 160
Bowser, Martha C.	1930	CHR 18 254
Bostick, Joseph F.	1928	CHR 18 274
Bouchelle, Byron	1924	CHR 18 440
Bowman, William S.	1931	CHR 18 452
Boyd, Ella C.	1932	AJG 19 19
Boyd, James F.	1933	AJG 19 113
Bordley, Sarah Elizabeth		AJG 19 225
Bonnett, Ernest W.	1925	AJG 19 433
Bodt, Wm. August	1922	AJG 20 67
Boarman, Horace	1921	AJG 20 187
Bond, Clinton	1938	AJG 20 259
Boarman, Corbin E.	1937	AJG 20 350
Boyd, Kate	1922	AJG 20 369
Boyd, Michael P.	1940	AJG 20 431
Bouldin, Mary Honora	1937	AJG 21 224
Bonhage, Annie	1935	AJG 21 419
Bond, Alice R. Johnson	1921	AJG 21 437
Bonnett, Adam	1948	RLW 22 207
Botts, Archer M.	1945	RLW 22 250
Boyd, Maggie C.	1947	RLW 22 374
Bouder, Joseph S.	1940	RLW 22 377
Bodt, Andrew P.	1919	RLW 22 419

17

Boyce, Lawrence D.	1954	RLW 23 303	
Boyd, Michael G.	1953	RLW 23 370	
Bowman, J. Webster	1953	RLW 23 405	
Botts, Daisy M.	1948	RLW 23 425	
Boggs, Nettie M.	1951	RLW 23 460	
Boyer, Henry H.	1946	RLW 23 493	
Borrell, Margaret Elizabeth	1954	TLA 24 159	
Boone, Rhoda B.	1954	TLA 24 197	
Boyle, Hanora	1958	TLA 24 222	
Boyle, Amanda A.	1958	TLA 24 272	
Bodt, Nellie C.	1959	TLA 24 462	
Bostic, James E.	1959	TLA 24 480	
Boiks, Sidor	1960	TLA 25 94	
Boarman, Bessye	1951	TLA 25 126	
Boruff, Conway	1959	WFNP	
Bosely, Arthur	1958	TLA 26 503	
Bowman, Cora A.	1960	TLA 26 532	
Boyd, Alvin J.	1944	TLA 26 597	

Brierly, Ann	1788	AJ 2 17	
Brown, James	1774	AJ 2 19	
Brice, Thomas	1776	AJ 2 29	
Bryerly, Robert	1779	AJ 2 33	
Brown, Garrett	1788	AJ 2 34	
Bryarly, Margaret	1781	AJ 2 45	
Brown, Joshua	1789	AJ 2 46	
Brown, Thomas	1785	AJ 2 47	
Brown, John	1786	AJ 2 51	
Brusebanks, Mary	1784	AJ 2 49	
Browning, William	1798	AJ 2 50	
Browne, Sarah	1780	AJ 2 55	
Brown, John	1782	AJ 2 64	
Brown, John T.	1794	AJ 2 66	
Bradin, Enoch	1791	AJ 2 56	
Bryarly, Nathaniel	1794	AJ 2 69	
Bryarly, Hugh	1799	AJ 2 76	
Brown, Soloman	1804	AJ C 197	
Brownley, Catharine	1811	AJ C 542	
Bryarly, Wakeman	1821	SR 1 245	
Bryarly, Priscilla E.	1825	SR 1 326	
Brown, Freeborn	1825	SR 1 355	

Brown, Mary B.	1829	SR 1 465
Brown, Joseph	1831	SR 1 529
Brown, Samuel	1835	TSB 5 219
Brown, Edward L.	1837	TSB 5 272
Brierly, William	1848	TSB 6 175
Bradford, George	1852	TSB 6 304
Brown, Aquila	1848	TSB 6 166
Brierly, Cordelia	1852	TSB 6 319
Brice, Benjamin	1856	CWB 7 105
Brown, Elizabeth	1858	CWB 7 162
Brookheart, Cassandra	1859	CWB 7 194
Brown, George W.	1866	BHH 8 3
Bradenbaugh, Jacob	1871	BHH 8 201
Brown, Mary	1873	BHH 8 320
Brown, Elizabeth M.	1876	WSR 9 101
Brendt, Lewis	1877	WSR 9 162
Bradley, Dennis	1879	WSR 9 397
Brown, Mary A.	1878	WSR 9 177
Bryant, Richarda	1880	WSR 9 312
Britton, Mary A.	1882	WSR 10 17
Bradley, Hannah	1885	WSR 10 124
Bradford, John H.	1887	WSR 10 200
Brierly, Richard	1883	WSR 10 350
Brown, Emory	1879	JMM 11 214
Brown, John W.	1893	JMM 11 302
Brown, Zelia	1888	JMM 11 405
Brazier, Thomas G.	1889	JMM 11 259
Brown, Philip A.	1897	GSN 12 74
Bradford, John W.	1900	GSN 12 315
Brown, Lewis	1902	GSN 12 420
Bryarly, John W.	1895	HTB 13 87
Bradford, Louisa	1905	HTB 13 233
Brand, William F.	1893	HTB 13 322
Brand, Sophia McHenry	1870	HTB 13 327
Brown, Augustus F.	1909	HTB 14 82
Brown, Augustus F.	1904	HTB 14 229
Brandt, Edward	1903	HTB 14 317
Brown, Morris	1906	HTB 14 369
Brown, Henry D.	1900	HTB 14 405
Bradenbaugh, Sidney E.	1896	JA 15 13
Brooke, H. Clay	1915	JA 15 152
Brown, George W.	1912	JA 15 195
Bradenbaugh, Thomas J.	1912	JA 15 347
Bradfield, Catherine R.	1920	JA 16 332

Brandt, Ella M.	1958	TLA 26 373
Breidenbaugh, Edward	1956	TLA 26 473
Broadwater, Lida J.	1955	WFNP 14 279
Bull, John	1782	AJ 2 16
Bull, Edmund	1776	AJ 2 28
Bussey, Thomas	1776	AJ 2 30
Butler, Joseph	1777	AJ 2 31
Bull, Susannah	1792	AJ 2 60
Bull, William	1791	AJ 2 62
Bull, William	1800	AJ C 11
Bull, Jacob	1803	AJ C 162
Bull, Sarah	1804	AJ C 243
Bussey, Edward B.	1807	AJ C 358
Butler, Mary	1808	AJ C 411
Butler, Thomas	1823	SR 1 298
Budd, Elizabeth	1828	SR 1 443
Bull, William	1834	TSB 5 162
Bull, Rachel	1841	TSB 5 512
Buckingham, James	1842	TSB 5 581
Butler, Jane	1842	TSB 5 594
Butler, Julian	1842	TSB 5 606
Bull, Sarah	1843	TSB 6 5
Bull, Sarah	1845	TSB 6 69
Bull, William	1853	CWB 7 6
Bull, James L.	1855	CWB 7 88
Bull, Elizabeth	1862	CWB 7 272
Burkins, Jacob	1869	BHH 8 112
Budd, Elizabeth	1872	BHH 8 268
Bull, Elizabeth	1874	WSR 9 29
Bull, William L.	1876	WSR 9 119
Butler, Walter B.	1877	WSR 9 143
Bull, James H.	1881	WSR 9 321
Butler, Clement	1882	WSR 9 343
Buchanan, John	1882	WSR 9 361
Burns, Alice	1886	WSR 10 165
Bull, James	1884	JMM 11 191
Bulett, John	1891	JMM 11 222
Butler, Thomas	1893	JMM 11 324
Bunce, Margaret A.	1894	JMM 11 424

Bull, Mary	1894	GSN 12 139
Burbank, Jesse	1891	GSN 12 180
Butler, Clement G.	1901	GSN 12 337
Burkins, George T.	1905	HTB 13 153
Burroughs, George H.	1913	JA 15 59
Buecker, Ferdinand	1917	JA 15 432
Burkins, Maggie R.	1921	JA 16 334
Burkley, Mary	1911	JA 16 281
Burkley, Frederick	1911	JA 16 282
Burgess, Eliza	1924	CSW 17 126
Burkins, Edith Frances	1931	CHR 18 409
Burrier, Serena E.	1929	AJG 19 308
Budnick, Albert J.	1935	AJG 19 492
Butterfield, Sara A.	1920	AJG 19 494
Bull, Milton	1928	AJG 20 57
Burkins, William	1937	AJG 20 120
Burkley, Catherine	1937	AJG 20 135
Butterfield, John	1938	AJG 20 394
Burkins, George M.	1937	AJG 20 417
Burns, Walter E.	1941	AJG 21 173
Burroughs, Henry C.	1939	AJG 21 310
Burns, R. Norris	1939	AJG 21 459
Buck, Laurance M.	1950	RLW 22 295
Buckley, Reba	1947	RLW 22 491
Bull, Adelaide M.	1928	RLW 23 98
Burns, Edith M.	1947	RLW 23 173
Buisson, George W.	1952	RLW 23 199
Burr, Stanley G.	1950	RLW 23 287
Bull, Charles A.	1953	RLW 23 382
Bunton, Horatio	1916	RLW 23 407
Burroughs, Susie Hays	1950	TLA 24 14
Butterfield, Carrie M.	1949	TLA 24 117
Burkins, Masena W.	1950	TLA 24 207
Burkins, Joseph A.	1958	TLA 24 262
Burkins, Carrie L.	1957	TLA 24 411
Bull, Alice S.	1948	TLA 24 416
Burns, Helen J.	1951	TLA 25 123
Burcham, James A.	1950	TLA 26 92
Burns, Winifred C.	1948	TLA 26 230
Budd, Joseph Adrien	1958	WFNP 14 096
Bull, Anna May	1956	TLA 27 1

Byard, Elizabeth	1887	WSR	10	416
Byrne, Lillian L.	1957	TLA	24	380

C

Cane, Dennis	1796	AJ 2 81
Carroll, John	1778	AJ 2 84
Campbell, John	1784	AJ 2 96
Carroll, James	1792	AJ 2 111
Carroll, Elizabeth	1792	AJ 2 115
Carlile, John	1802	AJ C 146
Carter, John	1805	AJ C 297
Cannon, Moses	1807	AJ C 350
Cannon, William	1813	AJ C 675
Cathcart, Joseph	1811	SR 1 144
Cariens, William	1818	SR 1 169
Calwell, David	1820	SR 1 231
Cain, John	1822	SR 1 254
Carlin, James	1827	SR 1 400
Cain, Elizabeth	1831	SR 1 533
Cavender, William	1827	SR 1 418
Carroll, Benjamin	1831	SR 1 553
Carlisle, John W.	1833	TSB 5 99
Caldwell, James	1841	TSB 5 534
Carman, Hester	1843	TSB 6 10
Carlin, William, Sr.	1847	TSB 6 152
Calwell, Margaret T.	1849	TSB 6 217
Carter, Joel	1856	CWB 7 106
Cariens, George	1858	CWB 7 180
Canon, Wm. Noble	1858	CWB 7 181
Cain, Matthew	1859	CWB 7 188
Calwell, Mary	1863	CWB 7 301
Cathcart, Joseph	1866	CWB 7 408
Campbell, John	1869	BHH 8 120
Carroll, Daniel	1871	BHH 8 197
Carter, Hannah G.	1872	BHH 8 280
Cairnes, Mary A.	1872	BHH 8 312
Cairnes, William	1874	WSR 9 10
Carlile, William A.	1878	WSA 9 169
Carroll, James	1880	WSR 9 257
Caldwell, Adeline	1880	WSR 9 262
Caddell, Theresa	1882	WSR 9 373
same		WSR 9 426
Carroll, William C.	1883	WSR 9 400

Carter, Dennis B.	1885	WSR 10 173
Carstor, Godfrey	1885	WSR 10 192
Carroll, Ellen	1886	WSR 10 198
Carroll, Bartholomew	1875	WSR 10 220
Carver, Joseph H.	1884	WSR 10 306
Calder, Lloyd	1883	WSR 10 320
Carver, Henry	1887	WSR 10 357
Calder, Martin	1889	JMM 11 52
Cairnes, Isaac H.	1889	JMM 11 103
Cahen, Louise	1890	JMM 11 118
Carman, Elizabeth	1895	JMM 11 441
Callahan, Timothy	1886	JMM 11 459
Carsins, Martha J.	1897	GSN 12 92
Calder, Preston M.	1898	GSN 12 196
Carroll, John W.	1901	GSN 12 339
Carman, David	1901	GSN 12 352
Callahan, Patrick	1902	GSN 12 411
Carroll, Margaret	1903	GSN 12 462
Calder, William	1894	HTB 13 34
Carver, John W.	1904	HTB 13 130
Cairnes, Sarah Elizabeth	1899	HTB 13 156
Carr, William W.	1907	HTB 13 331
Carroll, Thomas	1908	HTB 14 143
Carlile, David	1909	HTB 14 217
Cathcart, B. Franklin	1911	HTB 14 324
Calwell, Mary	1913	HTB 14 474
Carman, David A.	1914	JA 15 44
Carroll, W.J.	1914	JA 15 138
Calder, Naomi A.		JA 15 338
Cadwalader, George	1872	JA 15 413
Cadwalader, Frances	1879	JA 15 415
Carver, Geo. R.	1902	JA 16 26
Cairnes, Geo. A.	1916	JA 16 113
Carroll, Henry	1913	JA 16 115
Cathcart, Amanda	1911	JA 16 118
Carroll, Geo. E.	1919	JA 16 120
Cain, Elizabeth	1908	JA 16 143
Cathcart, Mary A.	1909	WFNP 1922
Cathcart, Geo. M.	1920	JA 16 264
Caulford, James	1920	JA 16 277
Carver, Josephine S.	1921	JA 16 363
Carlin, Josiah	1907	JA 16 260
Carr, Francis A.	1916	JA 16 152
Cassell, James M.	1924	CSW 17 129

Carr, Willard Grayson	1953	TLA 25 335
Campbell, James A.	1959	TLA 25 401
Carroll, V. Clyde	1953	TLA 26 320
Cadwalader, Mary Read	1957	TLA 26 348
Carr, Joseph Willis	1955	WFNP 14 284
Cerny, Joseph Lee	1942	AJG 21 304
Cerny, Mary	1940	AJG 21 374
Chaney, Richard	1781	AJ 2 90
Chauncey, George	1802	AJ C 90
Chisholm, Thomas	1805	AJ C 307
Chauncey, Gerrett	1813	AJ C 700
Chew, Thomas S.	1821	SR 1 234
Charlton, James	1830	SR 1 499
Chesney, William	1840	TSB 5 467
Chew, Cassandra M.	1848	TSB 6 54
Chapple, Robert	1849	TSB 6 228
Chalk, Hester Ann	1860	CWB 7 227
Chesney, Mary	1871	BHH 8 257
Chew, Edward M.	1878	WSR 9 175
Christie, Gabriel	1881	WSR 9 310
Chesney, James R.	1881	WSR 9 330
Chisham, Thomas	1879	WSR 10 59
Chatterton, Ann	1878	WSR 10 235
Chambers, James	1868	WSR 10 390
Chesney, Daniel B.	1888	JMM 11 219
Chase, Charles H.	1900	GSW 12 311
Charshee, Bennett	1902	GSN 12 454
Chapman, Fanny C.	1898	HTB 13 375
Chamberlaine, Pamelia H.	1900	HTB 14 213
Chenworth, Wm. H.	1912	HTB 14 367
Chamberlaine, Wilmer J.	1915	JA 15 91
Charshee, Catherine V.	1914	JA 16 1
Chambers, Emory	1906	JA 16 401
Chandlee, Rachel Ann	1912	CSW 17 224
Chambers, Paul	1926	CSW 17 357
Chew, Henrietta	1923	CSW 17 417
Chipchase, Ann Louisa M.	1885	CHR 18 1
Chapman, Christopher C.	1924	CSW 17 456

HARFORD COUNTY, 1774-1960

Clendening, Howard A.	1932	AJG 19 187
Clark, Chapman S.	1932	AJG 19 267
Close, Philip H.	1943	AJG 21 390
Clark, Florence Alma	1947	RLW 22 110
Clark, George R.	1947	RLW 22 150
Clark, Mamie A.	1944	RLW 22 328
Cloak, Elizabeth	1942	RLW 23 67
Clark, Nannie M.	1945	RLW 23 236
Clotworthy, Blanche	1952	RLW 23 469
Clapper, Simon K.	1946	TLA 24 497
Clift, George D.	1951	TLA 26 132
Cook, John	1780	AJ 2 88
Cowen, John	1781	AJ 2 90
Cox, William	1782	AJ 2 92
Coale, William	1784	AJ 2 97
Collins, Robert	1785	AJ 2 99
Copeland, George	1785	AJ 2 104
Corbit, William	1786	AJ 2 106
Cox, Mary	1790	AJ 2 109
Coale, Philip	1791	AJ 2 110
Cook, John	1797	AJ 2 123
Covenhaven, John	1797	AJ 2 124
Connelly, Donn	1800	AJ 2 126
Colby, Thomas	1802	AJ C 47
Coale, Margaret	1802	AJ C 58
Cooley, John	1807	AJ C 385
Cooper, Sebilla	1810	AJ C 518
Cole, William	1811	AJ C 597
Cowan, Eleanor	1812	AJ C 672
Coale, William	1812	AJ C 756
Coleman, John	1816	SR 1 82
Courtney, Jonas	1816	SR 1 108
Cox, Israel	1818	SR 1 151
Courtney, Thomas	1823	SR 1 315
Coale, Joseph H.	1825	SR 1 329
Coale, William	1825	SR 1 338
Cooper, Susanna	1827	SR 1 393
Coale, Elizabeth	1827	SR 1 406
Courtney, Sarah	1831	SR 1 526
Cole, James	1831	SR 1 546
Coale, Samuel	1832	TSB 5 8

Coale, Skepwith H.	1832	TSB 5	10
Cox, William	1833	TSB 5	93
Cooley, John J.	1837	TSB 5	268
Cooley, Sarah	1837	TSB 5	290
Cole, Catherine	1840	TSB 5	493
Cochlan, Dennis	1842	TSB 5	570
Coale, Richard	1844	TSB 6	33
Cowen, Samuel	1847	TSB 6	142
Cole, James C.	1851	TSB 6	275
Cochran, Charlotte	1851	TSB 6	276
Cox, Rachel	1852	TSB 6	320
Cordery, Philip	1855	CWB 7	57
Coale, Susan	1858	CWB 7	177
Cook, Elisha	1859	CWB 7	201
Courtney, Cyrus	1859	CWB 7	205
Cooper, William	1863	CWB 7	313
Cooper, Edward	1864	CWB 7	351
Connelly, Patrick	1865	CWB 7	384
Corrigan, Bartholomew	1866	CWB 7	405
Cordery, James M.	1866	BHH 8	10
Coale, James	1868	BHH 8	78
Coale, Gerard	1870	BHH 8	149
Coen, John	1871	BHH 8	199
Coulson, William	1872	BHH 8	264
Cook, George P.	1873	BHH 8	369
Cockey, Rebecca	1873	BHH 8	374
Cole, Jonas	1877	WSR 9	134
Coen, Sarah Ann	1877	WSR 9	150
Coates, Anna M.	1880	WSR 9	265
Cocklin, Daniel	1881	WSR 9	289
Coates, Phebe A. M.	1881	WSR 9	306
Courtney, Benjamin S.	1883	WSR 9	398
Conly, George W.	1883	WSR 9	443
Coale, John W.	1879	WSR 10	91
Connor, Ann	1882	WSR 10	109
Cook, Joel	1885	WSR 10	136
Cooper, Abraham	1887	WSR 10	348
Coale, Saml. Chase	1881	WSR 10	352
Cox, Levi	1888	WSR 10	430
Collins, Seymour	1889	WSR 10	469
Courtney, William A.	1884	JMM 11	111
Colgan, Elizabeth	1891	JMM 11	289
Coale, John B.	1888	GSN 12	3
Cook, William A.	1896	GSN 12	22

Coffey, Johanna	1896	GSN 12 95
Coulston, William G.	1896	GSN 12 175
Cox, Elisha	1890	GSN 12 250
Connaughton, Luke	1900	GSN 12 280
Cook, Conrad C. P.	1900	GSN 12 295
Cooper, Thomas J.	1901	GSN 12 382
Connaughton, Thomas	1904	HTB 13 34
Cooker, Levi	1899	HTB 13 43
Coale, Isaac W.	1899	HTB 13 168
Courtney, Hollis	1907	HTB 13 420
Coale, Isaac C.	1906	HTB 14 30
Cook, E, E.	1909	HTB 14 62
Collier, P. F.	1908	HTB 14 64
Conway, Mary Ann	1909	HTB 14 76
Courtney, Cyrus A.	1898	HTB 14 84
Cole, John W.	1908	HTB 14 162
Coale, Mary E.	1907	HTB 14 180
Copper, Kate E.	1909	HTB 14 190
Cooper, Evan B.	1906	HTB 14 258
Colwell, Mary	1913	HTB 14 474
Cook, William F.	1910	HTB 14 492
Coen, Mary Jane	1910	JA 15 22
Correri, Paul	1914	JA 15 54
Cole, Mary	1911	JA 15 194
Colder, Naomi	1916	JA 15 338
Cook, Catharine A.	1914	JA 15 388
Cooper, Margaret	1914	JA 15 448
Cooper, Mary E.	1915	JA 16 9
Cooper, William	1912	JA 16 173
Coe, Moses P.	1917	JA 16 178
Courtney, Susan E.	1919	JA 16 266
Coen, Daniel S.	1914	JA 16 279
Courtney, Harry M.	1911	JA 16 342
Collier, Abraham	1923	CSW 17 12
Cook, Melissa Briggs	1923	CSW 17 53
Cook, Alice V.	1923	CSW 17 56
Coomes, W. H.	1924	CSW 17 122
Cooney, John	1924	CSW 17 234
Coale, Emily	1917	CSW 17 156
Converse, Edmund Cogswell	1920	CSW 17 324
Courtney, Annie C.	1912	CSW 17 344
Cochran, William	1921	CSW 17 352
Cooper, Mary E.	1919	CSW 17 363
Corse, Frederick W.	1915	CSW 17 425

31

Cook, William P.	1927	CHR 18 13
Coe, Hanna E.	1925	CHR 18 125
Cohen, James W.	1914	CHR 18 134
Coale, John H.	1925	CHR 18 270
Coale, A. Lee	1926	CHR 18 458
Cochran, Clara	1932	AJG 19 62
Conrad, Conrad	1929	AJG 19 272
Conner, Rebecca J.	1926	AJG 19 442
Corbin, Johnson	1936	AJG 20 126
Colgan, Irene E.	1933	AJG 20 195
Coale, Ira V.	1913	AJG 20 227
Coale, Anna Mariah	1939	AJG 20 254
Copenhaver, Jefferson Davis	1927	AJG 20 300
Cooper, Nelson B.	1931	AJG 20 395
Cole, Oliver F.	1932	AJG 21 253
Cooper, Louisa	1913	AJG 21 307
Cochran, Ida M.	1942	AJG 21 318
Coe, Charles E.	1943	RLW 22 40
Coale, Joseph R.	1946	RLW 22 147
Corn, William H.	1949	RLW 22 193
Coe, George W.	1937	RLW 22 266
Coleman, Mary N.	1948	RLW 22 356
Cohee, Agnes M.	1952	RLW 22 496
Correri, Joseph H.	1944	RLW 22 497
Cooper, Winfield	1950	RLW 23 123
Corbin, Cora B.	1951	RLW 23 243
Courtney, Cecil C.	1954	RLW 23 258
Cottrell, Hilja	1941	RLW 23 445
Coale, William W.	1952	RLW 23 449
Cochran, Catherine S.	1950	TLA 24 61
Cole, Mary S.	1944	TLA 24 65
Collins, Charles A.	1954	TLA 24 72
Courter, Minnie A.	1950	TLA 24 114
Cooper, W. Ellsworth	1944	TLA 24 201
Connellee, Wm. J.	1953	TLA 24 186
Cowser, Maggie	1958	TLA 24 224
Coaliny, Claudia L.	1956	TLA 24 485
Coale, H. Edward	1959	TLA 25 161
Corns, James A.	1954	TLA 25 170
Cooper, Nelson	1958	TLA 25 436
Corona, Vincenza Leodora	1936	WFNP
Cotton, Jane	1953	TLA 26 58
Cobourn, Frederick Lee	1959	TLA 26 55
Cooney, Thomas D.	1960	WFNP 14 155

Cox, Charles C.	1959	TLA 26 391
Cochran, G. Wilbur	1959	WFNP 14 294
Crooks, William	1778	AJ 2 85
Crawford, Mordecai	1785	AJ 2 100
Crocket, Samuel	1785	AJ 2 103
Crawford, Alexander	1786	AJ 2 107
Cretin, John	1784	AJ 2 116
Craig, John	1797	AJ 2 118
Creswell, Isabella	1795	AJ 2 120
Crawford, Susannah	1797	AJ 2 121
Crocket, Benjamin	1796	AJ 2 122
Crawford, Mordecai	1815	SR 1 51
Criswell, Mary	1845	SR 1 54
Criswell, Elizabeth	1815	SR 1 102
Cronin, Margaret	1846	TSB 6 104
Crayten, Robert	1847	TSB 6 133
Cranston, Mary	1860	CWB 7 223
Cronan, William	1864	CWB 7 334
Criswell, William	1869	BHH 8 119
Crawford, Joseph	1874	WSR 9 21
Criswell, Temperance	1874	WSR 9 23
Cromwell, Charlotte	1876	WSR 9 89
Cresmer, Gotlieb	1877	WSR 9 156
Cronin, Patrick	1880	WSR 9 262
Crow, Miles	1887	WSR 10 298
Crevensten, Francis C.	1891	JMM 11 173
Creswell, Margaret	1890	JMM 11 175
Creswell, Mary Amanda	1895	JMM 11 191
Cross, William	1900	GSN 12 268
Cranston, Sarah A.	1900	GSN 12 285
Crawley, William W.	1901	GSN 12 375
Cranston, Robert	1821	GSN 12 392
Craig, John	1902	GSN 12 431
Crumlish, John J.	1911	HTB 14 268
Cross, Margaret	1905	JA 16 256
Cromwell, Henry A.	1923	CSW 17 349
Crothers, Lena A.	1922	CSW 17 367
Cronin, Cyrus C.	1924	CHR 18 129
Crew, J. Fred	1926	CHR 18 231
Cronin, Wm. H.	1902	CHR 18 282
Cronin, Jessie Baker	1929	CHR 18 309

Cromwell, Harriett	1912	AJG 19 30
Crow, Elizabeth	1934	AJG 19 264
Crumlish, Joseph	1935	AJG 19 317
Creelman, John F.	1933	AJG 19 491
Creswell, Mary F.	1938	AJG 20 411
Crew, Theodore H.	1938	AJG 21 168
Crow, John T.	1940	AJG 21 386
Creaghan, John T.	1947	RLW 22 472
Craig, Katie K.	1945	RLW 23 192
Crouse, Lawrence Francis	1954	RLW 23 494
Cronin, Ella	1953	TLA 24 11
Crowe, Katherine D.	1957	Filed not prob. 13 401
Crowe, Katherine D.	1957	TLA 25 193
Creswell, Catherine	1938	Filed not prob. 13 892
Cronin, T. Arthur	1952	TLA 26 519

Culver, Benjamin	1774	AJ 2 79
Cummins, John	1800	AJ 2 130
Curry, James	1808	AJ C 454
Cunningham, John	1812	AJ C 612
Curey, John	1832	TSB 5 13
Cullum, Richard	1843	TSB 6 12
Curran, Lewis	1843	TSB 6 20
Cunningham, Walter	1853	CWB 7 18
Cunningham, Eleanor	1855	CWB 7 89
Curry, Sarah Ellen	1883	WSR 9 395
Cunningham, Andrew	1882	WSR 9 435
Cunningham, B. C. W.	1872	WSR 10 411
Cull, Robert	1880	JMM 11 88
Cunningham, John A.	1888	JMM 11 234
Curry, Hannah C.	1893	GSN 12 31
Cummings, Hugh	1898	GSN 12 197
Cummings, Emily E.	1901	GSN 12 342
Curtiss, George G.	1901	GSN 12 357
Cullum, Jennie M.	1912	HTB 14 292
Curtis, Ellen M.	1903	HTB 14 415
Cullum, James F.	1919	JA 16 127
Cullum, Henry	1920	JA 16 210
Currier, Theodore W.	1919	JA 16 257
Cullum, Martha J.	1919	CHR 18 90
Cullum, Alice L.	1931	AJG 19 198
Curtis, George A.	1933	AJG 19 219

Cummings, Mary	1920	AJG 19 275
Curry, Anna M.	1933	AJG 20 9
Curtis, Isabelle	1934	AJG 20 49
Culp, Sarah A.	1931	RLW 22 163
Cummings, Mary F.	1949	RLW 22 240
Curry, Margaret V.	1945	TLA 24 476
Cullum, Emily F.	1955	WFNP 13 699
Curry, J. Lee	1940	TLA 26 4

D

Dale, John	1778	AJ 2 142
Davis, William	1774	AJ 2 136
Daugherty, George	1784	AJ 2 149
Day, John of Edward	1784	AJ 2 150
Dawes, Isaac	1789	AJ 2 164
Day, Mary Ann	1796	AJ 2 165
Day, John	1791	AJ 2 171
Davis, David	1801	AJ C 41
Dallam, Margaret	1801	AJ C 124
Dallam, Richard	1805	AJ C 264
Davis, John	1809	AJ C 467
Dallam, Josias W.	1821	SR 1 225
Day. Josiah	1821	SR 1 237
Davis, Joseph	1826	SR 1 381
Davis, Joseph	1828	SR 1 423
Dallam, Samuel W.	1828	SR 1 429
Davis, Elijah	1829	SR 1 480
Davis, Joseph	1831	SR 1 539
Davis, Ruben H.	1835	TSB 5 215
Davis, Susannah	1836	TSB 5 230
Davis, John	1839	TSB 5 385
Day, Goldsmith	1839	TSB 5 439
Davis, Susanna	1851	TSB 6 270
Davis, David S.	1852	TSB 6 337
Davidson, John S.	1853	TSB 6 355
Davis, John	1853	CWB 7 10
Davis, William I.	1854	CWB 7 74
Day, William G.	1854	CWB 7 42
Daugherty, Michael	1855	CWB 7 60
Davis, Martha	1855	CWB 7 76
Davis, Luther M.	1857	CWB 7 131
Davis, Julia Ann	1858	CWB 7 155
Davis, Ruth	1863	CWB 7 318
Davis, Samuel	1865	CWB 7 376
Dallam, Rush B.	1866	BHH 8 9
Daughton, Daniel	1867	BHH 8 39
Dameron, Charles B.	1868	BHH 8 95
Davidge, Rebecca	1873	BHH 8 358
Day, Thomas	1868	WSR 9 4

Davis, Robert H.	1877	WSR 9 138
Day, Amos	1881	WSR 9 288
Dallam, William H.	1882	WSR 9 401
Davis, Martha E.	1885	WSR 10 133
Davis, Jane	1880	WSR 10 356
Davis, Elisha	1887	JMM 11 168
Davidson, Jones	1887	JMM 11 188
Davis, William J.	1884	GSN 12 37
Dalton, John B.	1892	GSN 12 147
Dallam, John S.	1899	GSN 12 220
Dallam, Amanda M.	1898	GSN 12 221
Dallam, William	1899	GSN 12 253
Davis, Elizabeth	1900	GSN 12 275
Davis, Caroline L.	1900	GSN 12 286
Day, William N.	1900	GSN 12 323
Davison, William	1901	GSN 12 377
Dallam, Mary C.	1899	HTB 13 162
Dance, Caroline	1902	HTB 13 281
Day, Sallie E.	1905	HTB 13 290
Dampier, Sarah A.A.	1908	HTB 13 435
Davis, George W.	1912	HTB 14 398
Dance, Hannah S.	1912	HTB 14 401
Davis, S. Griffith	1904	HTB 14 448
Dawson, John H.	1912	HTB 14 462
Daugherty, John C.	1905	HTB 14 472
Dallam, Charles L.	1915	JA 15 127
Day, Samuel S.	1909	JA 15 161
Daugherty, Mary Carter	1916	JA 15 408
Dalton, J. Frank	1918	JA 16 41
Daugherty, Annie V.	1917	JA 16 48
Davison, Harriett	1919	JA 16 114
Daugherty, Catherine	1918	JA 16 254
Davis, Mary J.	1918	JA 16 412
Dance, Caroline	1902	HTB 13 281
Daugherty, T. Benton	1924	CSW 17 73
Davis, William B.	1921	CSW 17 371
Daugherty, J. Finney	1917	CSW 17 455
Davis, James W.	1911	AJG 19 37
Davis, Helen S.	1924	AJG 19 91
Dallam, William	1919	AJG 19 115
Davis, Elma J.	1922	AJG 20 30
Davis, Edward B.	1936	AJG 20 39
Day, Emory U.	1939	AJG 21 9
Davis, Gladden	1941	AJG 21 16

Davis, S. Griffith	1941	AJG 21 157
Daughton, B. Frank	1936	AJG 21 244
Davis, Eva M. H.	1941	AJG 21 382
Davis, Charles D.	1945	AJG 21 408
Daugherty, William S.	1946	AJG 21 425
Day, Willard Hammond	1923	AJG 21 464
Dalton, George S.	1951	RLW 22 355
Dallam, Benjamin R.	1947	RLW 22 465
Day, William H.	1945	RLW 23 101
Davis, Mercy A.	1948	RLW 23 113
Daughton, Harry F.	1916	RLW 23 156
Dallam, William H.	1947	RLW 23 170
Daugherty, George F.	1948	RLW 23 251
Daniel, Leslie A.	1937	RLW 23 339
Dawson, Lee	1955	RLW 23 364
Day, Nellie W.	1945	RLW 23 454
Daniel, Mary A.	1957	TLA 24 24
Davis, Enos Norris	1945	TLA 24 79
Dayhoof, Orlando L.	1945	TLA 24 279
Daughton, M. Frances	1955	Not recorded
Davis, G. Harry	1952	TLA 25 396
Davis, James Norman	1960	WFNP 14 148
Daugherty, Edna C.	1960	TLA 26 476
Davis, Clinton K.	1952	WFNP 14 280

Deacon, Stephen	1775	AJ 2 137
Debrular, Benjamin	1780	AJ 2 148
Denny, Simeon	1789	AJ 2 163
Denny, Margaret	1791	AJ 2 166
Deaver, Richard	1791	AJ 2 167
Dessaa, Jean	1797	AJ 2 176
Debrular, Frances	1792	AJ 2 178
Delaporte, Frederick F. C.	1797	AJ 2 181
Deaver, Hannah	1801	AJ C 35
Debrular, Sarah	1803	AJ C 181
Delaporte, Betsey H.	1803	AJ C 103
Dean, Samuel	1807	AJ C 399
Deaver, James	1812	AJ C 628
Demoss, John	1820	SR 1 221
Denbow, Thomas	1826	SR 1 374
Deaver, Mable	1827	SR 1 399
Denbow, Levi	1829	SR 1 463

Demoss, Thomas	1834	TSB 5 155
Deaver, Aquila	1835	TSB 5 234
Deaver, Aquila	1836	TSB 5 209
Delmas, Francis	1845	TSB 6 72
Dellam, Fanny	1846	TSB 6 103
Denbow, John	1850	TSB 6 257
Demose, David	1853	CWB 7 13
Deaver, Richard	1861	CWB 7 244
Devoe, John	1865	CWB 7 390
Dever, John	1868	BHH 8 67
Deets, Frederick	1869	BHH 8 137
Delmos, Theodore	1871	BHH 8 254
Dean, Nathan Sr.	1872	BHH 8 311
Denbow, Elizabeth	1880	WSR 9 252
Devoe, John	1883	WSR 10 155
Devoe, James	1890	JMM 11 195
De Lany, J. F.	1868	JMM 11 199
Deaver, Elizabeth	1886	JMM 11 311
Deiker, John H.	1894	JMM 11 411
Derickson, John P.	1893	GSN 12 6
Demoss, James	1886	GSN 12 179
DeBaugh, Adam	1899	GSN 12 261
Devoe, George V.	1901	GSN 12 338
Dean, James	1902	GSN 12 396
Dekka, Elizabeth	1905	HTB 13 218
Dence, Caroline	1902	HTB 13 281
Deets, Samuel	1903	HTB 13 287
DeCoursey, Isaiah	1903	HTB 13 350
Deckman, Alice A.	1906	HTB 13 394
Dennis, Sallie A.	1900	HTB 13 426
Dern, Charles P.	1907	HTB 13 434
DeCou, Richard	1909	JA 15 69
Deckman, Joseph T.	1915	JA 15 132
Devoe, Grafton	1916	JA 15 236
Denbow, Samuel S.	1916	JA 15 289
DeBaugh, Elizabeth	1909	JA 15 345
Deaver, Geo. W.	1916	JA 16 155
DeLany, Geo. L.	1918	JA 16 299
Dean, J. Edgar	1922	CSW 17 6
Derrickson, Catharine	1924	CSW 17 159
DeCourcy, Joel I.	1925	CSW 17 410
DeVoe, Rebecca E.	1925	CSW 17 437
Densby, Clara J.	1925	CHR 18 262
Dennison, Chas. A.	1911	CHR 18 268

De Haven, Olivia E.	1927	CHR 18 473
De Goll, Ann A.	1927	AJG 19 10
Delbridge, Clarence A.	1932	AJG 19 80
Delbridge, E. Genevieve	1932	AJG 19 80
Deckman, Florida F.	1934	AJG 19 279
De Baugh, John A.	1935	AJG 19 368
Dennison, Isaac	1931	AJG 20 2
Deets, Leona B.	1937	AJG 20 119
DeGruchy, Mary	1939	AJG 20 401
Dern, Rebecca J.	1941	AJG 20 499
Dempsey, Emma K.	1933	AJG 21 483
Dennison, John T.	1941	RLW 22 59
Dean, N. Howard	1932	RLW 22 319
Deppish, Carrie	1946	RLW 22 480
DeLand, Robert Edgar	1943	RLW 23 100
Dehaven, Edward	1952	RLW 23 140
Deckman, Jacob	1945	RLW 23 351
De Bonis, Pearl	1957	TLA 24 467
Dentry, Henrietta T.	1955	WFNP 13 582
De Bey, Albert Lee Gerard	1944	TLA 25 109
Deckman, Augusta	1949	TLA 25 270
Delorme, Frank F.	1953	TLA 25 341
De Marco, Adam	1953	WFNP 14 128
DeBord, Edgar G.	1959	WFNP 14 152
De Moss, Annie L.	1951	TLA 26 415

Dickson, David	1778	AJ 2 145
Dickenson, Gilbert	1857	CWB 7 139
Diffenderffer, Joseph T.	1862	CWB 7 285
Divers, Ananias	1871	BHH 8 236
Dixon, William, H.	1875	WSR 9 62
Dick, Charles, Sr.	1876	WSR 9 85
Diffenderffer, George M.	1882	WSR 9 344
Divers, William H.	1865	WSR 10 316
Dierker, John H.	1892	JMM 11 411
Divers, John	1899	GSN 12 258
Dierker, Annie M.	1895	HTB 14 118
Disher, George F.	1909	HTB 14 209
Dickinson, Mary E.	1917	JA 15 463
Dixon, Benjamin	1925	CSW 17 204
Disher, John	1927	CHR 18 48
Dick, Katherine M.	1930	CHR 18 255

Divers, William A.	1934	AJG 19 360
Diovidio, Carmine	1936	AJG 20 25
Dierker, Georgia M.	1937	AJG 20 109
Ditzel, Frank	1935	AJG 30 139
Dick, J. Lumsden	1941	AJG 21 3
Dick, Stella Hope	1947	RLW 22 118
Dinning, Ernest Lawrence	1946	RLW 22 119
Dick, May	1947	RLW 22 413
Dibb, Annie M.	1942	RLW 23 22
Dickinson, Susie Stump	1950	RLW 23 76
Diethelm, Rose	1954	RLW 23 487
Dill, Howard S.	1957	TLA 25 343

Dougherty, William	1777	AJ 2 139
Dorney, Thomas	1777	AJ 2 140
Doran, Hugh	1778	AJ 2 141
Dorsey, John	1785	AJ 2 153
Dorsey, Greenberry	1798	AJ 2 187
Doran, Philip	1818	SR 1 158
Dorsey, Ann	1819	SR 1 176
Doherty, Samuel	1822	SR 1 259
Dorney, Thomas	1844	TSB 6 27
Dorsey, Archibald	1847	TSB 6 142
Doddrell, James C.	1856	CWB 7 94
Dorsey, Sarah	1861	CWB 7 241
Dobson, Jesse	1862	CWB 7 275
Dorney, William	1866	CWB 7 407
Dougherty, Samuel	1871	BHH 8 226
Dorney, Mary A.	1873	BHH 8 317
Donahue, John	1885	JMM 11 141
Dougherty, Catherine	1891	JMM 11 200
Dorsey, Linda S.	1893	JMM 11 395
Dolan, Charles	1902	GSN 12 450
Donahoo, James L.	1892	HTB 14 79
Dollman, John G.	1911	HTB 14 436
Dorsey, Allen R.	1913	HTB 14 490
Dooley, Lyde	1924	CSW 17 290
Dooley, H. E.	1927	CHR 18 203
Dorrance J. Ford	1919	AJG 19 24
Donohue, Michael	1929	AJG 19 194
Donahue, Joseph	1936	AJG 20 81
Dorsey, Millie	1934	AJG 21 144

Donnelly, John	1943	AJG 21 315
Dorsey, Arthur	1937	AJG 21 332
Donahoo, Alverta	1939	AJG 21 418
Doyle, J. Franklin	1949	RLW 22 262
Dolce, Daniel D.	1954	RLW 23 222
Doukas, Potisha	1955	TLA 24 229
Dorrance, Maude B.	1954	TLA 24 310
Donnelly, Delia	1943	TLA 25 469
Dorsey, Evangeline J.	1952	TLA 26 273
Dorogi, Bejamin	1960	TLA 26 481
Dorsey, Laura Lee	1959	TLA 26 506
Drew, Anthony	1786	AJ 2 155
Drew, Henry	1787	AJ 2 158
Drew, Sarah	1791	AJ 2 174
Drew, Anthony	1797	AJ 2 184
Drew, Aquila	1817	SR 1 131
Drury, Elizabeth S.	1921	CSW 17 127
Drechsler, Margaret F.	1920	CHR 18 32
Drechsler, George E.	1933	AJG 19 192
Draper, J. A.	1919	AJG 20 275
Durbin, Daniel	1774	AJ 2 134
Durham, Mordecai	1778	AJ 2 144
Durham, Samuel	1787	AJ 2 159
Durban, Thomas	1782	AJ 2 161
Durbin, Samuel	1789	AJ 2 162
Durbin, Sian	1797	AJ 2 186
Durham, Elizabeth	1803	AJ C 78
Durham, David	1815	SR 1 48
Durham, Thomas	1840	TSB 5 456
Duffee, Bridget Ann	1845	TSB 6 73
Durham, Nathaniel	1847	TSB 6 147
Duncan, Jane	1849	TSB 6 209
Duncan, James	1857	CWB 7 132
Duncan, Joseph M.	1862	CWB 7 286
Duval, Mary Ann	1862	CWB 7 292
Durham, Abraham	1872	BHH 8 270
Durham, Abel	1875	WSR 9 39
Duncan, James	1879	WSR 9 211

Durham, Nathaniel	1879	WSR 9 230
Duncan, Catharine	1881	WSR 9 270
Dunnigan, Patrick	1888	JMM 11 68
Dubois, John	1885	JMM 11 69
Durbin, John H.	1898	GSN 12 243
Durham, Abraham	1901	GSN 12 381
Dunnigan, John	1903	HTB 13 150
Dunnigan, James	1914	JA 15 433
Durham, William	1920	JA 16 301
Dutton, Ellen J.	1922	JA 16 383
Duval, Mary	1924	CHR 18 28
Dunnigan, Catherine	1931	AJG 19 58
Dudek, Barbara J.	1934	AJG 19 425
Dunnigan, James P.	1937	AJG 20 371
Duncan, John J.	1940	AJG 21 431
Durham, Jacob G.	1945	AJG 21 432
Dubel, William S.	1943	AJG 21 477
Dunnigan, John	1940	RLW 22 83
Dudek, Frank J.	1947	RLW 22 339
Dunnigan, Alice Glackin	1947	RLW 23 189
Durham, Clifton L.	1955	RLW 23 388
Duffin, Ruth R.	1958	TLA 25 330
Durman, Margaret	1951	TLA 26 413
Dyer, Josiah	1780	AJ 2 146
Dyer, Joseph	1793	AJ 2 178
Dye, Sadie E.	1953	TLA 25 143

E

Eakins, Margaret	1787	AJ 2 193
Eaton, Hannah	1868	BHH 8 40
Earp, Thomas	1864	JMM 11 202
Easter, Euphemia S.	1902	HTB 13 209
Easter, William T.	1906	HTB 13 282
Ebersole, John M.	1935	AJG 19 469
Eclip, John R.	1871	BHH 8 222
Eckel, Mary	1882	WSR 9 444
Edin, William	1793	AJ 2 197
Eden, Joseph	1814	AJ C 747
Edge, Emma H.	1896	HTB 14 235
Edel, Saml. T.	1907	HTB 14 338
Edmonson, James Oliver	1927	CHR 18 237
Edel, John W.	1924	RLW 22 188
Edwards, William Bert	1950	RLW 23 195
Edwards, Orrin C.	1956	RLW 23 451
Edwards, Henderson C.		RLW 23 459
Ege, Elizabeth E.	1899	HTB 14 181
Eglin, William C. L.	1926	CHR 18 63
Eicholtz, H. Jane	1933	AJG 19 247
Eicholtz, George W.	1936	AJG 20 240
Eifert, Elsie A. L.	1957	TLA 26 44
Elliot, Thomas	1795	AJ 2 191
Elliot, James	1794	AJ 2 190
Ely, Thomas	1783	AJ 2 188
Ely, Hugh	1799	AJ 2 200
Elliott, Ann	1799	AJ C 7
Ely, Rachel	1803	AJ C 127
Ely, Thomas	1814	AJ C 729

Ely, Joseph	1819	SR 1 192
Ely, John	1825	SR 1 422
Elliott, William	1842	TSB 5 600
Ely, William	1852	TSB 6 334
Ely, Hannah	1890	JMM 11 129
Ely, Thomas	1890	JMM 11 130
Elliott, Catherine A.	1886	JMM 11 167
Elsner, John	1907	HTB 13 372
Ely, David C.	1904	HTB 14 92
Ellicott, Charles Lewis	1912	HTB 14 465
Elsner, Geo. W.	1920	JA 16 184
Ely, Mary Belle	1924	CSW 17 80
Ellicott, David B.	1913	CSW 17 235
Ely, William A.	1924	CHR 18 224
Elste, Anna D.	1927	AJG 19 15
Ely, Charles Edward	1931	AJG 19 218
Elsner, Harry W.	1933	AJG 19 406
Ely, James H.	1936	AJG 21 465
Elder, Wm. H.	1934	RLW 22 96
Elste, Sr., George W.	1950	RLW 23 149
Elsner, Robert C.	1949	RLW 23 386
Ellicott, David B.	1960	TLA 25 158
Elster, Frederick	1872	WFNP
Emmord, Frederick	1882	WSR 9 356
Emrick, Jacob	1908	HTB 14 93
Emmord, John H.	1927	CSW 17 493
Emrick, George	1954	RLW 23 365
Emigh, Edward W.	1960	WFNP 14 154
England, George	1828	SR 1 425
Enlows, Prudence	1838	TSB 5 322
Enlows, James	1844	TSB 6 41
England, Catherine	1846	TSB 6 108
Enlows, Temperance	1853	CWB 7 1
England, John	1858	CWB 7 172
Enlows, Rebecca	1867	BHH 8 15
Enlows, John	1874	WSR 9 18
Enlows, Harriet	1877	WSR 9 140
England, Hannah S.	1884	JMM 11 122
Engle, Sarah Elizabeth	1898	HTB 14 20
Ennis, Lydia A.	1908	JA 16 397

Ensinger, Jennie	1920	CSW 17 243
Enfield, Samuel P.	1926	CHR 18 180
Ennis, Samuel J.	1932	AJG 21 216
Ennis, Annie E.	1944	RLW 22 371
England, Joseph Townsend	1953	RLW 23 180
Ensor, Abram Gorsuch	1932	TLA 24 384
Ernst, John F.	1938	AJG 20 354
Erickson, Thora C.	1931	AJG 21 43
Ernst, Paul J.	1954	TLA 24 468
Erkenswick, Catherine Ann	1947	WFNP 14 233
Esterley, Ella D.	1931	AJG 20 8
Esley, Lillie S.	1944	AJG 21 320
Esterley, Frederick	1951	RLW 22 420
Eshleman, Mollie E.	1956	TLA 24 22
Estes, David M.	1957	TLA 24 293
Eubank, Robert W.	1894	GSN 12 11
Evans, Evan	1791	AJ 2 194
Evans, John	1791	AJ 2 196
Evatt, Willie	1794	AJ 2 198
Everitt, Amoss	1853	TSB 6 356
Everitt, Charity	1861	CWB 7 261
Everitt, Charlotte	1863	CWB 7 312
Everest, James	1863	CWB 7 325
Everist, Ephriam	1865	CWB 7 374
Evans, Jas. Cecil	1883	WSR 9 409
Evans, John T.	1881	WSR 9 419
Evans, John Wistar	1871	WSR 10 157
Everett, Sarah	1894	GSN 12 105
Evans, Daniel S.	1898	HTB 13 402
Evans, A. W.	1912	HTB 14 379
Everist, George Thomas	1913	JA 15 443
Everett, William W.	1929	AJG 21 169
Everding, John W.	1943	RLW 22 65
Evans, Gertrude I.	1945	RLW 23 29
Evans, Lilburn E.	1945	RLW 23 380
Everett, Hannah R.	1946	TLA 24 60
Evans, Augusta K.	1944	TLA 26 344

Ewing,	John	1820	SR 1 206
Ewing,	William	1867	BHH 8 15
Ewing,	Eliza	1868	BHH 8 55
Ewing,	William	1871	BHH 8 241
Ewing,	Charity Jane	1885	JMM 11 140
Ewing,	William H.	1891	JMM 11 235
Ewing,	George A.	1902	GSN 12 447
Ewing,	Elizabeth W.	1908	HTB 13 432
Ewing,	Harvey	1929	CHR 18 235
Ewing,	Carrie D.	1941	AJG 21 182
Ewing,	May Stewart	1945	AJG 21 444
Ewing,	J. M. Sharpless	1943	TLA 24 447

F

Farley, Patrick	1826	SR 1 385
Farmer, Richard	1839	TSB 5 378
Farnandis, Fanny	1873	BHH 8 342
Famous, Samuel R.	1881	WSR 9 273
Fantom, Emily S.	1874	WSR 9 8
Faulkner, Margaret A.	1878	WSR 9 194
Faulkner, Henry H.	1880	WSR 10 61
Famous, Joseph M.	1884	WSR 10 203
Famous, Sarah A.	1882	WSR 10 216
Farnandis, Mary E.	1876	WSR 10 374
Favour, John B.	1899	GSN 12 241
Farnandis, Henry D.	1900	GSN 12 271
Farnandis, James	1900	GSN 12 281
Faulkner, Arabella	1900	GSN 12 287
Farrand, Samuel	1874	HTB 13 353
Farrand, Hannah D.	1896	HTB 13 309
Famous, Mary W.	1890	HTB 14 223
Farley, John R.	1913	HTB 14 463
Farnandis, Bessie D.	1927	CSW 17 483
Fahey, James H.	1927	CHR 18 291
Farr, Francis M.	1917	CHR 18 430
Famous, Charles W.	1920	AJG 20 188
Fahey, Michael H.	1917	AJG 20 376
Fahey, Michael W.	1936	RLW 22 58
Famous, Clara K.	1946	RLW 22 340
Famous, Mary L.	1949	RLW 22 402
Famous, James P.	1938	RLW 23 292
Fabrizio, Achillo	1952	TLA 24 59
Farnum, Betty C.	1958	TLA 24 377
Fabrizio, James A.	1958	TLA 24 456
Few, John	1834	TSB 5 123
Fell, Francis G.	1848	TSB 6 161
Few, Geo. Washington	1872	BHH 8 287
Ferrell, Ida C.	1923	CSW 17 298
Fehrman, Margaret	1923	CSW 17 463
Ferguson, Jane	1928	CHR 18 157
Fehrman, Ernest H.	1927	AJG 19 416

Ferrell, Edward R.	1932	AJG 20 159
Ferrandisco, Francesco Angelo	1948	TLA 24 102
Fencil, Lulu C.	1959	TLA 26 337
Finney, Manassa	1778	AJ 2 206
Fisher, William	1779	AJ 2 202
Fitzgerald, John	1791	AJ 2 209
Fisher, James	1825	SR 1 332
Fisher, William	1835	TSB 5 207
Fitzcharles, Kathrine	1862	CWB 7 484
Fitzpatrick, John	1863	CWB 7 307
Finney, John	1889	JMM 11 174
Fife, Robert	1890	JMM 11 376
Fife, Ruth	1890	JMM 11 377
Fishel, Jacob G.	1913	JA 15 184
Field, Laura E.	1908	JA 15 273
Fisher, Wilhelmina	1907	JA 15 424
Fitzpatrick, Catherine	1915	JA 16 162
Finkernagel, John	1923	CSW 17 118
Finney, Elizabeth McCormick	1916	CSW 17 281
Fisher, Robert Alexander	1933	AJG 19 222
Fisher, Joe	1940	AJG 20 388
Fishel, Annie R.	1919	RLW 23 110
Finkernagel, George	1957	TLA 24 135
Fieger, Phebe Turner	1953	TLA 24 424
Finney, Eliza McCormick	1953	TLA 26 103
Fitzpatrick, Clark E.	1953	WFNP 14 025
Fletcher, John	1846	TSB 6 121
Flowers, Rhoda	1852	TSB 6 298
Fletcher, Septimus	1871	BHH 8 243
Flaharty, William H.	1891	JMM 11 227
Flaharty, Caroline	1904	HTB 13 192
Flottemesch, Heinrick	1908	HTB 14 57
Fletcher, John Calvin	1911	HTB 14 448
Flavin, Martin	1905	JA 15 19
Fletcher, Jane M.	1919	JA 16 129
Flaharty, John R.	1925	CSW 17 250
Fleury, Corinne C.	1913	CHR 18 412
Flavin, Johanna	1917	AJG 19 359
Fleury, Corinne C.	1913	AJG 21 148

Fletcher, Bevan D.	1945	RLW 23 280
Flannery, Burt Vaughn		RLW 23 358
Fletcher, Columbus F.	1958	TLA 24 235
Fleckinstein, George Henry	1957	will filed-not prob.
Ford, Mary	1794	AJ 2 211
Foster, Samuel	1793	AJ 2 210
Foster, Margaret	1794	AJ 2 212
Forwood, Samuel	1807	AJ C 353
Ford, Joseph	1807	AJ C 362
Forwood, John	1807	AJ C 396
Ford, Joshua	1811	AJ C 559
Foard, William	1817	SR 1 120
Foster, John	1818	SR 1 153
Forwood, Mary	1820	SR 1 209
Forwood, John	1835	TSB 5 604
Foard, Loyd J.	1839	TSB 5 400
Forwood, John	1842	TSB 5 187
Ford, William	1843	TSB 6 1
Forsythe, William	1855	CWB 7 78
Forwood, Harriet E.	1856	CWB 7 115
Forsythe, George	1863	CWB 7 324
Forsythe, George, Jr.	1864	CWB 7 334
Forsythe, William	1864	CWB 7 336
Forsythe, Alexander	1865	CWB 7 399
Forwood, Parker	1866	CWB 7 403
Forwood, Mary A.	1868	BHH 8 61
Foley, James	1873	BHH 8 329
Foard, William	1874	WSR 9 28
Forwood, Jacob	1876	WSR 9 88
Foard, James H.	1881	WSR 9 328
Forder, William	1882	WSR 9 374
Forwood, Isabella L.	1883	WSR 9 467
Forwood, James	1882	WSR 10 33
Foley, Richard R.	1885	WSR 10 228
Foreman, Joseph H.	1883	WSR 10 240
Foster, Henry	1880	WSR 10 290
Forwood, Mary	1889	JMM 11 71
Forwood, George W.	1890	JMM 11 159
Forsythe, Mary A.	1894	JMM 11 427
Foley, Elizabeth	1903	HTB 13 76
Forwood, Julia A.	1905	HTB 13 147

Ford, William H.	1905	HTB 13 368
Foreman, Mary F.	1907	HTB 14 23
Foster, Henry C.	1916	JA 15 268
Foard, Oliver S.	1913	JA 16 319
Forwood, Jemima	1916	JA 16 474
Foard, M. Adelia	1924	CSW 17 96
Forwood, Parker L.	1925	CSW 17 283
Forsyth, Sarah J.	1927	CHR 18 24
Foard, Mary R.	1925	CHR 18 454
Fox, Ida May	1936	AJG 20 48
Forsythe, Clara Lulla	1929	AJG 20 56
Ford, James T.	1937	AJG 20 112
Foreman, George A.	1940	AJG 21 231
Foard, Thomas R.	1941	AJG 21 238
Forwood, George Parker	1945	AJG 21 378
Ford, George S.	1942	RLW 22 113
Foy, Lewis Robert	1948	RLW 22 185
Forsythe, Martha Jane	1948	RLW 22 192
Foley, Charles J.	1954	TLA 24 19
Ford, Lena M.	1956	TLA 24 104
Ford, John T.	1949	TLA 24 121
Foard, Frank O.	1957	TLA 24 268
Ford, Albert K.	1953	TLA 24 362
Forbes, John Hamilton Chews	1949	TLA 25 383
Forwood, Priscilla F.W.	1945	WFNP

Frisby, Thomas P.	1781	AJ 2 204
Frisby, William H.	1811	AJ C 561
Frisby, Thomas P.	1814	SR 1 2
French, Ebenezer	1850	TSB 6 255
Frede, Francis H.	1890	JMM 11 282
Frey, M. Edward	1894	GSN 12 53
Frey, John W.	1898	GSN 12 193
Frederick, Eliza	1908	HTB 14 16
Frederick, William A.	1896	HTB 14 98
Frey, George	1911	HTB 14 261
Frederick, Cecilia A.	1911	JA 15 119
Frede, Anna	1915	JA 15 475
Franklin, Charles	1918	JA 15 495
Frey, Hannah	1916	JA 16 247
Frederick, Maud M.	1917	JA 16 153
Frederick, Mary Emma		CHR 18 226

Frasch, Bazzil	1931	CHR 18 327
Fraser, Martha	1914	CHR 18 383
Frasch, John M.	1932	AJG 19 104
French, Robert C.	1935	AJG 20 62
Fraley, William H.	1912	AJG 20 386
Fristoe, Franklin S.	1939	AJG 21 54
Francis, Freeland M.	1929	RLW 22 7
Free, Evans M.	1951	RLW 22 441
Frith, Mimilea L.	1951	RLW 23 246
Frey, Alexander	1954	RLW 23 324
Fruhling, Otto F.	1953	RLW 23 348
Frock, Oliver Dayton	1953	RLW 23 368
Fristoe, Hattie S.	1939	TLA 24 221
French, Rena T.	1955	TLA 24 253
Franckewitz, Joseph	1947	TLA 24 318
Frasch, John Harry	1959	WFNP 13 702
Franko, Stephen D.	1946	TLA 25 253
Fullerton, John	1813	AJ C 288
Fullard, Henry	1830	SR 1 500
Fulton, William	1830	SR 1 498
Fulford, William	1838	TSB 5 345
Fulton, James	1839	TSB 5 383
Fulton, Elizabeth	1815	CWB 7 73
Fulton, William J.	1885	WSR 10 130
Furlong, Anastesivas	1889	GSN 12 200
Fulford, Frank H.	1920	JA 16 343
Fulton, John A.	1926	AJG 19 444
Fulford, Alexander M. Jr.	1916	AJG 20 12
Fulford, Katharine B.	1943	AJG 21 363
Fulton, James Magee	1947	RLW 22 176
Fahrman, Harry E.	1950	RLW 22 251
Fuller, Frederick W.	1953	RLW 23 70
Fulton, Jean Snodgrass	1958	WFNP 13 579
Fulford, Georgia A.S.	1958	TLA 25 375
Fulker, Raymond A.	1960	TLA 26 327
Fye, Battis	1878	AJ 2 208

G

Gallion, James	1774	AJ 2 215
Gallion, John	1775	AJ 2 220
Garland, Henry	1777	AJ 2 222
Garrettson, Richard	1778	AJ 2 223
Garrettson, Susanna	1780	AJ 2 230
Garland, Frances	1781	AJ 2 232
Gale, William	1781	AJ 2 233
Garrett, Amos	1794	AJ 2 247
Garrettson, Garrett	1794	AJ 2 249
Garrett, Joseph	1793	AJ 2 257
Gallion, Elizabeth	1799	AJ 2 266
Garrettson, Frances	1806	AJ C 343
Garrettson, George	1807	AJ C 401
Garrettson, Garrett	1808	AJ C 438
Garrettson, James	1810	AJ C 486
Garrettson, Susanna	1811	AJ C 565
Garrison, James	1813	AJ C 693
Garrison, Philip	1814	AJ C 762
Garrison, Cornelius	1814	SR 1 6
Garrison, Susanna	1815	SR 1 62
Gallup, Thomas	1820	SR 1 223
Garrettson, Ruthen	1830	SR 1 519
Garrison, Ann	1841	TSB 5 556
Galbreath, John	1844	TSB 6 46
Garrison, Philip	1847	TSB 6 155
Gale, Margaret	1848	TSB 6 177
Garrison, James	1852	TSB 6 297
Garrison, John	1854	CWB 7 40
Garrison, Philip	1858	CWB 7 182
Gallup, Oliver	1862	CWB 7 270
Galloway, Sarah M. J.	1864	CWB 7 345
Gailey, Robert	1865	CWB 7 392
Gamball, Sarah	1873	BHH 8 353
Galbreath, John F.	1876	WSR 9 81
Gammill, Margaretta	1876	WSR 9 93
Galbreath, Alexander	1881	WSR 9 272
Galloway, Moses	1881	WSR 9 303
Galbreath, Hannah	1881	WSR 9 332
Garrettson, William E.	1883	WSR 9 414

Gable, Evelyn P.	1952	RLW 23 2
Galloway, Kate R.	1932	RLW 23 35
Galloway, Sallie P.	1944	RLW 23 37
Galloway, Rose B.	1944	RLW 23 39
Galloway, Elizabeth E.	1952	RLW 23 68
Galbreath, Samuel Wheeler	1955	TLA 25 106
Gaines, Oliver Ira	1958	(TLA 26 371
		(WFNP 14 140
Gamber, Harry Francis	1957	TLA 26 513
Gemmell, David	1840	TSB 5 452
Gemmill, Margaret	1846	TSB 6 105
George, John R.	1886	WSR 10 447
Gerting, Charles	1892	JMM 11 277
Gemmill, Alice Ann	1892	JMM 11 365
Gentry, William F.	1924	CSW 17 237
Getz, Solomon	1928	CHR 18 450
Getz, Simon	1923	AJG 21 15
Gerdom, Clarence	1925	AJG 21 88
German, Florence Grace	1930	RLW 22 140
Getzel, Barbara T.	1949	RLW 22 269
Gerhard, Frederick William	1956	TLA 25 174
Giles, Nathaniel	1775	AJ 2 219
Gilbert, Michael	1784	AJ 2 234
Giles, Jacob	1784	AJ 2 237
Gibson, Ann	1801	AJ 2 254
Gilbert, Charles	1794	AJ 2 256
Gilbert, Charles	1798	AJ 2 263
Gilbert, T. Martin	1797	AJ 2 265
Gilbert, Philip	1805	AJ C 266
Gilbert, Parker	1805	AJ C 294
Gibson, William	1828	SR 1 431
Giles, Sarah	1828	SR 1 437
Gilbert, Micah	1828	SR 1 441
Gilbert, Amos	1836	TSB 5 251
Gilbert, Martin	1837	TSB 5 305
Gilbert, Elizabeth	1845	TSB 6 83
Gilbert, Micah	1853	CWB 7 15
Giles, Cordelia	1853	CWB 7 17

Gilbert, Michael	1859	CWB 7 207
Gilbert, Cassandra	1873	BHH 8 330
Gill, Elcy S.	1876	WSR 9 92
Gilbert, Jane E.	1876	WSR 9 98
Giles, Deborah	1877	WSR 9 136
Gilbert, Eliza Ann	1878	WSR 9 200
Gibson, James L.	1883	WSR 9 458
Gilbert, George T.	1872	WSR 10 83
Gilbert, Jarrett	1884	WSR 10 110
Gilbert, Joel H.	1885	WSR 10 154
Gilbert, Parker	1887	WSR 10 267
Gilbert, A. Preston	1893	JMM 11 353
Giles, John B.	1902	GSN 12 429
Giles, Thomas	1903	HTB 13 25
Gier, Henry	1905	HTB 13 173
Gier, Caroline	1906	HTB 13 306
Gillings, Hester	1903	HTB 13 447
Giles, Rachel	1904	HTB 13 478
Giles, Mary A.	1910	HTB 14 159
Gillis, Margaret	1914	JA 15 163
Gilbert, K. Estelle	1919	JA 16 183
Gibson, James J.	1922	JA 16 453
Gillease, Rosa	1926	CSW 17 370
Gilbert, Zachary T.	1914	CHR 18 77
Gilbert, M. Olivia	1921	CHR 18 189
Gilbert, Daniel R.	1935	AJG 20 10
Gilbert, Harry A.	1932	AJG 20 276
Gibson, Ernest H.	1937	AJG 20 313
Gilbert, Margaret W.	1937	RLW 22 197
Gilpin, Grace H. M.	1927	RLW 22 218
Gilmor, Lily M.	1933	RLW 22 215
Gilbert, A. Mary	1950	RLW 22 317
Gillease, John F.	1951	RLW 22 387
Gibson, Samuel E.	1951	RLW 23 30
Gilbert, Susie A.	1928	RLW 23 49
Gibson, William I.	1953	RLW 23 164
Gilbert, Mary E.	1945	RLW 23 376
Gibson, E. Robena	1956	TLA 25 101
Gianforcaro, Frank	1958	TLA 26 81

Glasgow, James	1823	SR 1 291
Gladden, William	1829	SR 1 488
Gladden, Jacob	1832	TSB 5 28
Glenn, William	1839	TSB 5 415
Glenn, William	1860	CWB 7 235
Glenn, Nathan	1862	CWB 7 276
Glenn, Robert	1864	CWB 7 361
Gladden, Jacob	1867	BHH 8 41
Glenn, Susan	1875	WSR 9 38
Gleason, Michael	1876	WSR 9 151
Gladden, William	1883	WSR 10 50
Glenn, Orpah	1884	WSR 10 105
Glasgow, C. R.	1876	WSR 10 145
Glasgow, George B.	1890	JMM 11 106
Glasgow, George R.	1894	JMM 11 391
Glasgow, Mary A.	1893	GSN 12 69
Glass, Roberta B.	1900	GSN 12 292
Glenn, John L.	1903	HTB 13 143
Gleason, Patrick	1905	HTB 13 383
Gleen, John Gorsuch	1909	JA 15 111
Glassman, John	1911	JA 15 329
Gladden, Mary E.	1924	CSW 17 199
Glessic, Nettie E.	1926	CSW 17 430
Glenn, Fannie May	1934	AJG 20 177
Gladden, Thomas S.	1927	AJG 20 385
Gladden, S. Walter	1939	RLW 22 88
Gladden, Jacob Edgar	1942	RLW 23 43
Glasgow, Hester Amy	1955	RLW 23 463

Gover, Priscilla	1790	AJ 2 251
Gorrell, Abraham	1805	AJ C 134
Gover, Samuel	1814	SR 1 7
Gordon, William	1815	SR 1 40
Gorrell, Mary	1841	TSB 5 547
Goldsborough, Howes	1841	TSB 5 554
Gordon, Franklin	1866	CWB 7 408
Gordon, Andrew	1871	BHH 8 203
Gover, Charlotte	1884	WSR 10 62
Gover, Hagar	1866	WSR 10 355
Gorrell, Virginia D.	1886	JMM 11 29
Gorrell, James L.	1891	JMM 11 239
Gottschalk, Albert	1890	HTB 13 63

Grafton, Nathaniel	1820	SR 1 217
Grafton, Corbin	1820	SR 1 219
Griffith, Hannah	1822	SR 1 260
Grafton, Samuel	1831	SR 1 551
Grafton, James P.	1835	TSB 5 224
Grafton, John	1838	TSB 5 343
Griffith, Luke	1838	TSB 5 356
Gross, Jacob	1842	TSB 5 561
Greenland, Elisha	1845	TSB 6 67
Greme, Mary F.	1845	TSB 6 81
Grier, Ralph	1846	TSB 6 96
Grant, Jacob	1848	TSB 6 164
Greenland, Mary	1852	TSB 6 321
Greenland, Aquila	1855	CWB 7 71
Griffin, Thomas	1855	CWB 7 85
Greenfield, Samuel K.J.	1861	CWB 7 242
Green, Richard	1861	CWB 7 252
Griffin, John A.	1864	CWB 7 349
Grafton, Phebe	1865	CWB 7 391
Griffith, Edward	1867	BHH 8 21
Graves, Madera	1873	BHH 8 343
Grafton, Martin	1874	WSR 9 1
Grenawald, Adam	1876	WSR 9 117
Greme, I. Adaline	1877	WSR 9 158
Griffin, Harriet	1877	WSR 9 163
Green, Amy	1881	WSR 9 290
Grant, John	1888	WSR 10 413
Grafton, John D.	1889	JMM 11 190
Green, Joshua R.	1891	JMM 11 268
Grant, George W.	1896	JMM 11 492
Grafton, Richard M.	1886	GSN 12 45
Grafton, Eliza	1889	GSN 12 86
Green, Lyttleton	1896	GSN 12 115
Grail, Charles	1898	GSN 12 135
Greenland, Martha E.	1899	GSN 12 229
Gross, Jacob	1902	GSN 12 397
Grafton, Corbin	1902	GSN 12 400
Greenland, James	1903	GSN 12 466
Greenway, J. Henry	1903	GSN 12 482
Greenland, William	1903	GSN 12 492
Grafton, Corbin M.	1906	HTB 13 232
Griffith, Prscilla	1905	HTB 13 363
Grafton, William Thomas	1908	HTB 14 38
Grafton, William	1899	HTB 14 60

Grafton, Jno. H.	1902	HTB 14 111
Grafton, Barbara	1900	HTB 14 212
Grant, Margaret	1908	(HTB 14 298
		(HTB 14 323
Greenway, Kate	1904	HTB 14 456
Gross, Luther J.	1914	JA 15 150
Grafton, Nathan	1911	JA 15 156
Grafton, Hulda	1914	JA 15 301
Gross, Margaret	1907	JA 16 28
Gross, Amos L.	1918	JA 16 45
Greenland, Richard E.	1908	JA 16 85
Gross, Jacob	1914	JA 16 164
Green, Helen B.	1907	JA 16 202
Grafton, Basil	1904	JA 16 216
Grafton, Auguste Naomi	1916	JA 16 298
Grafton, Wm. O.	1916	JA 16 467
Greenbaum, Henry	1925	CSW 17 205
Green, Kate F.	1922	CSW 17 251
Grey, David	1908	CSW 17 301
Green, James M.	1926	CSW 17 379
Grevemeyer, Ernest S.	1914	CSW 17 407
Gross, M. Ella	1927	CHR 18 19
Greer, W. C.	1911	CHR 18 73
Grier, John P.	1920	CHR 18 88
Grinnage, William	1925	CHR 18 113
Gray, William H.	1924	CHR 18 218
Gross, William B.	1930	CHR 18 276
Greer, Mary E.	1928	CHR 18 297
Griffin, Robert	1928	CHR 18 381
Grafton, Elizabeth	1908	CHR 18 414
Gross, J. Thomas	1919	CHR 18 446
Gross, Richard	1930	CHR 18 466
Greer, Edwin D.	1931	CHR 18 478
Green, John E.	1930	AJG 19 47
Green, Jane	1916	AJG 19 150
Grail, Chas. Henry	1933	AJG 19 162
Grafton, W. Chas. M.	1925	AJG 19 215
Greenway, Annie S.	1935	AJG 19 377
Grafton, T. Burling	1923	AJG 19 484
Greenland, Ingram	1936	AJG 20 26
Griffith, John A.	1936	AJG 20 226
Galloway, Richard S.	1929	AJG 20 228
Galloway, Anna Louisa	1904	AJG 20 231
Greenway, Wilton	1938	AJG 20 237

Gross, R. Harvey	1911	AJG 21 90
Grier, Mary H.	1931	AJG 21 156
Grafton, Mary J.	1928	AJG 21 222
Griffin, Glenn A.	1942	AJG 21 246
Grafton, Charles N.	1942	AJG 21 438
Grey, Clara V.	1946	RLW 22 67
Greenleaf, R. Walter	1941	AJG 21 417
Grafton, Charles S.	1945	RLW 22 141
Graham, William	1948	RFW 22 415
Gross, Marian H.	1939	RLW 22 423
Gross, Mamie A.	1950	RLW 23 60
Gray, Fannie March	1953	RLW 23 257
Griffith, W. M.	1943	RLW 23 267
Grafton, Elizabeth Rebecca	1943	RLW 23 311
Grubb, Jr., John D.	1955	RLW 23 313
Grafton, Mary Ursula	1948	TLA 24 83
Gray, James K.	1956	TLA 24 122
Grubb, Violet Burd	1953	TLA 24 204
Graybeal, Ida N.	1957	TLA 24 401
Greene, William A.	1947	TLA 24 484
Greer, Laura Oliver	1957	TLA 25 220
Green, Elmer W.	1959	TLA 25 370
Groak, George S.	1951	TLA 25 493

Guyton, John	1783	AJ 2 231
Gudgeon, Sutton	1814	AJ C 623
Guild, Samuel	1821	SR 1 243
Guyton, Elizabeth	1823	SR 1 284
Guyton, Martha	1849	TSB 6 218
Guyton, Edward M.	1860	CWB 7 224
Guyton, James	1868	BHH 8 80
Guyton, Sarah R.	1872	BHH 8 277
Guyton, Robert	1877	WSR 10 63
Gugerty, Patrick	1887	WSR 10 392
Gunther, Emke L.	1893	JMM 11 361
Guy, Ruthie Rachel H.	1915	JA 15 300
Guillott, Eugene F.	1918	JA 16 40
Guilfoyle, Maggie E.	1899	JA 16 197
Guillott, Ella M.	1930	CHR 18 299
Guthoff, Harry A.	1943	RLW 22 432
Guild, Florence White	1945	TLA 24 314
Gunstensperger, Alfred Andrew	1953	TLA 24 370

H

Hall, John	1774	AJ 2 268
Harris, James	1777	AJ 2 273
Hall, Aquila	1779	AJ 2 274
Hall, John of Cranberry	1779	AJ 2 276
Hall, Sophia	1785	AJ 2 280
Hall, Hannah	1782	AJ 2 286
Hall, Cordelia	1782	AJ 2 288
Hawkins, John	1783	AJ 2 292
Hayhurst, James	1783	AJ 2 294
Hall, Barthia	1784	AJ 2 296
Hall, Edward	1788	AJ 2 306
Hay, John	1789	AJ 2 312
Hanson, John	1793	AJ 2 316
Hanson, John	1799	AJ 2 327
Hawkins, Robert	1802	AJ C 77
Hays, William	1802	AJ C 93
Harris, Robert	1802	AJ C 111 A
Hays, John, Sr.	1802	AJ C 131
Hall, John	1804	AJ C 206
Hall, Thomas	1804	AJ C 382
Hall, Thomas	1807	AJ C 245
Hays, Esther	1808	AJ C 421
Hall, James W.	1808	AJ C 429
Hawkins, Matthew	1814	AJ C 707
Hanson, Benjamin	1814	AJ C 726
Hawkins, Nicholas	1814	SR 1 41
Hall, William	1818	SR 1 171
Hanway, David	1820	SR 1 198
Hays, Abraham	1821	SR 1 232
Hall, Benedict Edwd.	1822	SR 1 256
Hanna, William	1823	SR 1 290
Hall, Edward	1827	SR 1 407
Hall, Sarah	1828	SR 1 427
Hall, Isabella	1828	SR 1 451
Hall, Anne M.	1828	SR 1 452
Harper, Samuel	1830	SR 1 492
Hall, Josias	1832	TSB 5 40
Hays, Cynthia	1835	TSB 5 174
Harris, Judy	1837	TSB 5 282

Harmer, Abraham	1837	TSB 5 284
Hardesty, John	1842	TSB 5 588
Harkins, Aaron	1842	TSB 5 610
Hatton, Chaney W.	1845	TSB 6 60
Hall, George J.O.	1845	TSB 6 76
Hawkins, Robert	1847	TSB 6 132
Harryman, Sarah A.	1850	TSB 6 239
Harkins, Joseph	1850	TSB 6 263
Harkins, Sarah	1851	TSB 6 265
Hall, Mary C.	1850	TSB 6 278
Hanna, John	1852	TSB 6 296
Hall, Henry	1854	CWB 7 52
Hamilton, Alexander	1855	CWB 7 57
Hall, John C.C.	1855	CWB 7 62
Hall, Martha P.	1855	CWB 7 81
Harrison, Thomas	1857	CWB 7 134
Harmer, Joshua	1857	CWB 7 154
Harlan, Reuben S.	1858	CWB 7 166
Hanway, Joseph	1861	CWB 7 247
Hays, Thomas A.	1861	CWB 7 256
Hamill, James	1861	CWB 7 247
Hartman, George	1861	CWB 7 264
Harrod, William	1862	CWB 7 275
Hanway, Thomas	1862	CWB 7 288
Hall, James W.	1862	CWB 7 296
Hays, Nathaniel W.S.	1863	CWB 7 308
Harlan, Esther	1864	CWB 7 353
Hall, Martha	1864	CWB 7 353
Hall, John Sydney	1864	CWB 7 355
Harry, Joel	1865	CWB 7 383
Halderman, Jacob F.	1865	CWB 7 394
Hall, George W.	1866	BHH 8 5
Haviland, Asahel	1866	BHH 8 17
Hall, Elizabeth P.	1868	BHH 8 62
Hall, Charlotte Jane	1868	BHH 8 68
Hart, Sarah	1868	BHH 8 71
Harmer, Mary	1868	BHH 8 58
Hall, Jehu	1868	BHH 8 91
Harryman, William W.	1869	BHH 8 140
Hardesty, Mary C.	1869	BHH 8 144
Hall, Aquila	1870	BHH 8 174
Hardesty, Richard C.	1870	BHH 8 188
Hanway, Eleanor	1871	BHH 8 194
Hall, Adeline B.	1872	BHH 8 288

Harry, Joel	1872	BHH 8 302
Hays, Harriet B.	1872	BHH 8 303
Hall, Sophia S.	1873	BHH 8 344
Hall, Ann G.	1873	BHH 8 373
Harrod, Martha	1873	BHH 8 382
Harwood, Samuel	1874	WSR 9 6
Hall, Juliana	1874	WSR 9 17
Hays, Frederick	1876	WSR 9 79
Hanna, William	1878	WSR 9 201
Hamilton, William T.	1879	WSR 9 212
Hamill, Mary	1879	WSR 9 216
Harper, Samuel	1879	WSR 9 228
Hamilton, Alexander	1880	WSR 9 241
Harmer, Catharine A.	1881	WSR 9 319
Hawkins, Frances M.	1881	WSR 9 336
Hanna, Robert N.	1882	WSR 9 345
Hall, Thomas W., Jr.	1884	WSR 10 29
Harry, James	1885	WSR 10 93
Harris, Mary Rebecca	1885	WSR 10 121
Harlan, Elizabeth	1886	WSR 10 263
Hall, Robert	1887	WSR 10 321
Harlan, Henry S.	1885	WSR 10 373
Harlan, Joseph	1887	WSR 10 383
Harper, Hannah	1881	WSR 10 271
Hanson, Thomas	1875	WSR 10 418
Harlan, Abagail A.	1888	JMM 11 4
Harry, Lydia T.	1889	JMM 11 20
Hall, Thomas W.	1880	JMM 11 23
Hawkins, William	1877	JMM 11 179
Hawkins, William	1877	JMM 11 186
Hanway, David	1886	JMM 11 362
Harlan, David	1887	JMM 11 337
Hanna, Mary Jane	1894	JMM 11 484
Hanna, Stephen B.	1883	GSN 12 48
Hall, Caroline A.	1895	GSN 12 76
Harkins, Dr. J.W.	1898	GSN 12 130
Hanway, Mary A.	1894	GSN 12 132
Hanna, John A.	1898	GSN 12 217
Hays, C. Susan	1899	GSN 12 222
Hanlon, John	1899	GSN 12 264
Hamilton, Carvil	1900	GSN 12 270
Harkins, Eveline	1900	GSN 12 296
Hanway, Sarah A.	1901	GSN 12 357
Hawkins, Gilbert S.	1902	GSN 12 415

Harry, David	1903	GSN 12 464
Harlan, Margaret R.	1898	HTB 13 3
Hart, Agnes	1899	HTB 13 61
Harwood, James C.	1897	HTB 13 95
Harris, Mary	1904	HTB 13 116
Hanna, Hannah N.	1895	HTB 13 128
Harkins, William J.	1892	HTB 13 239
Haley, Sara J.	1894	HTB 13 246
Hamby, James W.	1908	HTB 14 13
Hanway, Wm. E.	1909	HTB 14 106
Hanna, Annie M.	1902	HTB 14 220
Harris, John A.	1911	HTB 14 246
Hall, Alverda	1890	HTB 14 248
Harris, Hazzard	1911	HTB 14 253
Harward, W. T.	1911	HTB 14 254
Harkins, Sarah A.	1904	HTB 14 304
Haywood, Belle	1912	HTB 14 340
Hall, John	1912	HTB 14 352
Harvey, Frank	1912	HTB 14 371
Hawkins, Albert T	1896	HTB 14 420
Harkins, Nathan R.	1910	JA 15 24
Harkins, Thomas A.	1914	JA 15 46
Harkins, Joseph A.	1909	JA 15 51
Hamby, Elizabeth	1908	JA 15 175
Hayes, Dennis	1914	JA 15 176
Hall, Joshua	1915	JA 15 199
Harry, Rachael E.	1911	JA 15 245
Hall, Edward H.	1911	JA 15 307
Hall, Aquilla	1897	JA 15 317
Hall, Charlotte Ramsay	1905	JA 15 321
Haviland, John	1911	JA 15 390
Harkins, John W.	1914	JA 15 395
Hayward, Thomas J.	1909	JA 15 435
Harlow, Jas. H.	1902	JA 16 27
Hanway, Martha C.	1909	JA 16 116
Hays, Jacob	1919	JA 16 121
Hays, Geo. Thomas	1919	JA 16 165
Harrison, Ellen	1916	JA 16 229
Hanway, T. Littleton	1915	JA 16 250
Harryman, Victoria B.	1918	JA 16 302
Harward, Laura V.	1919	JA 16 416
Hammond, Martha	1923	CSW 17 51
Hayes, Hutchinson W.	1923	CSW 17 58
Hanway, Joseph B.	1923	CSW 17 70

Hawkins/Harkins, Lurenna	1924	CSW	17	82
Hanway, B. Frank	1924	CSW	17	83
Hatso, Thomas	1924	CSW	17	124
Harris, Sophia K.	1924	CSW	17	150
Harlan, Mabel Patterson	1924	CSW	17	174
Hanway, Harry D.	1919	CSW	17	218
Hawkins, William Amos	1917	CSW	17	231
Harkins, George Edward	1920	CSW	17	247
Haslach, Adam	1919	CSW	17	305
Halloway, Jacob	1917	CSW	17	315
Hammond, William H.		CSW	17	317
Hanna, Florence	1925	CSW	17	340
Hall, Phillips M.	1925	CSW	17	391
Harry, Mary H.	1912	CSW	17	413
Hamilton, Ella D.	1921	CSW	17	457
Harlan, Bessie W.	1921	CSW	17	472
Hanna, Cassie	1927	CSW	17	487
Hanway, Libbie A.	1921	CHR	18	55
Hanna, Frances	1929	CHR	18	155
Harvey, Susan E.	1928	CHR	18	156
Harkins, Harry E.	1926	CHR	18	168
Harper, Ella C.	1910	CSW	17	99
Harper, William W.	1902	CSW	17	103
Harrison, Amos D.	1922	CHR	18	175
Hall, Thos. W. of Edward	1923	CHR	18	198
Hanna, Rose E.	1911	CHR	18	216
Harman, Frank B.	1921	CHR	18	221
Haughay, John	1924	CHR	18	246
Harry, Lyda Anne	1928	CHR	18	331
Harry, John	1928	CHR	18	332
Hand, Winnifred A.	1928	CHR	18	347
Hammond, May D.	1931	CHR	18	444
Harrison, Caroline W.	1928	AJG	19	106
Hanlon, James	1921	AJG	19	108
Harkins, George A.	1933	AJG	19	148
Harrison, E. P. H.	1919	AJG	19	302
Hanway, Hazel Elizabeth	1933	AJG	19	342
Hall, Edward Walter	1924	AJG	19	389
Hall, Margaret A.	1908	AJG	19	412
Harris, Laura Virginia M.	1921	AJG	19	413
Hall, Thos. White	1924	AJG	19	498
Hartzell, Catheran O.	1936	AJG	20	43
Harlan, Wm. Beatty	1929	AJG	20	115
Hall, Edward Jr.	1918	AJG	20	222

Hanson, Herman W.	1932	AJG 20 232
Harward, William D.	1931	AJG 20 286
Harlan, Edwin H.W.	1939	AJG 20 291
Hays, George A.	1936	AJG 20 332
Hall, William A.	1936	AJG 20 333
Harward, Sidney C.	1939	AJG 20 384
Hawkins, Lida Elva	1918	AJG 20 463
Hand, Ira E.	1941	AJG 21 74
Hayward, Samuel D.	1942	AJG 21 154
Hackett, Robley	1936	AJG 21 162
Harlan, Henry D., Judge	1942	AJG 21 201
Hanna, Zenobia	1938	AJG 21 214
Harrison, Samuel R., Jr.	1943	AJG 21 227
Harlan, Ariel Webster	1942	AJG 21 359
Hamilton, Sallie J.	1946	AJG 21 453
Halliday, Sophy S.	1945	RLW 22 2
Hall, Sarah C.	1946	RLW 22 44
Hall, Jane	1937	RLW 22 81
Harlow, J. Hayward	1939	RLW 22 233
Hamby, Ella J.	1937	RLW 22 386
Hall, John T.	1952	RLW 23 99
Hanway, Charles Clifford	1951	RLW 23 148
Harris, Ellin M.	1948	RLW 23 230
Harry, Sr. David G.	1951	RLW 23 369
Haughay, Corene	1955	RLW 23 383
Hanway, R. Percy	1945	RLW 23 387
Hamilton, Stuart Adams	1954	RLW 23 419
Harkins, Thomas L.	1954	RLW 23 411
Harvey, Eleanor E.	1937	RLW 23 470
Harris, Millie Laura Moorman	1934	RLW 23 490
Hamburger, Selina	1953	TLA 24 106
Hands, Constance L.	1957	TLA 24 157
Haslach, Maude E.	1953	TLA 24 162
Harvey, Robert W.	1957	TLA 24 232
Haughay, Alfrida C.W.	1952	TLA 24 233
Harte, James W.	1953	TLA 24 236
Hawkins, Eva	1957	TLA 24 394
Harkins, Helen R.	1958	TLA 24 452
Hammond, Susie S.	1956	WFNP 13 883
Hale, Roy Robert	1943	WFNP 14 272
Hall, Charles	1938	TLA 27 46
Harris, George H.	1958	TLA 27 105

Henderson, Elizabeth	1782	AJ 2	285
Henry, Samuel	1786	AJ 2	300
Henderson, Frances	1804	AJ C	208
Henderson, Philip	1812	AJ C	643
Hendon, Benjamin	1811	SR 1	29
Herbert, Benjamin	1818	SR 1	160
Heaps, Robert	1819	SR 1	178
Herbert, Banjamin	1838	TSB 5	363
Heaps, Archibald	1841	TSB 5	514
Henderson, Jane N.	1841	TSB 5	524
Henderson, John	1846	TSB 6	95
Henderson, George	1847	TSB 6	154
Heaps, John	1852	TSB 6	300
Herbert, Joseph	1852	TSB 6	332
Henderson, Robert T.	1854	CWB 7	43
Henderson, Archibald	1856	CWB 7	107
Herbert, Sophia	1857	CWB 7	129
Henderson, Francis	1862	CWB 7	294
Heaton, John	1867	BHH 8	29
Hendon, Alice P.	1871	BHH 8	196
Herbst, Mina	1873	BHH 8	357
Hendon, Benjamin	1874	WSR 9	7
Hendon, Mary A.	1875	WSR 9	47
Heaps, Rachel K.	1879	WSR 9	210
Heaps, Archibald	1879	WSR 9	220
Heaps, Elijah	1881	WSR 9	309
Henderson, Alice A.	1883	WSR 9	433
Herbert, Nicholas	1882	WSR 10	112
Hener, Henrietta	1885	WSR 10	123
Hergenrother, John M.	1883	WSR 10	127
Henderson, John B.	1885	WSR 10	221
Hess, George	1878	WSR 10	268
Heil, John	1888	JMM 11	21
Herbert, Paulina R.	1889	JMM 11	63
Helmling, Mary Jane	1894	JMM 11	374
Heaps, Rebecca J.	1901	GSN 12	381
Hetrick, Adam	1902	GSN 12	418
Heaps, David H.	1902	GSN 12	427
Heck, S. Catherine	1903	HTB 13	30
Henderson, Archibald S.	1904	HTB 13	98
Heaps, Mary C.	1905	HTB 13	160
Henderson, Thomas	1899	HTB 13	200
Herbst, Louisa M.	1907	HTB 13	373
Herbert, Christopher	1906	HTB 13	494

Henry, Thomas H.	1909	HTB 14 117
Henderson, Rachel A.	1907	HTB 14 131
Henriques, Sarah B.	1901	HTB 14 189
Hemore, Mary J.	1904	HTB 14 211
Henderson, William F.	1904	HTB 14 278
Henderson, J. Wesley	1906	HTB 14 347
Hecht, Isaac	1911	HTB 14 421
Heaps, Hugh T.	1914	JA 15 96
Hergenrother, Joseph A.	1917	JA 15 332
Henderson, Upton B.	1896	JA 15 344
Henderson, Frances A.	1912	JA 16 204
Hess, Charles	1921	JA 16 341
Henson, Augustus	1922	JA 16 390
Heath, Frederic M.	1901	JA 16 417
Heaps, Maggie H.	1923	CSW 17 3
Hener, William W.	1907	CSW 17 374
Hecht, Elizabeth	1925	CHR 18 100
Hellings, Charles J.	1928	CHR 18 296
Heath, Chas. DeVol	1929	AJG 19 1
Hetrick, Janie E.	1925	AJG 19 16
Heine, Frederick	1925	AJG 19 71
Hetrick, Theodore J.	1934	AJG 19 398
Hein, Julius	1936	AJG 19 432
Heaps, I. Wallace	1935	AJG 20 193
Healy, Thomas J.	1936	AJG 20 296
Herrman, James F.	1940	AJG 21 497
Heighe, Robert H.	1946	RLW 22 3
Hecht, Lawrence W.	1940	RLW 22 38
Hebditch, John C.	1944	RLW 22 157
Hecht, Emanuel	1947	RLW 22 311
Heaps, Mary E.	1937	RLW 22 322
Heighe, Anne McElderry	1953	RLW 23 80
Heaps, Osborne H.	1942	RLW 23 84
Heaps, Nelson A.	1941	RLW 23 132
Henry, Carrie	1952	RLW 23 175
Herring, George R.	1919	RLW 23 208
Heaps, Martha Harry	1954	TLA 24 2
Hess, Harry F.	1946	TLA 24 109
Hendrix, Ernest C.	1955	TLA 24 111
Heaps, Newton E.	1946	TLA 24 136
Henning, Frederick	1959	TLA 24 409
Henderson, M. Corinne	1956	WFNP
Hedrick, Elmer T.	1953	TLA 24 481
Henson, Roger S.	1936	TLA 25 388

Herbert, Lillian E.	1952	TLA 26 30
Henderson, Ross C.	1960	TLA 26 565
Hill, Richard	1780	AJ 2 283
Hill, Aaron	1783	AJ 2 290
Hill, William	1783	AJ 2 291
Hitchcock, Asael	1792	AJ 2 314
Hicks, James	1808	AJ C 443
Hill, Thomas	1814	AJ C 741
Hill, John G.	1811	SR 1 14
Hitchcock, William, Jr.	1811	SR 1 16
Hipkins, Charles	1818	SR 1 137
Hill, James, Sr.	1819	SR 1 246
Hill, William R.	1822	SR 1 253
Hitchcock, William	1825	SR 1 330
Hitchcock, Asael	1832	TSB 5 18
Hipkins, Charles G.	1839	TSB 5 391
Hitchcock, Mary	1852	TSB 6 311
Hitchcockm Lysias	1861	CWB 7 262
Hicks, Rebecca	1862	CWB 7 297
Hitchcock, Ann	1872	BHH 8 291
Hine, Elisha S.	1875	WSR 9 37
Hitchcock, Charles B.	1875	WSR 9 51
Hildt, John	1881	WSR 9 313
Hilton, Isaac	1883	WSR 9 431
Hilton, Lloyd	1883	WSR 9 440
Hildt, William	1887	WSR 10 387
Hildt, Jacob	1891	JMM 11 430
Hines, William M.	1895	JMM 11 446
Hitchcock, Mary B.	1898	GSN 12 206
Hitchcock, Jessie	1912	HTB 14 312
Hitchcock, Mary E.	1917	JA 16 46
Hilditch, William T.	1927	CHR 18 109
Hilditch, Margaret Elizabeth	1924	CHR 18 475
Hildt, Philip I.	1932	AJG 19 28
Hirtriter (sometimes Herterter)		
Emma	1932	AJG 19 318
Hill, Melissa	1934	AJG 19 338
Hines, Mary E.	1920	AJG 21 263
Hildebrand, Harner H.	1943	AJG 21 333
Himes, Sr. W. Robert	1945	AJG 21 440
Hill, Warner L.	1943	RLW 22 70

Higgins, Ettie M.	1948	RLW 22 214
Hillcoat, Robert W.	1948	RLW 22 225
Hirshauer, Frances	1958	TLA 25 243
Hitchcock, M. Clyde	1959	TLA 25 357
Hollis, William	1786	AJ 2 301
Hopkins, Joseph	1784	AJ 2 298
Horney, Thomas	1787	AJ 2 303
Hollis, Amos	1789	AJ 2 311
Hopkins, William	1789	AJ 2 305
Hopkins, Gerrard	1789	AJ 2 313
Hopkins, Joseph	1795	AJ 2 318
Hopkins, Elizabeth	1795	AJ 2 321
Hopkins, Rachel	1795	AJ 2 321
Holland, Frances	1795	AJ 2 324
Horner, Jane	1798	AJ 2 325
Hopkins, Charles	1803	AJ C 101
Howard, Thomas G.	1806	AJ C 157
Horner, James	1808	AJ C 432
Howard, Leonard	1809	AJ C 471
Holtham, Elizabeth	1810	AJ C 497
Howlett, Andrew	1810	AJ C 503
Hope, Thomas	1811	SR 1 24
Hopkins, Samuel	1811	SR 1 76
Hope, Richard	1816	SR 1 109
Hollis, Clark of Wm.	1819	SR 1 180
Howlett, James	1819	SR 1 188
Hogstin, James	1822	SR 1 250
Howe, John	1822	SR 1 264
Hollis, William	1824	SR 1 294
Hollis, Amos	1824	SR 1 306
Hoopers, Ruth	1824	SR 1 392
Hoke, Peter	1829	SR 1 473
Hope, James	1830	SR 1 495
Hopkins, Samuel	1830	SR 1 521
Howlett, John	1832	TSB 5 61
Hope, Hannah	1832	TSB 5 84
Hollingsworth, Nathaniel	1834	TSB 5 142
Hopkins, Samuel	1839	TSB 5 396
Hoopman, Peter	1840	TSB 5 430
Holly, Sarah	1840	TSB 5 444
Hoskins, Nathaniel	1840	TSB 5 446

71

Hoskins, Edith	1840	TSB	5	498
Hopkins, Samuel	1842	TSB	5	585
Hopkins, Rachel	1848	TSB	6	167
Hopkins, Hannah P.	1848	TSB	6	188
Hopkins, Ephraim G.	1849	TSB	6	220
Hopkins, Joseph	1849	TSB	6	231
Hopkins, Richard	1854	CWB	7	44
Howard, Edward A.	1854	CWB	7	47
Howe, James	1857	CWB	7	163
Holloway, Charles C.	1860	CWB	7	221
Howe, Thomas	1860	CWB	7	222
Hobbes, Lawson	1863	CWB	7	314
Hollingsworth, Robert	1863	CWB	7	323
Holland, Sybil	1863	CWB	7	327
Hooper, Benjamin	1862	CWB	7	280
Hopkins, Joshua	1863	CWB	7	317
Horton, Lewis	1864	CWB	7	335
Hopkins, William of Saml.	1866	CWB	7	404
Holland, Robert W.	1866	BHH	8	3
Howlett, Andrew J.	1867	BHH	8	32
Howard, Thomas G.	1867	BHH	8	37
Holloway, Elizabeth	1868	BHH	8	73
Hopkins, John	1870	BHH	8	172
Hoopes, Charles	1870	BHH	8	187
Howlett, John S.	1874	WSR	9	12
Hollingsworth, John	1874	WSR	9	20
Hollis, Jarrett	1874	WSR	9	22
Holloway, William	1875	WSR	9	48
Hoke, Jacob	1876	WSR	9	73
Hoke, Ann B.	1876	WSR	9	75
Hoskins, Elizabeth	1876	WSR	9	76
Hope, Thomas	1876	WSR	9	108
Holland, Eliza C.	1878	WSR	9	170
Hopkins, Eliza C.	1879	WSR	9	234
Hoopes, Thomas	1880	WSR	9	302
Hopkins, Margaret H.	1881	WSR	9	317
Hooker, Hannah W.	1882	WSR	9	353
Hope, Joshua H.	1883	WSR	9	390
Hoopes, Pascul I.	1883	WSR	9	392
Holland, Miranda	1883	WSR	9	395
Holloway, John B.	1883	WSR	9	410
Hollingsworth, Amos	1882	WSR	10	24
Hopkins, Richard	1884	WSR	10	73
Horn, Adam	1884	WSR	10	113

Hopkins, Hannah R.	1880	WSR 10 115
Hollingsworth, Rachel	1886	WSR 10 188
Howard, Amanda Z.	1886	WSR 10 248
Hollingsworth, Abigail	1880	WSR 10 279
Howlett, A. H.	1886	WSR 10 287
Hopkins, Elizabeth	1886	WSR 10 292
Hoskins, Cheyney	1884	WSR 10 313
Hopkins, Charles W.	1887	WSR 10 331
Hollis, Annie	1888	WSR 10 465
Holloway, Richard	1889	JMM 11 58
Hooper, Affie	1885	JMM 11 331
Hollahan, John	1893	JMM 11 347
Howard, Margaret M.	1881	JMM 11 352
Hoke, Fanny	1891	JMM 11 447
Howard, Patrick	1893	JMM 11 458
Hopkins, Eliza	1890	JMM 11 463
Hopkins, Eliza Ann	1891	GSN 12 41
Hollingsworth, Hanna C.	1897	GSN 12 120
Hollingsworth, Nathaniel T.	1884	GSN 12 183
Hopkins, Wilson W.	1899	GSN 12 266
Horn, Charlotte H. S.	1900	GSN 12 311
Hobbs, Eliza J.	1900	GSN 12 325
Hollingsworth, Silas W.	1902	GSN 12 426
Hollingsworth, Lois P.	1903	GSN 12 476
Hopkins, Mary Ann	1889	HTB 13 20
Holloway, George W.	1900	HTB 13 99
Holland, James W.	1901	HTB 13 111
Hope, William	1904	HTB 13 224
Hollingsworth, Lydia	1906	HTB 13 304
Hoopes, Morris C.	1908	HTB 13 382
Holloway, Eliza D.	1906	HTB 13 395
Hood, Catherine A.	1901	HTB 13 414
Hollohan, Mary	1909	HTB 14 36
Homer, Vincent	1893	HTB 14 328
Hopkins, Ephraim	1912	HTB 14 335
Hopkins, Thomas C.	1912	HTB 14 364
Hopkins, Edward C.	1913	JA 15 15
Holloway, James H.	1908	JA 15 27
Hopkins, Samuel W.	1911	JA 15 104
Hopkins, Amanda W.	1912	JA 15 213
Hoskins, Margaret	1913	JA 15 229
Hopkins, William J.	1912	JA 15 243
Holloway, Iris	1912	JA 15 342
Hopkins, Rebecca W.	1901	JA 15 381

Horner, Charles C.	1910	JA 15	419
Hollingsworth, Edward	1893	JA 15	469
Holloway, Sarah Ann	1907	JA 15	479
Hopkins, Ellen E.	1901	JA 16	151
Holloway, Wm. R.	1911	JA 16	160
Hooker, John W.	1915	JA 16	189
Hollohan, Patrick W.	1920	JA 16	297
Hooper, John W.	1909	JA 16	318
Hopkins, Rachel Morris	1921	JA 16	325
Hooker, Catherine M.	1921	JA 16	376
Hopkins, J. Thomas	1905	JA 16	428
Hollingsworth, Rebecca G.	1915	JA 16	430
Hoopes, Joseph T.	1923	CSW 17	10
Hollingsworth, Eliza	1923	CSW 17	48
Holly, Irene E.	1923	CSW 17	69
Howlett, William S.	1924	CSW 17	115
Holland, Susan G.	1924	CSW 17	131
Hoopes, Mary A.	1924	CSW 17	137
Hopkins, Alan L.	1925	CSW 17	240
Holly, Wm. W.	1924	CSW 17	339
Hopkins, Johns & Jane E.	1915	CSW 17	342
Holly, John	1891	CSW 17	387
Hopkins, Annie C.	1920	CSW 17	388
Holly, John W.	1924	CSW 17	420
Holloway, Catherine M.	1927	CHR 18	6
Hopper, Katherine V.	1921	CHR 18	12
Hollingsworth, Lewis E.	1928	CHR 18	114
Hollingsworth, Rebecca	1926	CHR 18	164
Hoffman, Leon	1908	CHR 18	240
Holloway, Samuel S.	1925	CHR 18	242
Horn, Annie C.	1926	CHR 18	302
Howard, Rebecca N.	1908	CHR 18	360
Hoover, George W.	1918	CHR 18	416
Howard, L. Lee	1919	CHR 18	437
Hopkins, J. Lee	1925	CHR 18	482
Hoffman, Chas. A.	1928	AJG 19	170
Hopkins, Elizabeth	1930	AJG 19	190
Howlett, Ellie F.	1933	AJG 19	281
Hoffman, Abraham	1932	AJG 19	291
Holly, James T.	1933	AJG 19	315
Howard, Annie R.	1931	AJG 19	345
Horner, John	1926	AJG 20	42
Hopkins, W. Wylie	1920	AJG 20	123
Hopkins, Hannah R.	1933	AJG 20	124

Hoover, George W.	1918	AJG 20 130
Howard, Clarence M.	1928	AJG 20 198
Holland, E. Stanley	1933	AJG 20 379
Hoopes, Russell	1936	AJG 21 77
Hoffman, Sallie R.	1941	AJG 21 170
Hochstrasser, Morgan T.	1941	AJG 21 176
Holloway, Harry C.	1944	AJG 21 364
Hornberger, Charles E.	1945	AJG 21 400
Hoffman, Jennie Leota	1946	RLW 22 86
Hopkins, Thomas C.	1944	RLW 22 94
Hooper, Miriam	1943	RLW 22 170
Hollahan, Katherine J.	1941	RLW 22 268
Holland, George R.	1950	RLW 22 405
Hoopes, Wilmer P.	1944	RLW 22 461
Hornberger, Laura E.	1951	RLW 23 8
Hopkins, J. Fletcher	1953	RLW 23 108
Howard, Pearl B.	1953	RLW 23 183
Hoffman, Sophia	1950	RLW 23 196
Hopkins, William D.	1954	RLW 23 202
Houck, Eli H. J.	1937	RLW 23 357
Hoeter, Theresa M.	1948	TLA 24 153
Holly, Nettie E.	1955	TLA 24 269
Hopkins, John W.	1938	TLA 24 356
Hollister, Susan P.	1952	TLA 25 73
Hollander, Louis D.	1955	TLA 25 297
Hopkins, Norman E.	1956	TLA 25 332
Hoffman, Katheryn Ryan	1960	TLA 25 345
Hopkins, Jennie M.	1955	WFNP 13 843
Hopkins, J. Stephenson	1952	TLA 26 154
Houck, Mamie C.	1959	TLA 26 451

Hutchinson, James	1780	AJ 2 282
Hughes, William	1794	AJ 2 271
Hughes, Charles	1789	AJ 2 309
Hughston, John	1784	AJ 2 331
Hughes, John H.	1802	AJ C 101
Huskins, Thomas	1805	AJ C 270
Hughes, John	1805	AJ C 286
Hunter, William	1823	SR 1 286
Hughes, Aram	1823	SR 1 292
Hutchins, Richard	1826	SR 1 376
Husbands, Elizabeth	1825	SR 1 405

Hutchinson, David E.	1943	AJG 21 401
Hughes, A. Verdie	1943	AJG 21 405
Hughes, Anna M.	1941	RLW 22 146
Huber, Raymond O.	1948	RLW 22 265
Hulshart, William E.	1949	RLW 22 287
Hulshart, Henrietta	1939	RLW 22 479
Hutner, Aaron J.	1947	RLW 23 73
Hughes, Ellen J.	1954	RLW 23 157
Hughes, Belle Hunter	1947	RLW 23 327
Huff, Mary T.	1925	TLA 24 150
Hutchinson, Morton Clement, Jr.	1959	TLA 24 320
Hutson, William Henry	1954	WFNP 14 051
Hyne, Otto Walter	1949	TLA 25 420

I

Iddings, Arthur	1950	TLA 24 81
Iley, Jacob C.	1867	BHH 8 19
Ingram, John	1841	TSB 5 539
Ingalhart, Michael	1852	TSB 6 317
Ingram, Elizabeth	1856	CWB 7 118
Ingman, Mary	1885	WSR 10 135
Irwin, Michael	1859	CWB 7 191
Irwin, Ava E.	1924	CSW 17 429
Irwin, Dellia A.	1927	CSW 17 471
Isennock, Victorine	1949	RLW 23 482
Ivins, George H.	1911	JA 15 272
Ivins, Harry O.	1941	RLW 22 191

J

Jamison, William	1774	AJ 2 335
Jarrett, Abraham	1776	AJ 2 340
James, Richard	1777	AJ 2 344
James, Mary	1778	AJ 2 345
James, Walter	1782	AJ 2 354
James, John	1792	AJ 2 360
Jarrett, Eli	1794	AJ 2 364
Jay, Stephen	1796	AJ 2 368
Jarrett, Elizabeth	1825	SR 1 358
James, Aaron	1840	TSB 5 487
James, Frederick	1843	TSB 6 15
James, Joseph	1859	CWB 7 189
Jacobs, Hetty S.	1861	CWB 7 267
James, Santy	1864	CWB 7 360
Jarrett, Archer H.	1869	BHH 8 124
James, Jacob	1876	WSR 9 72
Jarrett, Jesse B.	1881	WSR 9 274
Jarrett, Sarah H.	1880	WSR 9 244
James, Samuel	1881	WSR 9 329
James, Joseph	1883	WSR 9 454
Jarrett, Abraham	1882	WSR 10 46
James, John M.	1884	WSR 10 68
Jarrett, Joseph	1886	WSR 10 212
Janney, Johns H.	1888	JMM 11 19
James, Mary R.	1889	JMM 11 56
Jackson, Henry	1890	JMM 11 154
Jay, Martha W.	1891	JMM 11 252
Jay, Sarah	1891	JMM 11 252
Jay, John	1890	JMM 11 261
Jarrett, Julia A.	1896	GSN 12 1
James, John A.	1896	GSN 12 42
Jarvis, Wm. Josiah	1899	GSN 12 265
Jackson, Eliza M.	1897	HTB 13 58
Jarrett, Joshua W.	1905	HTN 13 155
Jacobs, Georgie	1906	HTB 14 96
James, Abraham	1909	HTB 14 150
James, Lemuel C.	1914	JA 15 87
Jacobs, Rosa S.	1894	JA 15 90
James, Charles Henry	1911	JA 15 203

Jacobs, Eva A.	1915	JA 16 77
Jarrett, Martin L.	1915	JA 16 206
Jarrett, Mary V.	1918	JA 16 472
Jarrett, William H.	1924	CSW 17 106
James, William H.	1924	CSW 17 107
Jasper, Richard T.	1924	CSW 17 135
James, Samuel S.	1927	CHR 18 82
Jackson, Isaac	1913	CHR 8 217
James, Alverda H.	1923	CHR 18 279
Jackson, William	1932	AJG 19 54
James, Mary V.	1931	AJG 19 77
Jackson, Charles E.	1930	AJG 20 133
Jackson, Ida Watters	1928	AJG 20 247
Jacobs, Elizabeth S.	1939	AJG 20 262
Jackson, John	1936	AJG 20 343
Jacobs, Wm. F.	1936	AJG 20 348
Jamison, Frances	1931	AJG 20 473
Jamison, Mabel A.	1941	AJG 21 41
Jacobs, Susie M.	1937 & 1944	AJG 21 345
James, Paul C.	1937	AJG 21 456
James, George Willis	1947	RLW 22 43
James, J. C. Hagey	1947	RLW 22 61
Jastram, George Berlin	1947	RLW 22 75
James, George B.	1947	RLW 22 196
Jameson, Samuel Melvin	1947	RLW 22 337
James, C. Harry	1951	RLW 23 54
James, Harry R.	1959	TLA 24 397
Jackson, Lula I.	1956	TLA 26 317
Jaeger, Paul	1956	TLA 26 399
Jeffrey, Martha	1776	AJ 2 338
Jeffrey, Robert	1782	AJ 2 356
Jenkins, C. John	1784	AJ 2 357
Jeffery, Thomas	1833	TSB 5 58
Jewel, George	1820	SR 1 215
Jewett, John	1854	CWB 7 24
Jeffery, Wm. Mc.	1883	WSR 9 389
Jewens, William	1883	WSR 9 402
Jenkins, John W.	1883	WSR 9 412
Jeffrey, William V.	1883	WSR 10 40
Jeffrey, James	1874	WSR 10 225
Jennings, John	1871	WSR 10 409

Jewens, William E.	1895	JMM 11 466
Jewett, Hugh J.	1898	GSN 12 152
Jenkins, Henry C.	1899	GSN 12 237
Jeffrey, Jane A.	1902	GSN 12 445
Jenkins, Samuel Oliver	1910	HTB 14 175
Jewett, George M.	1915	JA 15 165
Jeffrey, Martha J.	1916	JA 15 295
Jeffery, William G.	1917	JA 16 100
Jeffery, Hortense R.	1911	JA 16 110
Jefferson, John W.	1924	
Jewett, Hugh J.	1926	CSW 17 312
Jenkins, J. Hillen	1916	AJG 19 232
Jewens, William A.	1922	AJG 19 350
Jenkins, Rebecca H.	1928	AJG 19 474
Jewens, Sallie D.	1939	AJG 20 260
Jeffery, Mary I.	1940	AJG 21 206
Jewell, Arthur E.	1937	AJG 21 426
Jeffers, Lena	1929	RLW 22 34
Jeffers, Sarah Rebecca	1915	RLW 22 76
Jeffery, Charles Wesley	1944	RLW 22 172
Jessop, Richard Owings	1960	TLA 25 156
Jersey, Albert	1931	TLA 25 289
Jibb, John	1807	AJ C 230
Jirsa, Albert	1914	JA 15 66
Johnson, John	1774	AJ 2 333
Johnson, Alice	1775	AJ 2 336
Jones, Joseph	1778	AJ 2 346
Johns, Richard	1780	AJ 2 348
Jones, John	1780	AJ 2 348
Jolley, John	1781	AJ 2 350
Johnson, Joseph	1781	AJ 2 352
Johnson, Archibald	1785	AJ 2 359
Johnston, Mary	1793	AJ 2 362
Jones, Benjamin	1794	AJ 2 363
Johnson, Moses	1796	AJ 2 366
Johns, Mary	1806	AJ C 314
Johnson, Thomas	1807	AJ C 347
Jones, William	1807	AJ C 367

Johns, Henry	1807	AJ C 391
Johnson, Barnett	1812	AJ C 603
Johnson, Elizabeth	1820	SR 1 205
Jolley, Edward	1822	SR 1 265
Johnson, Caleb	1823	SR 1 280
Jones, Aquila	1824	SR 1 297
Jones, Amos	1827	SR 1 416
Johnson, Martha	1842	TSB 5 575
Johns, Francis	1844	TSB 6 48
Jones, Daniel	1848	TSB 6 173
Johnson, James	1848	TSB 6 203
Johnson, Elizabeth	1849	TSB 6 230
Jordan, Sophia	1849	TSB 6 233
Jones, Stephen	1852	TSB 6 299
Jordan, Mary	1852	TSB 6 313
Jones, Ezekiel	1855	CWB 7 92
Jones, James	1860	CWB 7 225
Johnson, Aaron	1863	CWB 7 310
Johnson, William	1864	CWB 7 339
Jones, Hugh	1864	CWB 7 340
Johnson, Joel	1864	CWB 7 357
Jones, Priscilla C.	1864	CWB 7 359
Jones, Elias N.	1865	CWB 7 396
Jones, Benjamin H.	1868	BHH 8 86
Johnson, Jacob	1868	BHH 8 104
Jones, William	1869	BHH 8 127
Johnson, Elizabeth	1869	BHH 8 142
Jones, Jane J.	1872	BHH 8 305
Johnson, Sarah A.	1871	BHH 8 234
Johnson, Sarah	1872	BHH 8 286
Johnson, Caroline	1873	BHH 8 315
Jones, Susan H.	1875	WSR 9 56
Johnson, Leonard	1876	WSR 9 111
Jones, Ambler	1878	WSR 9 196
Jones, Aquila	1878	WSR 9 199
Johnson, Michael G.	1880	WSR 9 253
Johnson, Caroline	1880	WSR 9 238
Jones, Thomas W.	1880	WSR 9 268
Jones, Henry	1881	WSR 9 305
Johnson, Ruth S.	1883	WSR 9 453
Jones, Elizabeth	1872	WSR 10 82
Jones, Bradford A.	1885	WSR 10 140
Jones, Mary E.	1885	WSR 10 184
Johnson, Jane	1885	WSR 10 138

Jones, James C.	1887	WSR 10 312
Johnson, Francis J.	1888	WSR 10 399
Johnson, John W.	1889	JMM 11 67
Johnson, Benjamin	1889	JMM 11 76
Johnson, Robert	1892	JMM 11 251
Jones, Jno. Fletcher	1889	JMM 11 126
Jones, Eliza	1890	JMM 11 144
Johnson, James	1892	JMM 11 258
Jones, Joseph	1892	JMM 11 281
Jones, James W.	1877	JMM 11 297
Johnson, Martha	1882	JMM 11 310
Johnson, George A.	1892	JMM 11 351
Jones, Ebenezer	1889	JMM 11 421
Jones, Nancy	1890	GSN 12 124
Jones, William H.	1897	GSN 12 151
Johnson, George W.	1899	GSN 12 240
Jones, Rebecca J.	1899	GSN 12 247
Jones, John	1899	GSN 12 261
Johnson, Ann	1900	GSN 12 298
Jones, Jane R.	1902	GSN 12 405
Jones, Susanna B.	1902	GSN 12 452
Johnson, Shadrach	1903	HTB 13 25
Jones, Robert	1901	HTB 13 35
Jones, Jennie		HTB 13 132
Johnson, Esther	1896	HTB 13 166
Jones, Rachel Ann	1896	HTB 13 179
Jones, Martha J.	1901	HTB 13 220
Jones, Sarah R.	1902	HTB 13 319
Johnson, Thomas	1906	HTB 13 351
Jones, Ellen	1908	HTB 13 384
Jones, Daniel W.	1908	HTB 14 78
Jones, Hugh W.	1911	HTB 14 215
Jones, Austin	1898	HTB 14 388
Jones, Miss Georgianna	1913	HTB 14 418
Jones, J. Amos	1891	HTB 14 471
Johnson, Elisha	1911	JA 15 219
Jones, Foulk	1903	JA 15 280
Jones, Mary D.	1906	JA 16 97
Johnigan, Benjamin	1919	JA 16 180
Jones, Alfred T.	1917	JA 16 244
Johnson, George W.	1921	JA 16 378
Johnson, Uretta E.	1921	JA 16 410
Jones, James T.	1915	JA 16 493
Jordan, Catharine Hooper	1923	CSW 17 23

Johnson, William T.	1922	CSW 17 220
Johnson, James T.	1912	CSW 17 229
Johnson, Jacob	1922	CSW 17 271
Joesting, Henry	1905	CSW 17 498
Johnson, James Locher	1909	CSW 17 466
Jones, Andrew J.	1930	CHR 18 248
Jones, Christie Ann	1929	CHR 18 448
Johnson, Sophia	1933	AJG 19 181
Johnson, Mary Louisa	1926	AJG 19 372
Jourdan, Martha J.	1922	AJG 19 422
Johnson, W. Elmer	1940	AJG 20 467
Jones, Isaac O.	1940	AJG 21 17
Jones, Wm. Henry	1943	AJG 21 239
Johnson, Alice R.		AJG 21 437
Johnson, Henry A.	1924	RLW 22 33
Johnson, A. James	1946	RLW 22 72
Jorett, Philip	1949	RLW 22 152
Jones, Sallie	1944	RLW 22 254
Johnson, William W.	1928	RLW 22 258
Jones, Frederick C.	1944	RLW 22 376
Jones, Myrtle	1941	RLW 22 410
Jones, John W.	1929	RLW 22 466
Josenhans, Catherine	1934	RLW 23 152
Jobes, Alice A.	1955	RLW 23 281
Johnson, Charles W.	1947	RLW 23 398
Jourdan, Bernard G.S.	1954	RLW 23 474
Jones, B. Elizabeth	1955	RLW 23 479
Johnson, Stella B.	1950	TLA 24 101
Johnson, Annie Carty	1957	TLA 24 202
Jobes, Mary E.	1955	filed not prob.
Johnson, Joseph G.	1940	TLA 24 437
Jones, Allie Osborne	1957	TLA 25 233
Joesting, William	1960	TLA 25 398
Joseph, June L.	1959	TLA 26 100
Johnson, James Arthur	1956	TLA 26 255
Johnson, Robert J.	1950	TLA 26 300
Judd, John	1873	BHH 8 324
Judd, Maria Louisa	1899	GSN 12 225

K

Kathcart, Joseph	1818	SR 1 144
Kain, Edward	1833	TSB 5 96
Kane, John	1903	HTB 14 13
Kane, Margaret	1908	HTB 14 341
Kalmbacker, George	1913	HTB 14 485
Kalb, Conrad H.	1931	CHR 18 315
Kammerer, Charles H.	1906	CHR 18 319
Kammerer, Mary E.	1931	CHR 18 438
Kalb, Mary E.	1934	AJG 21 366
Kalal, Barbara	1940	AJG 21 379
Kahoe, Rose Lee	1931	RLW 22 153

Kennedy, Robert	1783	AJ 2 373
Kell, Thomas	1790	AJ 2 376
Kelly, Alexander	1794	AJ 2 379
Kennedy, James	1811	AJ C 576
Kell, Alesanna	1814	AJ C 759
Kennedy, John	1815	SR 1 4
Kent, Jessie	1815	SR 1 52
Kemble, John	1831	SR 1 545
Kerr, Robert	1832	TSB 5 25
Kelly, Michael	1834	TSB 5 153
Kent, John	1840	TSB 5 464
Kennard, Mathew	1846	TSB 6 112
Keen, Timothy	1848	TSB 6 158
Kean, John	1859	CWB 7 197
Kennedy, John	1860	CWB 7 234
Kennedy, James	1860	CWB 7 238
Keen, Aquila D.	1861	CWB 7 250
Keech, John R.	1862	CWB 7 271
Keen, George B.	1865	CWB 7 378
Keithley, John	1868	BHH 8 96
Kean, James	1871	BHH 8 218
Keithley, Edward F.	1872	BHH 8 281
Kent, Ann	1873	BHH 8 322
Keech, Susan P.	1875	WSR 9 32

Keathley, Jonathan	1880	WSR	9	250
Kelly, Mary	1881	WSR	9	290
Kent, Elizabeth B.	1881	WSR	9	297
Kennedy, William	1877	WSR	10	27
Kellogg, Ebenezer H.	1880	WSR	10	187
Kennedy, Thomas	1886	WSR	10	189
Kean, Chloe	1870	WSR	10	257
Kennard, Howard	1878	WSR	10	426
Kenley, Lewis	1887	JMM	11	54
Kenley, Lelia M.	1892	JMM	11	240
Kenny, Mary A.	1890	JMM	11	176
Keuchel/Kenchel, Anthony	1890	JMM	11	183
Kennedy, Silas	1889	JMM	11	238
Kennard, Catherine	1887	JMM	11	265
Kenley, George W.	1890	JMM	11	271
Kessler, Henry	1890	JMM	11	341
Kearney, Bridget	1893	JMM	11	360
Kelly, William J.	1890	JMM	11	409
Kell, Robert	1895	JMM	11	486
Kenley, Louisa Rebecca	1895	GSN	12	59
Kelly, Matilda	1900	GSN	12	288
Kent, Grier B.	1900	GSN	12	322
Kennedy, John T.	1901	GSN	12	351
Kelly, James	1890	HTB	13	15
Keith, John H.	1903	HTB	13	23
Keith, Mary	1903	HTB	13	48
Kelly, Alice	1904	HTB	13	221
Kearney, Francis	1900	HTB	13	228
Kelly, Julia M.	1899	HTB	13	266
Kennedy, Eliza E.	1899	HTB	14	208
Kenney, Catharine T.	1911	HTB	14	240
Kelly, Catharine Keough	1907	HTB	14	351
Kenny, James A.	1913	HTB	14	470
Keighler, Rosa Neilson	1911	HTB	14	481
Keane, Ellen	1912	JA	15	85
Kennedy, Johns	1910	JA	15	232
Kelley, Thomas J.	1917	JA	15	356
Kelly, Richard	1913	JA	15	485
Kelley, John L.	1917	JA	10	84
Keatley, Clifton G.	1920	JA	16	226
Kennedy, Wm.	1920	JA	16	232
Kell, Geo. E.	1921	JA	16	336
Keen, Lycurgus	1923	JA	16	489
Kennedy, Elmira	1924	CSW	17	182

HARFORD COUNTY, 1774-1960

Name	Year	Reference
Kennedy, Rosa M.	1930	CHR 18 325
Keithley, Emily F.	1930	CHR 18 382
Kellogg, Mary	1918	CHR 18 486
Kenly, Emma Bay	1928	AJG 19 67
Kennedy, Samuel L.	1923	AJG 19 163
Kennedy, Annie V.	1933	AJG 19 321
Kelly, Elizabeth B.	1935	AJG 19 417
Kelly, James M.	1928	AJG 19 418
Kennedy, Thomas A.	1916	AJG 19 486
Kendle, Mary Ellen	1932	AJG 20 152
Kenyon, Clara V.	1936	AJG 20 243
Keller, George C.	1942	AJG 21 264
Kelly, Mary Jane	1942	AJG 21 335
Kent, Alice Catherine	1918	RLW 22 132
Kelsey, Stella B.	1928	RLW 22 117
Kelly, William J.	1951	RLW 23 338
Keech, Betty Wharton	1954	RLW 23 462
Kennedy, Clara Owens	1948	TLA 24 116
Kell, Susan Elizabeth	1956	TLA 24 313
Kelly, Louise M.	1955	TLA 24 455
Kent, Robert Harrington	1958	TLA 25 188
Kelly, Andrew P.	1950	TLA 26 366
Kelly, William Norment		WFNP 14 232
Kimble, James	1780	AJ 2 369
Kidd, John	1782	AJ 2 371
Kimble, Stephen	1784	AJ 2 371
Kitely, Rachel	1799	AJ 2 381
Kimberly, John	1806	AJ C 339
Kirkwood, Robert	1810	AJ C 500
Kirkwood, Robert	1829	SR 1 494
Kimble, Stephen	1834	TSB 5 121
Kirkwood, Robert	1843	TSB 6 2
Kinsey, Seth	1852	TSB 6 314
King, Jane	1856	CWB 7 99
King, Thomas	1883	WSR 10 41
Kirkwood, Richard H.	1886	WSR 10 270
Kilgore, Mary	1887	WSR 10 359
Kimble, Alfred W.	1892	JMM 11 373
Kirk, Jacob	1894	JMM 11 379
Kirk, George W.	1895	GSN 12 15
Kimes, Rachel A.	1908	HTB 13 380

Kieferle, Frederick A.	1908	HTB 13 405
King, Martha E.	1908	HTB 14 113
Kilroy, Patrick	1909	HTB 14 288
Kirk, Samuel J.	1908	HTB 14 438
Kirk, J. Hall	1913	HTB 14 466
King, William H.	1914	JA 15 93
Kieffer, Edwin H.	1904	JA 15 274
Kirkwood, James H.	1904	JA 16 144
Kinhart, Catherine	1920	JA 16 347
Kirk, Mary E.	1919	JA 16 368
Killingsworth, Annie P.	1923	JA 16 468
Kirk, Elijah	1922	JA 16 492
Kielty, Maria	1927	CSW 17 479
Kirk, Susie Jane	1929	CHR 18 138
Kimble, Robert E.	1926	CHR 18 159
Kirk, Walter B.	1932	AJG 19 185
Kissick, Daniel	1935	AJG 20 58
Kirkland, Elizabeth Green	1930	AJG 20 493
King, Phoebe	1918	AJG 21 306
King, William A.	1948	RLW 22 144
Kinhart, Fannie O.	1943	RLW 22 320
Kinnamon, Ella May	1949	RLW 22 488
Kilby, Roby	1950	RLW 23 119
King, Mary A.	1953	RLW 23 283
Kirkwood, Stuart R.	1953	TLA 25 20
Kirby, Wilton G.	1960	TLA 25 129
Kinhart, Dora Jane	1958	TLA 26 333
King, Maude E. & Frank B. Sr.	1943	TLA 27 5

Klinefelter, Peter	1838	TSB 5 149
Klemper, Belle	1918	JA 16 58
Klair, Edwin H.	1923	CHR 18 287
Klair, Louis H.	1929	RLW 22 494
Klair, Cora B.	1953	RLW 23 227
Klitch, Eleanor G.	1934	TLA 24 381
Klein, Wm. Charles, Jr.	1960	WFNP 14 303

Knox, Eving	1833	TSB 5 102
Knight, Aquila	1835	TSB 5 164
Knight, Thomas	1848	TSB 6 190
Knight, John W.	1849	TSB 6 219

Knight, Sarah	1854	CWB 7 48
Knopp, Joseph	1860	CWB 7 225
Knight, John B.	1865	CWB 7 397
Knopp, Elizabeth	1875	WSR 9 122
Knight, William	1897	GSN 12 138
Knofler, August	1905	HTB 14 136
Knight, Cora Alverda	1918	JA 16 93
Knight, Wm. H.	1922	JA 16 425
Knight, John W.	1926	CHR 18 79
Knight, Oliver	1923	CHR 18 449
Knight, Juliet S.	1928	AJG 19 477
Knopp, George W.	1937	AJG 20 38
Kirkland, Elizabeth Green	1930	AJG 20 493
Knight, Elsie Smith	1942	RLW 22 77
Knopp, Joseph Enos	1933	RLW 22 122
Knight, Thomas W.	1932	RLW 23 42
Knight, William G.	1950	RLW 23 271
Knight, Ralph O.	1959	TLA 24 374
Knopp, Christopher	1931	TLA 26 641
Knapp, Pearl Fern	1951	TLA 27 61

Koomes, Nathaniel	1840	TSB 5 459
Kolk, Geo. Adam	1856	CWB 7 98
Kolk, Gotfried	1877	WSR 9 144
Koenigswald, Frank	1912	JA 15 39
Kotras, Cyrill	1956	WFNP
Kohlbus, William Henry	1958	WFNP
Kotras, Cyrill	1956	TLA 25 411
Kowadla, Harry	1956	WFNP 14 301

Kruson, Nicholas	1786	AJ 2 374
Kroeson, Derrick	1818	SR 1 185
Kreag, Frederick	1887	WSR 10 349
Krouse, Conrad	1905	HTB 13 180
Kraft, Regina	1914	JA 15 220
Kropff, John Owen	1939	AJG 20 346
Krapiunik, Frank	1948	RLW 23 377
Knapp, Leonard, Sr.	1952	RLW 23 414
Kroh, George W.	1945	RLW 23 429

L

Lammott, Henry	1798	AJ 2 408
Lancaster, Benjamin	1826	SR 1 385
Lancaster, Jesse	1833	TSB 5 109
Lahiff, Andrew	1864	CWB 7 333
Lampkin, Benjamin	1871	BHH 8 244
Larkin, Edward	1883	JMM 11 180
Lagan, Andrew	1892	JMM 11 249
Lancaster, John O.	1897	GSN 12 111
Lamm, Charles	1905	HTB 13 204
Lantz, J. G. Frederick	1906	HTB 13 369
Lagan, Jane	1909	HTB 14 17
Langreader, Aug.	1901	HTB 14 198
Larncour, Wm. M.	1909	JA 16 13
Lambden, Edward F.	1918	JA 16 62
Langreder, Mary E.	1911	JA 16 345
Larner, John C.	1920	CHR 18 92
Lancaster, William E.	1924	CHR 18 433
Lay, Charles	1926	CHR 18 469
Lay, August	1928	CHR 18 487
Lantz, Emma C.	1930	AJG 19 53
Lantz, Walter J.	1929	AJG 19 133
Lawson, Mary E.	1931	AJG 19 259
Lasher, James L.	1927	AJG 19 265
Lawder, E. Roxanna	1924	AJG 19 381
Lacey, James V.	1926	AJG 19 385
Lanius, John Henry	1934	AJG 20 271
Lay, Catharine	1937	AJG 20 316
Lambright, Wm. Amoss	1940	AJG 21 64
Lancaster, William A.	1942	AJG 21 119
Lacey, Robert C.	1927	AJG 21 143
Lavenstein, Charles Henry	1925	RLW 23 151
Lachmann, Charles W.	1951	RLW 23 260
Lackey, Ernest	1955	RLW 23 389
Lancaster, Ella Irene	1953	RLW 23 475
Lawson, Mary Aiken	1951	RLW 23 489
Lamb, Emerson H.	1955	TLA 24 152
Lackey, Lottie	1958	TLA 24 375
Languis, Catherine	1951	TLA 25 10
Lackey, Amy Ross	1954	WFNP

Lanius, Adelaid F.	1953	TLA 26 34
Laye, John C.	1960	TLA 26 152
Lawder, Henry C., Jr.	1957	TLA 26 644
Lee, James	1778	AJ 2 384
Lee, James	1786	AJ 2 396
Legore, Elizabeth	1787	AJ 2 397
Letimore, John	1790	AJ 2 399
Lee, Samuel	1798	AJ 2 400
Leonard, Barney	1806	AJ C 321
Lister, Norris	1810	AJ C 506
Lee, David	1816	SR 1 72
Lee, William	1822	SR 1 267
Leech, James	1827	SR 1 398
Lee, William D.	1828	SR 1 455
Lee, Parker Hall	1829	SR 1 475
Lee, James	1840	TSB 5 483
Lee, Richard D.	1842	TSB 5 578
Lemmon, George	1845	TSB 6 88
Lee, Walter B.	1849	TSB 6 210
Lee, Elizabeth	1853	CWB 7 6
Levy, Sarah	1858	CWB 7 165
Lee, Deborah	1859	CWB 7 192
Lee, Mary	1860	CWB 7 219
Lee, Ralph S.	1862	CWB 7 273
Lewis, Elisha	1868	BHH 8 49
Lee, Hannah	1868	BHH 8 63
Lewin, John	1868	BHH 8 89
Lemmon, George	1874	WSR 9 12
Lewin, Amos I.	1875	WSR 9 60
Lewis, Hannah S.	1876	WSR 9 101
Levering, Mary A.	1880	WSR 9 246
Lewis, Joseph H.	1880	WSR 9 256
Lee, Mary Rebecca	1881	WSR 9 323
Lee, Bryarly	1882	WSR 9 348
Lee, Charles W.	1882	WSR 9 372
Lee, D. Wilson	1883	WSR 10 16
Levering, Alexander T.	1884	WSR 10 256
Levering, A. J.	1887	WSR 10 319
Lewin, Lydia	1879	WSR 10 367
Lee, Mary Elizabeth	1879	WSR 10 369
Lee, Mary	1888	JMM 11 30

Lee, Deliverance H.	1887	JMM 11 93
same (Agreement)	1890	JMM 11 106
Lee, James C.	1890	JMM 11 106
Lee, Elizabeth G.	1887	JMM 11 318
Leithiser, Nathaniel	1893	JMM 11 322
Lewis, Ann E.	1895	JMM 11 489
Lee, Clarence	1895	GSN 12 18
Lee, Parker H.	1888	GSN 12 30
Lening, Charles	1885	GSN 12 207
Lee, William D.	1902	GSN 12 404
Lee, Joseph	1902	GSN 12 423
Levering, Howard A.	1899	HTB 13 32
Lee, Samuel M.	1896	HTB 13 112
Lee, Mary P.	1904	HTB 13 144
Lee, James C.	1887	HTB 13 194
Levering, Sarah R.	1904	HTB 13 273
Lee, Henry W. A.	1909	HTB 14 102
Leight, Thomas W.	1916	JA 15 240
Lee, James	1913	JA 15 291
Lee, Mary P.	1909	JA 15 360
Lee, Bettie	1913	JA 15 373
Lee, Cassandra W.	1884	JA 15 396
Lewis, Eloiza S.	1916	JA 15 462
Lee, Otho S.	1911	JA 16 18
Lear, Geo. W.	1907	JA 16 182
Lee, Jupiter	1908	JA 16 388
Lee, Josephine V.	1919	JA 16 407
Lee, Isaac S.	1930	CHR 18 491
Leffler, Elizabeth	1930	AJG 19 21
Leffler, Elizabeth	1932	AJG 19 23
Leight, James Buchanan	1935	AJG 19 376
Lejeune, Augustine L.	1926	AJG 19 383
Lewis, A. Nelson	1935	AJG 19 447
Lee, Elizabeth R.	1933	AJG 20 46
Lee, Mary E.	1932	AJG 20 175
Leonardi, Vincenzo	1940	AJG 20 324
Lee, Francis L.	1923	AJG 21 82
Lee, Elizabeth Dallam Wingfield	1941	AJG 21 145
Lejune, John Archer, Lt. Gen.	1942	AJG 21 188
Lewis, Genelia E.	1942	AJG 21 242
Lewis, Allan C.	1947	RLW 22 201
Leight, Joseph T.		RLW 22 332
Lee, Norman J.	1947	RLW 22 403
Lee, John L. G.	1945	RLW 22 452

Lee, S. Cassandra	1943	RLW 23 127
Lee, Helen Murray	1950	RLW 23 295
Levaskevich, Serge	1955	RLW 23 294
Leydecker, Philip L.	1951	RLW 23 316
Lewis, Gladys R.	1955	RLW 23 360
Lee, Edward K.	1952	TLA 24 88
Lewis, Oscar E.	1957	TLA 24 150
Lewis, Zachary R.	1954	TLA 24 255
Levy, Bernhardt	1951	TLA 25 52
LeHardy, Chas. William	1955	TLA 25 265
Leatherman, Martin	1957	TLA 25 291
Lemmon, Ida B.	1959	TLA 25 367
Lee, David	1957	TLA 25 415
Lewis, Jessie Vass	1954	TLA 26 216
Leithiser, Richard H.	1957	TLA 26 311
Leishman, Gilford James, Sr.	1959	WFNP 14 302

Lingan, Thomas	1781	AJ 2 391
Lightl, Elizabeth	1784	AJ 2 394
Litton, John	1793	AJ 2 402
Little, George	1810	AJ C 222
Lilly, Thomas	1858	CWB 7 160
Littig, Sarah Jane	1876	WSR 9 126
Linaburger, Mary A. D.	1880	WSR 9 251
Livezey, Priscilla	1881	WSR 10 26
Lisby, John	1900	GSN 12 314
Little, James	1908	HTB 13 436
Livesey, Joseph	1899	HTB 13 479
Littig, Philip W.	1890	HTB 14 24
Livezey, Jacob	1910	HTB 14 247
Litzinger, William B.	1912	HTB 14 376
Livezey, Sylvania	1924	CSW 17 167
Lisby, Charles H.	1925	CSW 17 287
Livezey, Robert S.	1911	CSW 17 496
Lilly, Robert H.	1932	AJG 19 203
Lines, Daniel W.	1929	AJG 20 91
Little, Mary A.	1938	AJG 20 407
Livezay, Robert	1943	AJG 21 185
Lieske, Henry E.	1947	RLW 23 48
Livingston, Nellie Josephine	1942	RLW 23 428
Livezey, Thomas Nice	1953	TLA 24 417
Lips, Nannette B.	1957	TLA 25 25

Lindenstruth, William M.	1954	TLA 25 182
Livezey, Maude M.	1951	TLA 26 50
Lloyd, Margaret	1903	HTB 13 86
Lloyd, Thomas J.	1905	HTB 14 468
Llewellyn, Hayden E.	1952	RLW 23 262
Lockhard, Samuel	1791	AJ 2 378
Love, John	1793	AJ 2 404
Loe, Deborah	1793	AJ 2 407
Love, Robert	1803	AJ C 144
Loney, Mary	1819	SR 1 190
Long, John	1819	SR 1 195
Logue, George	1833	TSB 5 100
Love, Margaret	1837	TSB 5 274
Love, Bennet	1852	TSB C 287
Loflin, Daniel A.	1859	CWB 7 196
Low, Jeremiah	1871	BHH 8 247
Love, Elizabeth	1871	BHH 8 250
Lodge, Abel	1879	WSR 9 227
Lochary, Catharine	1881	WSR 9 298
Loflin, Richard	1870	WSR 10 48
Lowe, Jeremiah	1888	JMM 11 86
Lochary, George	1883	JMM 11 161
Lowe, Robert	1890	JMM 11 451
Love, Daniel B.	1902	GSN 12 438
Lovett, Sallie E.	1902	GSN 12 439
Lovett, Sarah J.	1902	HTB 13 13
Lowery, Lewis C.	1903	HTB 13 29
Logan, Harriet	1903	HTB 13 31
Lomyer, Margaret	1889	HTB 13 123
Lochary, Julia B.	1901	HTB 13 135
Loudan, Ann W.	1904	HTB 13 329
Love, Samuel T.	1911	HTB 14 279
Lomyer, Robert	1912	HTB 14 483
Lochary, Thomas	1914	JA 15 129
Lochary, John	1915	JA 15 379
Lowe, Ammon D.	1915	JA 16 335
Lowe, Laban	1925	CSW 17 461
Lowe, Mary Jane	1922	CHR 18 173

95

Lynch, John	1777	AJ 2 388
Lyon, Jonathan	1784	AJ 2 389
Lyttle, Elizabeth	1784	AJ 2 394
Lytle, James	1814	AJ C 735
Lytle, George	1814	SR 1 5
Lytle, Avarilla	1815	SR 1 26
Lytle, Rachel	1828	SR 1 448
Lytle, James	1848	TSB 6 87
Lytle, James	1864	CWB 7 339
Lyon, George Taylor	1890	JMM 11 218
Lynch, John	1890	JMM 11 264
Lynch, James P.	1894	JMM 11 439
Lytle, George W.	1882	JMM 11 380
Lytle, John H.	1883	GSN 12 16
Lytle, Maria R.	1900	HTB 13 38
Lynch, Thomas H.	1904	HTB 13 52
Lytle, Mary S.	1908	HTB 13 450
Lytle, William K.	1900	HTB 14 179
Lynch, Daniel J.	1912	JA 15 210
Lytle, Jos. F.	1923	JA 16 476
Lynch, Daniel P.	1922	JA 16 499
Lyon, Georgia T.	1924	CSW 17 108
Lyon, Eliza P.	1924	CSW 17 161
Lynch, Mary H.	1933	AJG 19 298
Lyon, A. Lincoln	1942	AJG 21 136
Lynch, John	1915	AJG 21 476
Lytle, Florence Taylor	1953	TLA 24 471

M

Maxwell, James	1782	AJ 2 426
Mathews, John	1782	AJ 2 428
Mather, James	1786	AJ 2 436
Mathews, Bennet	1790	AJ 2 444
Mathews, Milcha	1795	AJ 2 469
Mathews, Levin	1795	AJ 2 470
Maxwell, Jacob	1798	AJ 2 474
Maxwell, Moses	1805	AJ C 302
Marsh, John	1805	AJ C 311
Mathews, Bennet	1805	AJ C 317
Maddon, Mary	1805	AJ C 326
Maden, James	1807	AJ C 372
Maulsby, David	1807	AJ C 376
Mathews, Roger	1810	AJ C 495
Mahon, John	1812	AJ C 631
Martin, William	1813	AJ C 719
Macatee, Leonard	1820	SR 1 212
Mason, John	1822	SR 1 255
Marshall, Samuel	1823	SR 1 274
Martin, Robert	1824	SR 1 310
Malsby, David	1830	SR 1 497
Malsby, Wheeler	1830	SR 1 509
Mackey, Mary	1831	SR 1 536
Marshall, William	1832	TSB 5 21
Marche, John	1837	TSB 5 303
Martin, Mary	1839	TSB 5 402
Massey, Rigbie	1841	TSB 5 540
Maxwell, William	1842	TSB 5 543
Martin, Moses	1842	TSB 5 590
Martin, Oliver P.	1845	TSB 6 59
Macatee, Ann	1848	TSB 6 172
Massey, Aquila	1851	TSB 6 268
Mathews, Naomi	1851	TSB 6 280
Maynadier, Catharine S.	1851	TSB 6 277
Martin, Thomas	1852	TSB 6 310
Maddon, James	1852	TSB 6 318
Magness, James	1852	TSB 6 325
Macatee, Harry	1852	TSB 6 328
Magness, William	1853	TSB 6 341

Macatee, George I.	1853	TSB 6 352
Maynadier, William M.	1854	CWB 7 45
Macatee, Elizabeth	1860	CWB 7 234
Maulsby, Jane	1864	CWB 7 331
Maulsby, Jane	1864	CWB 7 332
Mason, George	1869	BHH 8 114
Massey, Hannah M.	1872	BHH 8 298
Martin, Elizabeth S.	1873	BHH 8 345
Maris, Sarah W.	1874	WSR 9 8
Macatee, Ignatius G.	1875	WSR 9 66
Magaw, Samuel	1875	WSR 9 71
Macatee, Clement	1876	WSR 9 121
Maul, David	1876	WSR 9 197
Maxwell, Amos	1880	WSR 9 254
Martin, John	1883	WSR 9 408
Martin, William G.	1883	WSR 10 1
Mairs, Jesse J.	1860	WSR 10 98
Mackin, Cornelius	1885	WSR 10 106
Mahan, Susan	1888	WSR 10 406
Magness, Lee A.	1888	JMM 11 9
Magraw, James M.	1888	JMM 11 18
Malcolm, Elizabeth A.	1894	JMM 11 452
Markel, Adam	1895	JMM 11 472
Mahan, Catharine	1896	GSN 12 4
Maxwell, David	1890	GSN 12 27
Mahan, William H.	1898	GSN 12 143
Martin, John	1898	GSN 12 189
Makinson, William T.	1899	GSN 12 232
Mahan, James P.	1899	GSN 12 245
Martin, Patrick	1899	GSN 12 256
Martin, Catharine	1900	GSN 12 267
Martin, Samuel H.	1902	GSN 12 430
Maguire, Francis	1903	GSN 12 474
Mathews, Lemuel E.	1903	GSN 12 494
Mayes, Susannah A.	1902	HTB 13 2
Maxwell, George D.	1902	HTB 13 37
Mason, Mary A.	1905	HTB 13 182
Martin, John T.	1904	HTB 13 188
Magness, Mary E.	1899	HTB 13 421
Mason, Amanda V.	1906	HTB 14 169
Marsteller, John	1911	HTB 14 204
Mathiot, Annie M.	1898	HTB 14 241
Macpherson, Charles L.	1911	HTB 14 343
Matthews, Ruth H.	1911	HTB 14 383

Mahan, Cassir A.	1913	HTB 14 479
Maslin, Frank S.	1913	HTB 14 495
Martin, Margaret E.	1907	HTB 14 496
Mason, Samuel	1882	JA 15 1
Martin, E. Jennie	1915	JA 15 192
Mardew, Jacob W.	1913	JA 15 231
Massey, James R.	1909	JA 15 351
Martin, Moses	1899	JA 15 378
Maulsby, John Joshua	1903	JA 15 460
Martin, Susie D.	1917	JA 15 489
Macattee, Henry	1905	JA 15 498
Martin, Frank Michael	1918	JA 16 35
Matthews, Montraville O.	1919	JA 16 278
Martin, James Polk	1917	JA 16 454
Mars, Wm. S.	1921	JA 16 490
Martin, Edwin E.	1924	CSW 17 226
Mayes, Howard L.	1922	CSW 17 382
Martin, Frankanna	1923	CHR 18 83
Markline, John N.	1926	CHR 18 89
Markley, L. Cordelia	1927	CHR 18 93
Marshall, Margaretta Taylor	1931	CHR 18 312
Maloney, William	1929	CHR 18 334
Maxwell, Ellen H.	1931	CHR 18 378
Mahan, Sarah Jane	1901	AJG 19 69
Marshall, J. Henry	1921	AJG 19 210
Malatesta, Dutonia	1933	AJG 19 324
Maddox, Margaret E.	1934	AJG 20 53
Martin, Frank	1934	AJG 20 95
Magness, John T.	1938	AJG 20 297
Mackin, Thomas	1937	AJG 20 308
Martin, August	1928	AJG 20 317
Mason, John T.	1914	AJG 20 412
Mahan, Sarah Jane	1927	AJG 21 105
Mahan, Chas. Alfred	1927	AJG 21 107
MacIntire, Benjamin Gould	1937	AJG 21 167
Maslin, Jackson W.	1935	AJG 21 183
Martin, Wiley P.	1943	AJG 21 226
Martin, Clarence W.	1945	AJG 21 404
Macklem, Mary A.	1946	AJG 21 487
Marvin, George C.	1927	RLW 22 80
Mahoney, Ella V.	1942	RLW 22 108
Maslin, Sallie H.	1933	RLW 23 15
Magness, Edward W.	1949	RLW 23 134
Martin, Harry M.	1947	RLW 23 150

Macklem, Bessie V.	1954	RLW 23 279
MacNabb, Charles H.	1950	RLW 23 284
Magness, William Luke	1953	RLW 23 319
MacNabb, V. Catherine	1955	RLW 23 391
Maulsby, David L.	1907	RLW 23 395
Maulsby, D. Lee	1924	RLW 23 397
Magness, Samuel S.	1948	RLW 23 436
Marx, John H.	1955	RLW 23 499
Mason, Samuel, Jr.	1951	RLW 23 496
Matthews, C. Hollis	1956	TLA 24 3
Martin, Arthur F.	1951	TLA 24 64
Mason, B. Carola	1958	TLA 24 173
Maulsby, Florence Y.	1951	TLA 24 240
Mavin, R. T.	1881	TLA 24 312
Mash, Anna L.	1958	TLA 24 393
Martin, Mary F.	1960	TLA 24 463
Martin, J. T. Bascom	1953	TLA 24 477
Macklem, Rebecca J.	1955	TLA 25 70
Martin, Alma M.	1960	TLA 25 151
Macklem, Lavinia D.	1955	WFNP 13 700
Magness, Wm. Harry	1957	TLA 25 196
MacLaughlin, John Andrew	1942	TLA 25 218
MacAllister, Grace Robinson	1957	TLA 25 262
Masek, Marie	1956	TLA 25 427
Maxwell, E. Stahler	1953	TLA 26 10
Martin, Stephen, J.	1947	WFNP 14 074
Martell, Natale	1957	TLA 26 384
Markline, George Adam	1957	WFNP 14 318

McAtee George	1788	AJ 2 5
McDonald, Cornelius	1787	AJ 2 156
McNair, James	1778	AJ 2 414
McComas, Benjamin	1778	AJ 2 415
McCrackin, James	1778	AJ 2 416
McClure, Robert	1780	AJ 2 421
McComas, Solomon	1781	AJ 2 424
McComas, Daniel of W.	1785	AJ 2 431
McGaclin, Patrick	1786	AJ 2 435
McComas, Martha	1786	AJ 2 438
McCartie, Sarah	1787	AJ 2 439
McComas, James	1781	AJ 2 449
McClaskey, Patrick	1791	AJ 2 451

McComas, Hannah	1796	AJ 2 454
McCord, Arthur	1793	AJ 2 457
McComas, Moses	1794	AJ 2 460
McComas, James	1794	AJ 2 462
McMath, Samuel	1794	AJ 2 471
McClintick, Mathew	1797	AJ 2 472
McComas, Alexander	1800	AJ 2 477
McAdow, John	1801	AJ C 74
McCowen, Frances	1803	AJ C 122
McComas, Aaron	1805	AJ C 255
McGill, Joseph	1810	AJ C 527
McComas, Daniel	1811	AJ C 567
McGilligan, Thomas	1811	AJ C 574
McElhaney, Michael	1815	SR 1 36
McFaddon, John	1811	SR 1 68
McGay, James	1817	SR 1 112
McComas, John of Danl.	1820	SR 1 210
McComas, John of Alex.	1826	SR 1 364
McMath, William	1823	SR 1 270
McComas, John	1826	SR 1 365
McComas, Elizabeth	1826	SR 1 370
McCoy, William	1833	TSB 5 76
McClaskey, James	1834	TSB 5 128
McNutt, William	1836	TSB 5 256
McClaskey, David	1838	TSB 5 334
McVey, James	1842	TSB 5 559
McFadden, William	1842	TSB 5 56?
McCracken, James	1842	TSB 5 567
McGaw, James	1842	TSB 5 612
McComas, Francis H.	1843	TSB 6 14
McAdow, Andrew	1844	TSB 6 49
McConnell, Samuel	1844	TSB 6 51
McComas, Aaron	1845	TSB 6 70
McGaw, Elizabeth	1846	TSB 6 93
McClaskey, Elizabeth	1847	TSB 6 148
McComas, Jacob	1849	TSB 6 216
McComas, Solomon	1849	TSB 6 235
McComas, Elizabeth	1851	TSB 6 273
McComas, James S.	1853	CWB 7 11
McFeely, Bernard	1854	CWB 7 46
McComas, Cassandra	1856	CWB 7 97
McFaddon, Jane	1856	CWB 7 101
McComas, John C.	1856	CWB 7 112
McCormick, Elizabeth	1856	CWB 7 123

McComas, William	1857			CWB 7 141
McComas, Martha	1858			CWB 7 161
McComas, Ellen	1859			CWB 7 208
McCracken, Mary	1860			CWB 7 226
McComas, William	1861			CWB 7 262
McGaw, John	1863			CWB 7 309
McFaddon, John	1864			CWB 7 330
McComas, Barnet	1864			CWB 7 366
McCoy, John C.	1865			CWB 7 387
McKendless, Sophia	1865			CWB 7 388
McCommons, John	1867			BHH 8 18
McComas, Charlotte A.	1867			BHH 8 35
McConkey, James	1868			BHH 8 65
McCourtney, Elvira Mary	1871			BHH 8 193
McCabe, Patrick	1877			WSR 9 148
McGaw, Robert	1878			WSR 9 166
McGaw, Robert F.	1878			WSR 9 189
McCoy, David G.	1881			WSR 9 271
McCabe, Rosa	1881			WSR 9 295
McComas, Gabriel A.	1882			WSR 9 349
McAtee, Harriet	1882			WSR 9 366
McFaddon, Mary A.	1883			WSR 9 441
McComas, Louisa	1883			WSR 10 144
McGeoch, John	1887			WSR 10 314
McCreary, Rebecca N.	1888			WSR 10 456
McCausland, Thomas J.	1875	see	(	JMM 11 12
McCausland, Maria C.	1875	also	(	JMM 11 12
McCausland, Louisa I.	1875	GSN	(	JMM 11 12
McCausland, Eliza	1875	12	(	JMM 11 12
McCausland, Mary A.	1875	folio	(	JMM 11 12
McCausland, Jane	1875	467	(	JMM 11 12
McComas, John E.	1889			JMM 11 14
McCormick, Elizabeth B.	1890			JMM 11 156
McFadden, Robert	1891			JMM 11 196
McFadden, William J.	1892			JMM 11 247
McKindless, Alice Ann	1890			JMM 11 312
McGaw, Susan G.	1889			JMM 11 233
McOlvain, Jeremiah	1889			JMM 11 330
McAfee, James	1891			JMM 11 405
McComas, Joshua	1896			GSN 12 43
McLaughlin, Elizabeth	1894			GSN 12 88
McNabb, David G.	1899			GSN 12 262
McNutt, Richard S.	1900			GSN 12 309
McCausland, Thomas J.	1875			GSN 12 467

McCausland, Jane	1875	GSN 12 467
McCausland, Eliza	1875	GSN 12 467
McCausland, Maria C.	1875	GSN 12 467
McCausland, Louisa I.	1875	GSN 12 467
McCausland, Mary A.	1875	GSN 12 467
McSparran, William	1903	GSN 12 471
McCloskey, Martha F.	1901	GSN 12 478
McCann, Ephriam	1903	HTB 13 51
McGaw, Sallie J.	1903	HTB 13 90
McDoon, John	1904	HTB 13 161
McNutt, Mary	1904	HTB 13 235
McGuigan, John	1901	HTB 13 259
McKee, Mary J.	1906	HTB 14 15
McComas, William A.	1909	HTB 14 31
McComas, Rachel A.	1906	HTB 14 70
McCall, George B.	1909	HTB 14 87
McCormick, Mary J.	1905	HTB 14 166
McNutt, Hugh J.	1910	HTB 14 188
McDoon, Laura L.	1908	HTB 14 251
McElwain, Martha M.	1900	HTB 14 319
McConkey, William Henry	1912	HTB 14 345
McCreery, Andrew B.	1909	HTB 14 424
McLaughlin, Sarah A.	1912	HTB 14 455
McDonald, Catherine	1913	JA 15 56
McCubbin, Maggie Roney	1914	JA 15 60
McCurdy, Hannah S.	1911	JA 15 124
McCombs, Abram P.	1915	JA 15 208
McIlvain, Annie C. M.	1911	JA 15 215
McComas, Rebecca J.	1899	JA 15 238
McCombs, Maria C.	1916	JA 15 246
McCommons, Joseph T.	1915	JA 15 251
McGorroy, Thomas B.	1914	JA 15 382
McDonald, Nelson W.	1917	JA 15 423
McClung, Ephraim B.	1910	JA 15 456
McCommons, Edward	1889	JA 15 486
McVey, Wm. H.	1917	JA 16 24
McKee, Chas B.	1919	JA 16 105
McFadden, Joseph M.	1916	JA 16 130
McCoy, William G.	1914	JA 16 141
McNutt, Wm. F.	1920	JA 16 268
McClung, Hannah A.	1920	JA 16 380
McKivitt, Eliz. Jane	1922	JA 16 429
McConkey, Mary Elizabeth	1924	CSW 17 133
McCommons, William T.	1924	CSW 17 152

McIlvain, Rachel	1924	CSW 17	172
McGuire, Elizabeth A.	1924	CSW 17	277
McIlvaine, John Morton	1910	CSW 17	294
McNabb, J. Martin	1924	CSW 17	346
McRoy, S. Etta	1926	CSW 17	350
McGaw, Charles A.	1909	CSW 17	359
McEwing, F. W.		CSW 17	369
McCommons, Ely F.	1915	CSW 17	393
McConkey, Edward E.	1926	CSW 17	441
McIlwain, Mary E.	1927	CSW 17	468
McLaughlin, Sarah Retta	1902	CSW 17	475
McLaughlin, Anna Mary	1902	CSW 17	477
McComas, George W.	1901	CHR 18	99
McNabb, James W.	1922	CHR 18	140
McDonald, Catherine	1929	CHR 18	227
McLaughlin, Truston P.	1927	CHR 18	258
McNulty, Annie V.	1914	CHR 18	267
McCurdy, John A.	1927	AJG 19	5
McCann, Albert L.	1931	AJG 19	32
McPhee, Christina D.	1931	AJG 19	119
McNutt, John T.	1909	AJG 19	151
McDoon, Rose	1933	AJG 19	177
McCoy, Helen R.		AJG 19	183
McGaw, Ella J.	1926	AJG 19	330
McGuigan, Sylvester A.	1933	AJG 19	400
McCann, Nelson	1934	AJG 20	6
McGonigall, Josephine	1936	AJG 20	20
McFadden, William G.	1937	AJG 20	108
McDonald, Thomas V.	1931	AJG 20	165
McCommons, Roberta	1932	AJG 20	475
McElhinney, Thomas J.	1940	AJG 20	477
McCully, William N.	1940	AJG 21	23
McCormick, Martha G.	1937	AJG 21	93
McCloskey, Margaret	1938	AJG 21	139
McCann, Edward P.	1942	AJG 21	177
McComas, William N.	1937	AJG 21	212
McCormick, P. Henderson	1938	AJG 21	217
McLhinney, Margaret M.	1940	AJG 21	243
McMaster, Wilhemina W.	1943	AJG 21	257
McFadden, Charles W.	1939	AJG 21	308
McMaster, George	1934	AJG 21	343
McCommons, Clarence A.	1935	AJG 21	380
McClung, Columbus P.	1945	AJG 21	413
McKenzie, Clara M.	1947	RLW 22	95

McCarney, Mary C.	1949	RLW 22 238
McClintock, Emma N.	1948	RLW 22 458
McCauley, Paul K.	1953	RLW 23 97
McGrady, Milly Cdelia	1952	RLW 23 145
McClung, J. Samuel	1952	RLW 23 159
McGaw, Abbie V.	1953	RLW 23 187
McCann, R. Lamar	1948	RLW 23 290
McCommons, Mary M.	1953	RLW 23 372
McCommons, John E.	1939	RLW 23 418
McCully, Ethol C.	1955	RLW 23 442
McCommons, Mary C.	1948	RLW 23 476
McLean, James	1944	RLW 23 478
McCormick, J. Lawrence	1953	TLA 24 6
McKelvey, Abbie M.	1958	TLA 24 123
McEwing, James	1957	TLA 24 170
McGaw, Robert F., Jr.	1923	TLA 24 271
McFatridge, Elva Mary	1958	TLA 24 458
McSpodden, Hardy L.	1955	TLA 26 19
McGuigan, Annie N.	1949	TLA 26 115
Mead, Benjamin	1787	AJ 2 440
Meads, James	1817	SR 1 128
Megay, John	1840	TSB 5 441
Mechem, Francis	1841	TSB 5 526
Mechem, Isaac	1859	CWB 7 195
Meads, Elisha	1865	CWB 7 379
Merritt, Abraham	1882	WSR 9 370
Mechem, Lydia G.	1872 & 1875	WSR 10 95
Mechem, William	1885	WSR 10 385
Mercer, Singleton A.	1866	JMM 11 136
Meeds, Mary E.	1899	GSN 12 263
Meads, James B.	1907	HTB 14 34
Metzel, Alice Ann	1892	JA 16 63
Metzel, Jacob B.	1918	JA 16 68
Meiers, Henry	1892	JA 16 161
Merryman, Henry S.	1910	JA 16 483
Meehan, Henry	1911	CHR 18 247
Meigs, Robert R.	1927	AJG 19 13
Mead, J. Gladiss	1914	AJG 19 27
Merryman, Nelson O.	1926	AJG 19 39
Mechem, Cassandra M.	1930	AJG 19 401
Meehan, Mary A.	1940	AJG 20 392

Meigs, Montgomery C.	1944	AJG 21 337
Melvin, William	1937	AJG 21 421
Meredith, Clarence S.	1948	TLA 24 155
Meiers, Frederick H.	1936	TLA 24 440
Merryman, H. Clayton	1933	TLA 24 483
Mitchell, Edward	1779	AJ 2 418
Miles, John	1779	AJ 2 420
Mitchell, Thomas	1782	AJ 2 422
Miles, Jane	1786	AJ 2 434
Miles, Margaret	1790	AJ 2 446
Mills, Thomas	1781	AJ 2 448
Mitchell, Kent	1793	AJ 2 458
Miller, John	1800	AJ 2 476
Miller, Joseph	1800	AJ C 67
Middleton, William	1805	AJ C 272
Mitchell, Sarah	1805	AJ C 333
Michael, John	1805	AJ C 341
Mitchell, Aquila	1807	AJ C 365
Mitchell, Parker	1812	AJ C 653
Miller, Ann F.	1817	SR 1 122
Miles, Aquila	1818	SR 1 139
Mitchell, Gabriel	1828	SR 1 439
Mitchell, Thomas	1830	SR 1 504
Michael, Ann	1834	TSB 5 134
Miller, James	1840	TSB 5 470
Mitchell, William	1842	TSB 5 582
Mitchell, Jane	1845	TSB 6 74
Mitchell, Ezekiel	1846	TSB 6 101
Mitchell, Thomas	1849	TSB 6 212
Mitchell, Kent	1850	TSB 6 240
Michael, Jacob	1853	TSB 6 338
Mitchell, Elizabeth	1853	TSB 6 343
Michael, Daniel	1853	CWB 7 2
Mitchell, Sarah	1854	CWB 7 21
Mitchell, Alfred	1854	CWB 7 28
Mitchell, Richard	1856	CWB 7 121
Mitchell, Sarah	1857	CWB 7 127
Michael, William	1857	CWB 7 138
Mitchell, Hannah	1861	CWB 7 239
Michael, Owen	1871	BHH 8 223
Mitchell, Evan	1873	BHH 8 319

Miller, Thomas	1873	BHH 8 325
Miller, Joseph	1873	BHH 8 348
Miles, Rachel	1877	WSR 9 160
Michael, Wm. Emory	1880	WSR 9 247
Mitchell, Clemency	1882	WSR 9 367
Milton, Louisa C.	1883	WSR 9 440
Mitchell, James R.	1884	WSR 10 276
Middleton, Allen	1886	WSR 10 393
Middleton, C. W.	1881	JMM 11 33
Mitchell, John	1890	JMM 11 162
Mitchell, Edmund	1891	JMM 11 224
Miller, Fannie A.	1890	JMM 11 182
Michael, Jacob J.	1880	JMM 11 254
Middleton, Jane P.	1893	JMM 11 394
Miller, Solomon	1897	GSN 12 47
Mitchell, Ann Eliza	1899	GSN 12 243
Miller, Jacob O.	1900	GSN 12 289
Mitchell, Frederick O.	1900	GSN 12 301
Mitchell, Amos A.	1901	GSN 12 355
Mitchell, Joseph G.	1902	GSN 12 453
Milton, Griffith T.	1890	HTB 13 94
Mitchell, George Van	1904	HTB 13 124
Michael, Henry C.	1904	HTB 13 411
Mitchell, John Parker	1907	HTB 14 108
Mitchell, Caroline P.	1898	HTB 14 177
Minnick, Eliza Ann	1910	HTB 14 252
Michael, Charles W.	1897	JA 15 103
Mitchell, J. Henry	1913	JA 15 134
Minnick, Martha C.	1903	JA 15 348
Miller, John Joseph	1912	JA 15 377
Michael, Ann M.	1910	JA 15 446
Milton, Sallie R.	1899	JA 16 122
Mitchell, Henry F.	1919	JA 16 149
Mitchell, Hannah S.	1920	JA 16 258
Mitchell, Solomon T.	1919	JA 16 293
Michael, John M.	1921	JA 16 315
Mitchell, Eliza A.	1917	JA 16 322
Milton, Isabella P.	1920	JA 16 404
Mitchell, William	1921	JA 16 423
Mitchell, Geo. Alfred	1920	JA 16 448
Mitchell, Samuel Houston	1923	CSW 17 21
Mitchell, Evans Lewis	1916	CSW 17 341
Michael, Susanna Rebecca	1921	CSW 17 426

Middendorf, J. Henry	1913	CSW 17 448
Mink, Mary	1930	CHR 18 250
Mitchell, Robert O.	1929	CHR 18 386
Mitchell, Robert Lewis	1930	CHR 18 391
Mitchell, John T.	1932	AJG 19 60
Mitchell, Henry L.	1925	AJG 19 101
Mick, Lonnie E.	1927	AJG 19 103
Mitchell, Edward M.	1933	AJG 19 327
Michael, Charles O.	1935	AJG 19 387
Miles, Joseph H.	1935	AJG 19 392
Miller, Kate V.	1934	AJG 19 429
Miller, Sidney H.	1922	AJG 20 66
Miller, James Ramon	1923	AJG 20 97
Minnick, T. Alford (Alfred)	1915	AJG 20 98
Michael, Ida M.	1937	AJG 20 154
Mitchell, Frederick O'Neill	1934	AJG 20 256
Miller, Fannie Bell	1916	AJG 20 279
Mitchell, Anna Elizabeth	1938	AJG 20 334
Mitchell, Mary Emma	1935	AJG 20 403
Minnick, Florence M.	1939	AJG 21 70
Mitchell, Raymond	1938	AJG 21 97
Mitchell, Malvine	1924	AJG 21 103
Mitchell, Robert H.	1937	AJG 21 118
Michael, Orion C.	1939	AJG 21 249
Mitchell, Estelle Archer	1935	AJG 20 221
Mitchell, Ada May	1938	AJG 20 224
Michael, Annie F.	1939	AJG 21 296
Minnick, Millard Glyndon	1944	AJG 21 370
Mitchell, Mary A.	1944	RLW 22 4
Mitchell, Malcolm W.	1943	RLW 22 49
Mitchell, Maude R.	1946	RLW 22 165
Mitchell, Fannie E.	1942	RLW 22 181
Mitchell, Lillie E.	1942	RLW 22 202
Michael, Clara V.	1942	RLW 22 421
Mitchell, Alonzo Edward	1950	RLW 23 11
Michael, Charles W.	1931	RLW 23 10
Michael, Mary Florence	1945	RLW 22 493
Michael, J. Calvin	1953	RLW 23 129
Mitchell, Jennie	1954	RLW 23 174
Mitchell, Lillie N.	1954	RLW 23 242
Minnick, Stevenson Archer	1956	RLW 23 465
Mitchell, Annie M.	1944	TLA 24 1
Mitchell, Parker, Sr.	1952	TLA 24 138
Mitchell, Minnie G.	1942	TLA 24 163

Miller, James P.	1944	TLA 24 277
Miller, J. Harry	1958	TLA 24 398
Mitchell, Mary E.	1926	TLA 24 412
Miller, William L.	1958	TLA 24 415
Mitchell, McHenry	1924	TLA 24 427
Mitchell, Julian F.	1959	TLA 24 442
Miller, Kate L.	1959	TLA 24 444
Miller, J. Herbert	1957	WFNP
Miller, James	1946	TLA 25 79
Miller, Edward F.	1958	TLA 25 87
Mitchell, Amanda Raymond	1952	WFNR
Mitchell, Anna H.	1949	TLA 25 225
Mitchell, Mary B.	1957	TLA 25 236
Mitchell, Evan M.	1960	TLA 25 255
Miller, John G.	1959	TLA 25 319
Minnick, Elizabeth C.	1938	TLA 25 393
Miller, Emma C.	1942	TLA 25 429
Mitchell, H. Kemp	1953	TLA 26 275
Michael, Hazel M.	1954	TLA 26 394
Miller, Donald W.	1952	WFNP
Michael, Beatrice P.	1947	TLA 26 594

Morgan, Edward	1775	AJ 2 411
Morris, Richard	1777	AJ 2 413
Montgomery, Thomas	1785	AJ 2 432
Morgan, William	1795	AJ 2 463
Morris, James	1791	AJ 2 479
Morgan, Roelef	1805	AJ C 257
Monk, Richard	1805	AJ C 328
Monk, William	1812	AJ C 600
Montgomery, John	1815	SR 1 59
Morris, Israel	1818	SR 1 162
Morgan, Robert	1819	SR 1 182
Morgan, Robert	1819	SR 1 193
Montgomery, Thomas	1822	SR 1 246
Moore, Joseph	1826	SR 1 383
Monks, John	1827	SR 1 421
Morrison, Mathew	1835	TSB 5 158
Montgomery, Juliet	1835	TSB 5 212
Moores, Mary	1835	TSB 5 228
Montgomery, Thomas	1837	TSB 5 307
Montgomery, William B.	1838	TSB 5 370

Moulton, Mathew	1843	TSB 6 18
Morgan, Margaret	1846	TSB 6 99
Moore, John R.	1847	TSB 6 146
Morse, Elijah M.	1848	TSB 6 170
Moores, James	1853	TSB 6 349
Moores, Aquila P.	1853	TSB 6 351
Moore, Joseph	1853	TSB 6 354
Morrison, Emmor	1854	CWB 7 22
Morris, William	1854	CWB 7 37
Morgan, Susanna E.	1858	CWB 7 157
Morgan, Thomas H.	1862	CWB 7 279
Morgan, William H.	1864	CWB 7 363
Moore, Isaac	1866	BHH 8 11
Morrison, John	1868	BHH 8 75
Morrison, Margaret P.	1869	BHH 8 118
Morgan, Ann B.	1869	BHH 8 132
Morrison, Mary	1871	BHH 8 245
Mordew, Jacob W.	1913	JA 15 231
Moore, Benjamin P.	1875	WSR 9 58
Moores, Elizabeth	1877	WSR 9 161
Moffett, John T.	1882	WSR 9 377
Morris, Isaac	1883	WSR 9 437
Morrison, Daniel	1885	WSR 10 117
Moore, Patrick	1886	WSR 10 254
Morgan, Thomas H.	1862	WSR 10 363
Moseman, Margaret	1867	WSR 10 449
Moores, Annie L.	1889	JMM 11 6
Moore, Elizabeth	1887	JMM 11 8
Morse, Elizabeth	1873	JMM 11 157
Moulsdale, Elizabeth	1885	JMM 11 212
Morrison, Alexander	1873	JMM 11 307
Monses, Otto	1894	JMM 11 426
Monks, James H.	1889	JMM 11 482
Monks, Hampton	1896	JMM 11 490
Moore, Mary G.	1892	GSN 12 24
Morris, William	1897	GSN 12 104
Morrison, Emmor	1890	GSN 12 177
Morgan, Jane	1899	GSN 12 228
Moore, Amelia	1899	GSN 12 255
Morris, Isaac E.	1901	GSN 17 379
Morrison, Catherine E.	1902	GSN 12 388
Moore, Deborah H.	1900	GSN 12 276
Moses, John	1902	GSN 12 456
Moitz, Gabriel	1901	HTB 13 22

Morrison, Hannah J.	1902	HTB 13 138
Morris, Elenor	1903	HTB 13 244
Morgan, William	1908	HTB 14 9
Moore, J. Wilson	1903	HTB 14 33
Moulsdale, Thomas	1904	HTB 14 157
Moore, Mary Dixon	1902	HTB 14 222
Moulsdale, Eleanor Louisa	1909	HTB 14 270
Moores, John	1890	HTB 14 274
Morse, George W.	1909	HTB 14 349
Moore, Martha J.	1917	JA 15 392
Moores, Edward P.	1918	JA 16 215
Monks, Gertrude R.	1917	JA 16 392
Moore, Caleb J.	1921	JA 16 433
Morkovsky, John	1924	CSW 17 154
Morris, Katharine Louise	1923	CSW 17 253
Monell, Ambrose	1917	CSW 17 323
Moore, E. Ross		CSW 17 355
Moore, E. Estelle	1923	CSW 17 494
Moitz, Adelina E.	1906	CHP 18 70
Moore, Charles Byron	1915	CHR 18 75
Moulsdale, Keziah O.	1930	CHR 18 338
Morison, Elizabeth H.	1912	CHR 18 369
Moore, Lillie M.	1928	AJG 19 46
Moore, W. Osborne	1928	AJG 19 209
Morlok, Fred	1935	AJG 19 375
Moore, James O.	1937	AJG 20 149
Morrison, William H.	1932	AJG 20 336
Morgan, Isabella	1918	AJ 20 458
Moore, Harry R.	1941	AJG 21 30
Moxley, John R.	1941	AJG 21 92
Morgan, John T.	1934	AJG 21 259
Morgan, John Pierpont	1942	AJG 21 266
Moore, Leo M.	1945	AJG 21 409
Moulsdale, Mary A.	1945	RLW 22 180
Mosle, Anne Brackenridge	1951	RLW 22 424
Monk, Mary E.	1954	RLW 23 346
Moore, Lillian M.	1952	TLA 24 17
Morgenstern, Charles	1954	TLA 24 132
Moore, Smith L.	1932	filed not rec. 13 345
Moxley, Allen L.	1952	TLA 24 436
Monro, Randolph	1956	TLA 24 439
Moulsdale, Christine	1947	TLA 25 231
Moore, Smith L.	1932	TLA 26 435
Morris, Daniel L.	1959	TLA 26 591

Murphy, James	1788	AJ 2 443	
Murray, Elizabeth	1824	SR 1 312	
Murphy, John	1854	CWB 7 53	
Murphy, William	1871	BHH 8 229	
Murphy, Thomas I.	1873	BHH 8 363	
Murray, James	1874	WSR 10 182	
Musser, Lydia	1893	JMM 11 369	
Murphy, John	1902	HTB 13 91	
Munnikhuysen, Leila	1892	HTB 13 148	
Mullineax, Joseph H.	1902	HTB 13 183	
Murphy, Mary	1910	HTB 14 161	
Munnikhuysen, Mary Howard,	1915	JA 16 253	
Murphy, Mary E.	1918	JA 16 358	
Murray, William Edward	1923	CSW 17 59	
Murphy, Owen	1924	CSW 17 119	
Murphy, John T.	1924	CSW 17 214	
Munnikhuysen, Annie F.	1924	CSW 17 264	
Munnikhuysen, Olivia Jane	1923	CSW 17 405	
Munnikhuysen, Elizabeth Dallam	1928	CHR 18 106	
Munnikhuysen, Ann Lee	1928	CHR 18 470	
Murphy, Cornelius F.	1911	AJG 19 155	
Munnikhuysen, Frances	1932	AJG 19 325	
Munnikhuysen, Wakeman B.	1930	AJG 21 303	
Munnikhuysen, Bryarly	1928	AJG 21 371	
Murray, Bertha M.	1945	RLW 22 190	
Munnihuysen, Edith	1945	RLW 22 499	
Murphy, Margaret M.	1952	RLW 23 12	
Murphy, Lee L.	1953	RLW 23 107	
Munnikhuysen, Henry D. F.	1955	RLW 23 275	
Munnikhuysen, Francis Lee	1919	RLW 23 452	
Murphy, Louise	1957	TLA 24 53	
Myer, Charles M.	1887	GSN 12 72	
Myers, Mary E.	1907	HTB 13 342	
Myer, Margaret J.	1908	HTB 13 390	
Myers, Sarah Elizabeth	1910	HTB 14 407	
Myers, Eliza Rebecca	1916	CSW 17 385	

N

Nagle, Daniel S.	1894	JMM 11 387
Nagle, Thos. F.	1922	JA 16 497
Nevill, Rachel	1787	AJ 2 487
Nelson, Jane V.	1815	SR 1 28
Nelson, Robert	1818	SR 1 141
Nevill, Simon	1820	SR 1 208
Nelson, Aquila	1827	SR 1 387
Nelson, Jarrett	1832	TSB 5 31
Nelson, William	1851	TSB 6 266
Nelson, James	1853	CWB 7 14
Neville, Cassandra	1855	CWB 7 72
Neville, John	1861	CWB 7 267
Nelson, George	1863	CWB 7 305
Nelson, James	1866	CWB 7 402
Neville, Elizabeth	1874	WSR 9 1
Nelson, Nicholas H.	1875	WSR 9 30
Neville, Susan	1888	JMM 11 105
Newell, McFadden A.	1892	JMM 11 355
Nelson, Elizabeth B.	1886	JMM 11 393
Neilson, Rosa	1903	HTB 13 70
Nelson, Horatio	1889	HTB 13 114
Newmeyer, Solomon	1903	HTB 13 480
Nelson, Susan R.	1913	JA 15 130
Nelson, Wm. B.	1921	JA 16 355
Nelson, Margaret S.	1921	JA 16 478
Nelson, John Thomas	1924	CSW 17 132
Nelson, William H.	1924	CSW 17 138
Nelson, Elizabeth A.	1922	CSW 17 307
Nelson, Elizabeth S.	1923	CHR 18 406
Nelson, Nicholas	1909	AJG 19 257
Nehrer, Caroline	1920	AJG 19 339
Neeper, Samuel J.	1914	AJG 20 409
Newmeyer, Hannah	1936	AJG 21 398
Nelson, Thomas Rush	1942	RLW 22 131
Neary, Frank B.	1946	RLW 23 53
Nehrer, Mary B.	1952	RLW 23 185

Newmeyer, Emanuel	1945	RLW 23 239
Newman, Maxwell C.	1956	TLA 26 376
Nizer, Samuel H.	1916	JA 16 42
Nicholson, Hopper Emory	1920	JA 16 245
Nicoll, Thomas Y.	1921	CHR 18 104
Nickas, Sam.	1959	WFNP 13 559
Norris, Joseph	1795	AJ 2 484
Norris, Sarah	1780	AJ 2 485
Norrington, Mary	1792	AJ 2 488
Norris, Edward	1793	AJ 2 490
Norris, James	1798	AJ 2 493
Norris, Daniel	1804	AJ C 222
Norton, Stephen	1815	SR 1 46
Norris, Clarissa	1822	SR 1 251
Norris, Aquila	1825	SR 1 334
Norris, Mary	1825	SR 1 345
Norris, John	1829	SR 1 491
Norris, Otho	1830	SR 1 502
Norris, John	1835	TSB 5 197
Norris, William	1837	TSB 5 291
Norris, Edward	1839	TSB 5 388
Norris, Sarah	1851	TSB 6 17
Norris, Vincent	1849	TSB 6 220
Norris, Rhesa	1852	TSB 6 306
Noble, Elizabeth	1856	CWB 7 124
Norton, Thomas	1863	CWB 7 315
Norris, John	1864	CWB 7 358
Norris, Cassandra	1865	CWB 7 381
Norris, James	1872	BHH 8 267
Norris, Elizabeth	1872	BHH 8 300
Norris, Alexander	1873	BHH 8 351
Norris, Sophia E.	1873	BHH 8 377
Norris, Edward	1875	WSR 9 55
Norris, Cardiff D.	1876	WSR 9 75
Norris, David Lee	1883	WSR 10 13
Norris, Fannie L.	1884	WSR 10 45
Norris, Jane D.	1883	WSR 10 97
Norris, David	1885	WSR 10 190
Norris, Salem	1888	WSR 10 443
Norton, Thomas P.	1890	JMM 11 152

O

O'Brien, Mary	1850	TSB 6 261
O'Brien, Louisa Dallam	1905	HTB 14 384
O'Connor, Susan F.	1891	GSN 12 234
O'Donnell, Thomas	1854	CWB 7 31
O'Donnell, Edward O.	1858	CWB 7 177
Oelds, Henrietta	1881	WSR 10 56
Offley, Annie E.	1919	JA 16 53
Offley, Martha M.	1919	JA 16 446
Oliver, Caroline	1886	WSR 10 242
Oldfield, William	1902	GSN 12 443
Oldfield, Nathan H.	1905	HTB 14 122
Oliver, William	1889	HTB 14 289
Oldfield, John F.	1903	CHR 18 176
Oldfield, Laura E.	1938	AJG 20 148
Oldfield, Martha E.	1929	AJG 21 122
Oliver, G. F.	1918	AJG 21 178
Oliver, James	1945	AJG 21 407
Oliver, Mary Magdalene	1945	RLW 22 330
Onion, Zacheus	1781	AJ 2 498
Oneil, Francis	1804	AJ C 251
O'Neill, John	1838	TSB 5 326
O'Neill, Esther	1883	WSR 9 423
Onion, Edward D.	1904	HTB 13 164
Oneill, Henry E.	1917	JA 16 139
O'Neill, Johanna	1925	CSW 17 276
Onion, William S.	1923	CHR 18 34
O'Neill, J. William	1928	CHR 18 306
Onion, James B.	1943	RLW 22 261

Opperman, Richard F.W.	1919	JA 16 150
Orsburn, Benjamin	1880	WSR 9 255
Orr, Sarah E.	1907	HTB 13 415
Orr, J.K.	1909	HTB 14 68
Orr, John A.	1936	AJG 20 423
Orem, Frederick S.	1937	AJG 21 193
Orr, William R.	1944	AJG 21 488
Orr, Susie Morgan	1956	RLW 23 427
Orem, Marie W.	1953	TLA 25 209
Osborn, William	1779	AJ 2 494
Osborn, James	1780	AJ 2 496
Osborn, Jane	1787	AJ 2 502
Osborn, Lawrence	1789	AJ 2 504
Osborn, Cyrus	1798	AJ 2 504
Osborn, Ann	1803	AJ C 142
Osborn, Semelia	1811	SR 1 1
Osborn, Bennet	1815	SR 1 38
Osborn, Elizabeth	1833	TSB 5 114
Osborn, Amos	1841	TSB 5 529
Osborn, James H.	1865	CWB 7 385
Osborn, Bennett	1868	BHH 8 70
Osmond, Jacob Sr.	1899	HTB 13 17
Osborn, Eliza Lavinia	1905	HTB 13 175
Osborn, Lucy Belle	1903	HTB 13 279
Osborn, Rachel	1907	JA 16 75
Osborn, Luther Stewart	1917	JA 16 399
Osborn, Esther N.	1919	AJG 19 309
Osmond, Clarence R.	1941	AJG 21 58
Osmond, Margaret H.	1946	RLW 22 6
Osborn, Mary A.	1951	RLW 23 71
Osborn, S. Mitchell	1954	TLA 24 124
Osborn, Margaret L.	1959	TLA 24 278
Osborn, Carroll S.	1955	TLA 24 389
Osborn, O. Percival	1959	WFNP
Osborn, J. Howard	1944	WFNP 13 781
Osborn, Ulysses G.	1959	TLA 26 292
Osborne, Charles Lester	1957	WFNP 14 350

Otto, Catherine	1897	HTB 13 92
Ould, Mary S.	1903	HTB 13 242
Owings, Eleanor A.	1873	BHH 8 378
Owens, Owen W.	1883	WSR 9 432
Owens, John H.	1896	CSW 17 241
Owens, M. Loula	1927	AJG 20 405
Oyster, Geo. M., Jr.	1918	JA 16 303

P

Patrick, John	1783	AJ 2 510
Paca, Aquila	1783	AJ 2 513
Paca, John	1785	AJ 2 517
Pain, Bever	1788	AJ 2 525
Parker, Martain	1801	AJ C 37
Paul, Thomas	1815	SR 1 11
Patterson, Avarilla	1819	SR 1 177
Patterson, William	1827	SR 1 411
Parker, Joseph	1840	TSB 5 473
Pannell, James	1854	CWB 7 50
Pannell, Susan	1862	CWB 7 280
Paul, James	1863	CWB 7 304
Payne, Willis Minor	1868	BHH 8 54
Parry, Rowlam	1869	BHH 8 107
Payne, Ellen	1870	BHH 8 161
Parish, Daniel H.	1871	BHH 8 204
Parry, David	1875	WSR 9 45
Parry, William	1876	WSR 9 106
Patton, William H.	1880	WSR 9 260
Pannell, William F.	1881	WSR 9 338
Parker, Eliza	1882	WSR 9 380
Pannell, Mary L.	1883	WSR 10 12
Palmer, Mary E.	1880	WSR 10 65
Patterson, John N.	1883	WSR 10 171
Payne, Charity	1887	WSR 10 318
Parry, John, Sr.	1888	WSR 10 440
Payne, Jos. Bosley	1889	WSR 10 463
Patterson, Mary A.	1890	JMM 11 291
Palmer, Walter M. H.	1883	JMM 11 317
Parker, Sarah	1890	JMM 11 325
Parker, Joseph C.	1880	JMM 11 357
Palmer, Elizabeth G.	1891	JMM 11 435
Parker, Lucie	1901	GSN 12 344
Parker, Robert S.	1901	GSN 12 389
Palmer, Isabella E.	1904	HTB 13 285
Parker, Edward	1901	HTB 13 379
Paca, James W.	1916	JA 15 269
Patterson, James H.	1914	JA 15 325
Parker, Mariana	1916	JA 16 179

Page, Robt. S.	1920	JA 16 241
Patterson, M. Margaretta	1917	JA 16 292
Parry, Thomas	1926	CSW 17 380
Pancoast, Laura T.	1924	CHR 18 185
Page, Sarah Elizabeth	1908	CHR 18 229
Paca, Martha C.	1919	CHR 18 335
Parrish, Wm. C.	1931	AJG 19 147
Palmer, Beadie E.	1932	AJG 20 88
Parker, Annie A.	1933	AJG 20 179
Patrick, James Robert	1942	RLW 22 187
Parrott, Telitha	1941	RLW 23 25
Patterson, Charles Edwin	1935	RLW 23 65
Patterson, V. Blanche	1951	RLW 23 85
Papachrist, Christina	1945	RLW 23 384
Pascuzzi, Mary	1941	Filed not prob. 13, 361
Palmer, Lenora	1951	TLA 24 317
Patterson, Joseph	1952	TLA 24 493
Pacholik, Frank	1954	TLA 24 492

Perdue, Walter	1792	AJ 2 526
Perkins, Soloman	1801	AJ C 85
Perine, James	1804	AJ C 240
Perkins, Elizabeth	1816	SR 1 104
Perryman, Isaac	1831	SR 1 537
Perine, Ann	1835	TSB 5 204
Pennington, Cassandra	1840	TSB 5 480
Peaker, Cupid	1847	TSB 6 144
Pearce, Luke Wyle	1848	TSB 6 162
Pennington, John M.	1849	TSB 6 232
Pennington, Eliza A.	1867	BHH 8 31
Peters, Elizabeth	1868	BHH 8 57
Perryman, Juliana J.	1873	BHH 8 354
Peaco, Robert	1881	WSR 9 320
Penniman, Anna M.	1887	JMM 11 64
Pennington, Catherine	1885	JMM 11 401
Peiper, Henry	1893	GSN 12 40
Pennington, Mary E.	1900	GSN 12 309
Pearce, Mary E.	1908	HTB 14 234
Perkins, Nathan E.	1906	HTB 14 282
Penning, O. Parker	1912	HTB 14 395
Pearce, George	1913	JA 15 289
Pearce, Ethel S.	1919	JA 16 70

Pennell, John J.	1923	CSW 17 1
Pearson, Irene L.	1914	CHR 18 126
Pearson, Edwin E.	1930	CHR 18 495
Pennington, Carrollton	1920	AJG 19 249
Perry. John B.	1940	AJG 21 163
Peters, Evelyn Willing	1946	AJG 21 466
Pennington, M. Lareine	1945	AJG 21 473
Peterson, John W.	1944	RLW 22 1
Pennington, George T.	1947	RLW 22 28
Pennington, Robert R.	1948	RLW 22 138
Perry, Elisabeth W.	1953	RLA 23 304
Pearce, Alice A.	1950	TLA 24 363
Pennington, Kate	1958	TLA 24 386
Peters, Irene Ellen	1956	TLA 25 228
Peters, Zula E.	1960	(TLA 25 424
		(TLA 26 283
Perey, Arthur Garfield	1956	WFNP14 071
Pfeltz, Gustavus A.	1892	GSN 12 238
Philips, James	1803	AJ C 168
Philips, Martha	1829	SR 1 467
Philips, Ezra E.	1887	WSR 10 304
Phillips, James M.	1888	GSN 12 83
Phillips, Albert M.	1921	JA 16 284
Phillips, James R.		CHR 18 183
Phelps, Alfred S.	1938	AJG 20 153
Phillips, Geo. Thomas	1942	AJG 21 104
Phillpotts, Joseph	1952	TLA 24 27
Phillips, Mary P.	1953	TLA 25 214
Phillips, George B.	1953	TLA 25 216
Pitcock, Benjamin	1853	TSB 6 353
Pinkney, James	1867	BHH 8 30
Pitt, Peter	1871	BHH 8 255
Pickelberg, Frederick	1880	JMM 11 89
Pinion, William	1898	HTB 13 1
Pinkney, James	1905	JA 15 497

Pinkney, Sarah A. C.	1913	JA 16 147
Pinyon, Josephine E.	1910	JA 16 174
Picker, J. Milton	1950	RLW 23 167
Pitts, Cornelius Edward	1956	RLW 23 412
Pitcock, John H.	1956	TLA 25 62
Pinion, Carrie Jane	1958	TLA 25 97
Plunket, Susey	1784	AJ 2 516
Plowman, Ephriam	1877	WSR 9 154
Plowman, Jacob H.	1897	GSN 12 101
Plowman, Ida B.	1900	HTB 14 80
Pleasants, Henry	1928	CHR 18 145
Poteett, Thomas	1824	SR 1 285
Poteett, Thomas	1823	SR 1 317
Porter, Hugh	1829	SR 1 487
Poteet, Corbin	1837	TSB 5 280
Poteet, Thomas	1846	TSB 6 125
Pocock, David	1852	TSB 6 285
Poteet, James	1854	CWB 7 36
Powell, Miranda	1867	BHH 8 34
Pope, Daniel	1868	BHH 8 100
Polk, William I.	1872	BHH 8 274
Pounder, Mary	1873	BHH 8 384
Pocock, Salem	1876	WSR 9 96
Poole, John	1879	WSR 9 209
Powell, Anna D.	1882	WSR 9 365
Poteet, Elizabeth	1881	WSR 10 167
Poultney, June T. E.	1884	WSR 10 281
Pomeroy, Eugene H.	1907	HTB 13 339
Poteet, Thomas Howard	1913	JA 15 88
Poplar, William H.	1924	AJG 19 146
Powell, Hartley Carr	1936	AJG 20 250
Post, Alfred Philip	1908	AJG 20 322
Poole, Virgie A.	1937	AJG 21 68
Poole, Hannah Agnes	1943	RLW 22 294
Pons, Adolph	1949	RLW 22 394
Poteet, James Howard	1947	RLW 22 450
Poplin, Jettie E.	1951	RLW 23 220
Pohl, Margaret V.	1951	RLW 23 342
Poole, Howard L.	1960	WFNP14 340

Preston, Wm. Henry	1894	JMM 11 429
Price, Edward C.	1898	GSN 12 141
Prigg, Laura A.	1899	GSN 12 259
Prevost, Eliza W.	1900	GSN 12 298
Pretzman, Charles W.	1900	GSN 12 315
Presbury, John Henry	1905	HTB 13 226
Pritchett, E. H.	1907	HTB 13 365
Preston, James H.	1914	JA 15 166
Price, William I.	1905	JA 15 216
Pritchard, Christiana	1905	JA 15 247
Preston, Harriet H.	1905	JA 15 252
Preston, Ella O.	1918	JA 15 455
Pritchard, Joshua Rawhouser	1905	JA 16 60
Proctor, Jeremiah B.	1905	JA 16 220
Preston, Celia Harward	1918	CSW 17 93
Pritchard, Morgan Elliott		CSW 17 409
Price, David E.	1924	CHR 18 192
Price, James Henry	1929	CHR 18 272
Prigg, Clara L. C.	1924	CHR 18 443
Pritchard, Cora A.	1931	AJG 19 34
Preston, Robert S.	1928	AJG 19 51
Prigg, Henry	1934	AJG 19 269
Presbury, Nelson	1935	AJG 19 415
Preston, Mary Elizabeth	1924	AJG 20 50
Prigg, Devereux S.	1920	AJG 20 151
Presbury, Eliza J. F.	1924	CSW 17 170
Proctor, George M.	1924	AJG 20 357
Presberry, Eliza J. F.	1924	AJG 21 84
Pritchard, Missouri Jackson	1934	AJG 21 125
Preston, Columbus	1932	AJG 21 186
Price, Thomas K.	1941	AJG 21 217
Preston, Mary Elizabeth	1948	RLW 22 134
Preston, Walter W.	1941	RLW 22 344
Price, Sadie Harriett	1948	RLW 22 359
Prigg, Vrith L.	1937	RLW 22 384
Pritchard, William S.	1942	RLW 23 46
Price, Cadwaladr	1944	RLW 23 66
Preston, Mary C.	1951	RLW 23 178
Presberry, James O.	1950	TLA 24 395
Price, Mary Estelle	1956	TLA 24 406
Preston, Agnes V.	1952	TLA 24 430
Price, Matilda	1952	TLA 24 473
Preston, Edna S.	1955	TLA 25 121
Price, George A.	1958	WFNP14 033

Pritchard, Margaret Ellen	1960	WFNP 14 361
Preston, Warren E., Sr.	1958	WFNP 14 374
Puttee, Lewis	1779	AJ 2 508
Pue, Michael E.	1882	JMM 11 145
Pusey, Clarence Crane	1922	JA 16 414
Purcell, Martin J.	1925	CSW 17 310
Pue, Cornelia D.	1928	AJG 19 347
Pusey, Mattie Parker	1935	AJG 21 1
Putnam, Walter A.	1946	AJG 21 472
Pyle, Ralph	1803	AJ C 171
Pyle, Sarah	1804	AJ C 230
Pybus, John	1817	SR 1 35
Pyle, John	1834	TSB 5 131
Pyle, William	1842	TSB 5 615
Pyle, Isaac	1849	TSB 6 238
Pyle, Ann	1857	CWB 7 140
Pyle, Nathan	1857	CWB 7 153
Pyle, William H.	1871	BHH 8 210
Pyle, David	1879	WSR 9 205
Pyle, Nathan	1881	WSR 9 291
Pyle, John C.	1872	WSR 10 23
Pyle, Joshua H.	1878	JMM 11 418
Pyle, Sarah Ann	1894	GSN 12 46
Pyle, Eli	1892	HTB 13 10
Pyle, Herman T.	1903	HTB 14 489
Pyle, Rachel Ann	1916	JA 16 36
Pyle, Elisha R.	1927	CHR 18 50
Pyle, Thomas L.	1932	AJG 19 76
Pyle, George Milton	1927	AJG 19 253
Pyle, Florence B.	1930	AJG 19 355
Pyle, William S.	1933	AJG 20 90
Pyle, Martin W.	1938	AJG 21 25
Pyle, Floyd A.	1952	RLW 23 207
Pyle, Herman B.	1923	RLW 23 217
Pyle, Harry S.	1955	RLW 23 301
Pyle, Bertha C.	1958	TLA 26 79

Q

Quinlan, Catharine	1803	AJ C 152
Quarles, Charlotte	1862	CWB 7 272
Quigley, Hugh	1862	CWB 7 291
Quinlan, Susanna	1867	BHH 8 35
Quigley, Rebecca	1883	WSR 9 438
Quinlan, Daniel	1879	WSR 9 224
Quinby, Frank H.	1886	WSR 10 445
Quinby, James H.	1887	JMM 11 284
Quirk, Margaret	1914	JA 16 212
Quigley, William A.	1923	CSW 17 401
Quillen, R. W.	1934	AJG 19 287
Quirk, James J.	1941	AJG 21 411
Quirk, Catherine	1945	RLW 23 51

R

Ramsey, William	1800	AJ C 26
Ramsey, Mary	1807	AJ C 374
Raine, Samuel	1808	AJ C 427
Rampley, James	1817	SR 1 125
Rampley, James	1858	CWB 7 158
Raitt, Cassandra A.	1870	BHH 8 154
Ramsay, Henry B.	1881	WSR 9 275
Rampley, Mary S.	1882	WSR 9 359
Raymond, Mary L. F.	1885	WSR 10 141
Ramsay, Maria	1885	WSR 10 146
Ramsay, Samuel J.	1885	WSR 10 195
Ramsay, John C.	1885	WSR 10 272
Rawhouser, Joshua	1890	JMM 11 285
Raitt, Laura C.	1899	GSN 12 246
Ramsay, Susanna G.	1901	GSN 12 332
Rauscher, Frederick	1902	GSN 12 440
Ramsay, W. W.	1880	HTB 13 176
Rampley, Martha Jane	1906	HTB 13 258
Ramsay, H. C.	1902	HTB 14 119
Randow, Lena	1910	HTB 14 460
Ranson, Robert	1916	JA 15 270
Rahll, Mary	1916	JA 16 248
Radebaugh, Zoe	1922	CSW 17 258
Rawhouser, Wm. H., Sr.	1929	CHR 18 290
Ramsay, Elmer E.	1926	AJG 19 4
Ramsay, John R.	1930	AJG 19 44
Raymond, M. Priscilla	1931	AJG 19 276
Rasmussen, Anton	1926	AJG 19 290
Ramsay, T. Cooper	1913	AJG 19 479
Rampley, Philip N.	1938	AJG 20 191
Rampley, H. Elizabeth	1940	AJG 20 466
Rampley, William S.	1924	AJG 21 11
Rampley, Robt. Nelson, Sr.	1940	AJG 21 13
Rasmussen, Anton	1926	AJG 21 40
Raftes, Charles Arthur	1950	TLA 24 263
Rauscher, Anne	1956	TLA 24 495

Renshaw, Thomas	1774	AJ R 1
Renshaw, Thomas	1784	AJ R 16
Reese, Joseph	1803	AJ C 175
Reese, Abraham	1803	AJ C 178
Renshaw, Joseph	1809	AJ C 474
Renshaw, Cassandra	1812	AJ C 617
Renshaw, Joseph	1830	SR 1 507
Rees, Emmor	1848	TSB 6 196
Reynolds, Harriet A.	1858	CWB 7 170
Redding, Andrew	1860	CWB 7 232
Reid, Upton	1861	CWB 7 266
Reynolds, Edward	1862	CWB 7 277
Reed, Rebecca	1863	CWB 7 311
Rearick, Adam	1863	CWB 7 328
Reynolds, Harmon	1869	BHH 8 115
Reasin, Samuel H.	1872	BHH 8 295
Reese, Philip B.	1880	WSR 9 243
Reese, George	1882	WSR 9 364
Reese, Rebecca A.	1883	WSR 9 451
Renshaw, Cassandra	1883	WSR 10 1
Reasin, Emily M.	1882	WSR 10 107
Reasin, Jas. Frank	1883	WSR 10 226
Reed, Mary M.	1877	WSR 10 262
Reed, David	1887	WSR 10 428
Reynolds, David	1887	JMM 11 42
Reigle, Frank L.	1890	JMM 11 232
Reynolds, Martha Jane	1893	JMM 11 386
Reasin, Fannie M.	1892	GSN 12 56
Reynolds, Esther J.	1897	GSN 12 99
Reddington, John	1899	GSN 12 184
Reckord, Julia A.	1901	GSN 12 362
Reasin, William F.	1890	HTB 13 256
Rembold, Charles	1903	HTB 13 347
Reynolds, Thomas	1902	HTB 13 406
Redding, Timothy	1914	JA 15 11
Reese, Sallie J.	1900	JA 15 108
Reynolds, Martha A.	1914	JA 15 264
Reynolds, W. W.	1916	JA 15 309
Reasin, Jr., William H.	1914	JA 15 384
Reckord, John G.	1917	JA 16 21
Reasin, Annie E.	1924	CSW 17 87
Rembold, Rebecca V.	1930	CHR 18 265
Rembold, Anna Matilda	1926	CHR 18 400
Rembold, John	1920	AJG 19 35

Reeder, Howard E.	1933	AJG	19	81
Reid, William G.	1932	AJG	19	111
Reynolds, Louisa C.	1931	AJG	19	427
Reasin, Emily B.	1938	AJG	20	117
Reasin, Samuel Russell	1931	AJG	21	66
Rembold, Augustine Sr.	1927	AJG	21	115
Reedy, Rebecca J.	1947	RLW	22	391
Redding, Dora Rigdon	1945	RLW	23	63
Rees, Adele Bailey	1951	RLW	23	135
Reeves, Mary J.	1918	TLA	24	108
Reynolds, William L.	1945	TLA	24	99
Reginaldi, Mary	1953	TLA	24	134
Reginaldi, Anthony Joseph	1958	TLA	24	176
Reasin, Harry J.	1958	TLA	25	57
Read, Francis K.	1959	TLA	26	583

Richardson, William	1775	AJ	R	3
Rigbie, Sabina	1779	AJ	R	8
Rigbie, Nathan	1784	AJ	R	18
Richardson, Thomas	1784	AJ	R	20
Richardson, Benjamin	1785	AJ	R	21
Rilly, Barney	1785	AJ	R	23
Rigdun, Baker Thomas	1789	AJ	R	28
Rigbie, James	1791	AJ	R	31
Rigdon, Ann	1797	AJ	R	34
Ricketts, Samuel	1799	AJ	R	36
Richardson, William	1799	AJ	R	37
Richardson, Samuel	1807	AJ	C	369
Richardson, Hannah	1808	AJ	C	409
Richardson, Thomas	1808	AJ	C	446
Richardson, Henry	1812	AJ	C	657
Rigdon, Alexander	1820	SR	1	201
Rigdon, Baker	1820	SR	1	220
Ricketts, Samuel	1823	SR	1	275
Rigdon, Thomas B.	1824	SR	1	302
Richardson, William	1825	SR	1	348
Rigdon, Benjamin	1829	SR	1	461
Richardson, William	1834	TSB	5	151
Rigdon, Stephen	1837	TSB	5	262
Richardson, Elizabeth	1840	TSB	5	?
Rigdon, Benjamin	1849	TSB	6	211
Richardson, Benjamin	1850	TSB	6	240

Ricketts, Samuel	1853	CWB 7	5
Rigdon, Robert A.	1855	CWB 7	59
Riffle, Elizabeth	1855	CWB 7	86
Rigby, Sarah	1861	CWB 7	246
Riley, William	1862	CWB 7	287
Richardson, Margaret E.	1864	CWB 7	352
Rider, George	1865	CWB 7	368
Rigdon, Stephen	1865	CWB 7	371
Rice, William	1867	BHH 8	38
Riley, James	1868	BHH 8	88
Rigdon, George W. S.	1878	WSR 9	184
Riley, Margaretta	1882	WSR 10	71
Richardson, Sophia M.	1861	JMM 11	279
Richardson, Francis	1861	JMM 11	279
Richardson, E. Hall	1887	JMM 11	296
Richardson, Phebe	1889	JMM 11	72
Rigdon, Oliver F.	1897	GSN 12	96
Rickey, Samuel B.	1897	GSN 12	178
Ringland, Mary	1899	GSN 12	231
Richardson, Ezekiel J.	1900	GSN 12	283
Riley, Mary Ann	1901	GSN 12	374
Ringgold, Frederick S.	1903	GSN 12	483
Rigdon, Eli S.	1905	HTB 13	177
Richardson, J. L.	1886	HTB 13	345
Riley, Patrick	1904	HTB 14	141
Richardson, Alice A.	1899	HTB 14	240
Richardson, Lewis	1913	HTB 14	486
Richardson, J. Wiley	1914	JA 15	57
Rigdon, George B.	1913	JA 15	201
Richardson, Jessie Deborah	1908	JA 15	225
Riley, Harry S.	1920	JA 16	190
Ringgold, George	1924	CSW 17	114
Richardson, Japhet	1924	CSW 17	170
Riley, Henry	1924	CSW 17	194
Ridgely, Martin Eichelberger	1923	CSW 17	274
Richardson, Annie E.	1921	CSW 17	314
Rigdon, Virginia	1924	CHR 18	121
Richards, Leonard	1919	CHR 18	463
Rigney, Charles H.	1929	AJG 19	236
Ripken, Affena	1936	AJG 20	266
Riegel, Jennie	1940	AJG 20	359
Rigdon, Summerfield	1934	AJG 20	465
Richardson, J. Woodley	1924	AJG 20	470
Richardson, Nannie E.	1941	AJG 21	55

Richardson, W. H.	1921	AJG 21 59
Riley, John Archer	1939	AJG 21 134
Rickey, Elizabeth M.	1942	AJG 21 251
Rimmey, Sylvia C.	1943	AJG 21 482
Richards, Lena M.	1945	RLW 22 54
Ricketts, Oneda L.	1943	RLW 22 104
Riley, Lillian M.	1942	RLW 22 116
Richardson, Isabel E.	1941	RLW 22 161
Richardson, George O.	1954	RLW 23 241
Richardson, Elizabeth K. H.	1948	RLW 23 296
Rigdon, Edward L.	1937	RLW 23 308
Richardson, Ella Mae Spicer	1954	RLW 23 471
Richardson, Alfred	1954	TLA 24 16
Riddle, Helen Grote	1942	TLA 24 67
Richardson, Virginia H.	1953	TLA 24 177
Riddle, J. Frank	1957	TLA 24 319
Richardson, Letcher A.	1957	TLA 24 360
Rider, Blanche V.	1931	TLA 24 396
Ricci, Frank	1954	TLA 24 410
Richardson, Lewis E.	1960	TLA 25 327
Richardson, Charles R.	1960	WFNP
Ritrosi, Angelo	1953	TLA 26 47
Rice, John	1957	WFNP 14 010
Roberts, Richardson	1777	AJ R 6
Robinson, William	1778	AJ R 7
Roberts, John	1780	AJ R 10
Roberts, Stephen	1782	AJ R 15
Robinson, Edward	1787	AJ R 27
Rodgers, Samuel	1815	SR 1 20
Rodgers, Rowland	1817	SR 1 134
Rodgers, Joseph	1819	SR 1 184
Roberts, John	1827	SR 1 390
Rockhold, Lances Todd	1828	SR 1 449
Rogers, Joseph	1832	TSB 5 1
Rockhold, Sarah	1835	TSB 5 171
Roberts, Ann	1838	TSB 5 353
Robinson, Joseph	1839	TSB 5 381
Robinson, William	1841	TSB 5 549
Roberts, Thomas H.	1843	TSB 6 9
Robinson, George	1852	TSB 6 331
Rogers, Samuel	1854	CWB 7 41

Rogers, Catharine	1855	CWB	7	60
Robinson, Joseph G.	1855	CWB	7	70
Robinson, Sarah	1855	CWB	7	90
Robinson, George W.	1854	CWB	7	32
Robinson, John	1856	CWB	7	102
Robinson, Samuel	1858	CWB	7	157
Rogers, Mary	1859	CWB	7	203
Robinson, Mary	1861	CWB	7	240
Robinson, Charles	1863	CWB	7	299
Rockhold, Elijah	1863	CWB	7	310
Rogers, Elijah B.	1864	CWB	7	355
Rogers, John O.	1865	CWB	7	400
Robinson, John	1867	BHH	8	21
Robinson, Thomas S.	1871	BHH	8	190
Robinson, Ann	1871	BHH	8	207
Rogers, Joseph	1863	BHH	8	272
Rouse, Christopher C.	1872	BHH	8	278
Robinson, Martha S.	1875	WSR	9	34
Ross, A.T.	1875	WSR	9	59
Robinson, James C.	1878	WSR	9	100
Rodgers, John	1881	WSR	9	281
Rodgers, Minerva	1881	WSR	9	282
Roberts, Jane P.	1881	WSR	10	5
Roberts, Hugh	1870	WSR	10	36
Ross, William	1874	WSR	10	332
Rodham, William	1886	WSR	10	245
Robinson, Elizabeth	1880	WSR	10	450
Robinson, Lewis Bolivar	1888	JMM	11	102
Roe, John B.	1891	JMM	11	184
Robinson, Joseph E.	1890	JMM	11	216
Rodgers, Robert S.	1863	JMM	11	221
Rodgers, R. John	1891	JMM	11	237
Robinson, Joseph	1879	JMM	11	314
Rodgers, Grace S.	1891	JMM	11	433
Roberts, Mary E.	1894	JMM	11	440
Roberts, Lewis	1892	GSN	12	2
Roussey, Edwin H.	1896	GSN	12	13
Robinson, James C.	1897	GSN	12	67
Robinson, Sarah	1892	GSN	12	91
Rogers, Sarah E.	1896	GSN	12	149
Rockhold, Lysias	1900	GSN	12	300
Rockhold, Jemima	1900	GSN	12	319
Rogers, James M.	1901	GSN	12	363
Rowland, William B.	1885	GSN	12	412

Rogers, Dorleskea	1903	GSN 12 469
Rogers, Mary E.	1899	HTB 13 7
Robinson, T.J.	1896	HTB 13 19
Roach, Edward	1904	HTB 13 140
Rodgers, Sarah P.	1892	HTB 13 202
Robinson, Marion I.	1903	HTB 13 311
Robinson, Alphonso	1895	HTB 13 326
Roe, Mary J.	1896	HTB 14 124
Rouse, Stephen W.	1908	HTB 14 227
Ross, L.L.	1906	HTB 14 373
Robinson, Joseph M.	1888	HTB 14 413
Robinson, James Harry	1906	JA 15 31
Robinson, John K.	1903	JA 15 121
Roberts, Susanna Davis	1913	JA 15 123
Roach, Mary C.	1908	JA 15 308
Robinson, Wm. T.	1915	JA 16 50
Robinson, Robt. K.	1913	JA 16 157
Rockhold, Elizabeth	1918	JA 16 195
Roberts, Richard	1919	JA 16 419
Rouse, Harriett B.	1922	JA 16 479
Robinson, Daniel Percy		CSW 17 110
Rodgers, John		CSW 17 376
Robinson, Arlena	1925	CSW 17 422
Ross, Hugh	1921	CSW 17 444
Roberts, Thomas H.	1919	CSW 17 451
Rote, Sallie	1915	CHR 18 15
Robinson, Martha Rebecca	1924	CHR 18 80
Robinson, Thomas J.	1912	CHR 18 167
Robey, Anna R.	1927	CHR 18 171
Robinson, Thomas H.	1920	CHR 18 271
Robinson, Lena	1928	CHR 18 300
Robinson, John C.	1927	CHR 18 484
Rodgers, John A.	1931	AJG 19 87
Robinson, Alphonso P.	1929	AJG 19 173
Rodgers, Robert Perry	1926	AJG 19 206
Robbins, Jonathan M.	1925	AJG 19 301
Robinson, William E.	1934	AJG 19 304
Roszyk, Michael	1933	AJG 19 404
Roberts, William W.	1914	AJG 19 488
Rowe, Dorsey F.	1929	AJG 20 14
Robinson, Martha Rebecca	1928	AJG 18 80
Rogers, Wallis O.	1932	AJG 20 258
Roe, Chas. Albert	1936	AJG 20 263
Robinson, Mary Pitts	1937	AJG 20 309

Roberts, Pauline L.		AJG	20	203
Rockey, Charles Franklin	1917	AJG	20	415
Robinson, George W.	1939	AJG	20	427
Robinson, Mildred Catherine	1939	AJG	21	132
Roszyk, Antonina	1933	AJG	21	140
Rogers, Frank G.	1927	AJG	21	146
Roberts, Robert L.	1940	AJG	21	180
Roth, Chas. E. M. D.	1936	AJG	21	321
Rodgers, Elizabeth B. C.	1941	AJG	21	322
Robinson, Howard T.	1932	AJG	21	362
Rogers, Clara L.	1936	AJG	21	424
Rodenmayer, Ella V.	1931	AJG	21	470
Ross, Robert	1941	AJG	21	475
Robinson, Clara C.	1944	AJG	21	489
Robinson, Susie N.	1947	RLW	22	127
Rolph, Mary Eliza	1942	RLW	22	111
Rogers, Gertrude	1947	RLW	22	272
Rodia, Angelina	1942	RLW	22	324
Roth, Martha	1949	RLW	22	326
Rollins, James M.	1941	RLW	22	331
Rossiter, Jennie A.	1943	RLW	22	439
Roux, George P.	1928	RLW	23	87
Roux, Amelia Pelayo	1937	RLW	23	91
Robinson, A. Scott	1952	RLW	23	105
Robinson, Charles Richard	1952	RLW	23	146
Rollins, Martha C.	1951	RLW	23	169
Rouse, Harry J.	1951	RLW	23	177
Rosemer, Christopher J.	1954	RLW	23	273
Rogers, J. Thomas	1955	RLW	23	423
Robinson, John A.	1943	RLW	23	455
Roloson, Gertrude M.	1958	TLA	24	199
Ross, Alberta E.	1957	TLA	24	428
Robinson, Laura V.	1958	TLA	25	7
Roszyk, Frank M.	1957	TLA	26	149
Roland, Elihu G.	1958	WFNP	14	167
Robinson, Alverta	1957	TLA	26	569

Russell, Robert	1775	AJ	R	4
Ruth, Moses	1781	AJ	R	11
Ruth, Ester	1786	AJ	R	25
Ruff, John	1800	AJ	R	40

Rutledge, John	1800	AJ C 13
Ruff, Hannah	1801	AJ C 634
Rumsey, Benjamin	1808	AJ C 415
Ruff, Richard	1812	AJ C 634
Ruff, Henry	1815	SR 1 21
Rutledge, Ruth	1816	SR 1 78
Ruff, Mary	1820	SR 1 213
Ruff, Richard	1823	SR 1 269
Rutledge, Joshua	1825	SR 1 350
Rutledge, William	1836	TSB 5 232
Rush, Arnold	1844	TSB 6 31
Ruth, Susan O.	1833	TSB 5 107
Ruff, Henry	1845	TSB 6 65
Rush, John C.	1847	TSB 6 130
Rutledge, Hannah	1845	TSB 6 85
Rutledge, Adeline	1871	BHH 8 198
Russell, Thomas	1876	BHH 8 227
Rutledge, John W.	1873	BHH 8 334
Rutledge, Abraham	1875	WSR 9 52
Rutledge, Ignatius	1875	WSR 9 68
Rutledge, Mary A.	1880	WSR 9 240
Rutledge, A. Charles S.	1882	WSR 9 385
Russell, Avarilla	1878	WSR 10 284
Rutledge, Julia A.	1889	JMM 11 48
Rutledge, Caroline V.	1885	JMM 11 151
Rutledge, Joshua	1892	JMM 11 270
Ruth, Elizabeth	1887	JMM 11 79
Rutledge, Martha R.	1891	GSN 12 94
Rutledge, Phebe S.	1901	GSN 12 340
Rutledge, Patrick H.	1902	GSN 12 434
Rutledge, Henrietta M.	1904	HTB 13 79
Rutledge, Monica Ann	1907	HTB 14 199
Ruff, Elizabeth T.	1904	HTB 14 318
Rutledge, E. Randolph	1912	JA 15 80
Rutledge, Martha J.	1913	JA 16 313
Russell, Robert	1925	CSW 17 211
Russell, John H.	1921	CSW 17 217
Ruff, James H.	1906	CSW 17 278
Rutledge, John R.	1924	CSW 17 286
Rutledge, William S.	1919	CSW 17 474
Russell, John A.	1924	CHR 18 244
Russell, Catherine C.	1934	AJG 19 364
Russell, Robert C.	1929	AJG 20 23
Rush, Jacob H.	1934	AJG 20 167

Runan, Rachel Elizabeth	1910	AJG 20 248
Rumsey, George	1932	AJG 20 280
Rutledge, Mary Wallace	1935	AJG 21 133
Ruff, Jesse H.	1927	AJG 21 218
Rumsey, Margaret	1943	RLW 22 417
Ryan, Martin	1872	BHH 8 296
Ryan, Thos. W.	1921	JA 16 354
Ryan, Florence E.	1939	AJG 21 114

S

Saunders, Robert	1785	AJ R 78
Saunders, James	1790	AJ R 85
Saunders, Thomas	1790	AJ R 86
Saunders, Robert	1812	AJ C 619
Saunders, John	1812	AJ C 688
Saunders, Elizabeth	1821	SR 1 248
Sappington, Richard	1824	SR 1 311
Sanders, John	1839	TSB 5 425
Sappington, Cassandra	1852	TSB 6 336
Sawyer, William	1857	CWB 7 125
Saunders, Maria	1863	CWB 7 303
Sappington, John K.	1868	BHH 8 81
Saunders, John C.	1872	BHH 8 275
Sample, Sarah	1869	BHH 8 126
Sargable, Michael	1877	WSR 9 137
Saunders, Mary H.	1881	WSR 9 311
Sanders, Ralph	1881	WSR 9 322
Sadler, Thomas	1883	WSR 10 371
Savin, Patrick C.	1882	JMM 11 75
Sappington, Mary Ann	1885	JMM 11 114
Sawyer, Benjamin	1891	JMM 11 198
Salik, John C.	1899	HTB 13 118
Sawyer, William T.	1905	HTB 13 483
Sargable, Michael	1909	HTB 14 32
Salik, Lydia	1909	HTB 14 104
Sawyer, Octavia G.	1920	JA 16 251
Savin, Edward F.	1901	CSW 17 215
Sallada, Mary	1926	CHR 18 72
Sawyer, Mary M.	1903	CHR 18 195
Sanner, Basil P.	1929	CHR 18 211
Sanders, Margaret A.	1918	AJG 21 53
Savin, Mary J. I.	1924	AJG 19 88
Saunders, S. N.	1918	AJG 21 174
Sappington, Purnell F.	1936	AJG 21 248
Santi, Katharine	1943	RLW 22 264
Sadtler, Florence P.	1947	TLA 24 70
Salik, John J.	1958	TLA 24 212
Sampson, Richard W., Jr.	1959	WFNP 13 847

Scott, Benjamin	1782	AJ	R	59
Scott, Ann	1783	AJ	R	61
Scott, Robert	1784	AJ	R	66
Scott, Susanna	1798	AJ	R	107
Scarff, Henry, Sr.	1801	AJ	C	60
Scarff, Henry, Jr.	1800	AJ	C	63
Scarff, John	1801	AJ	C	88
Scarborough, Isaac	1815	SR	1	49
Scarborough, William	1823	SR	1	277
Scott, Daniel	1828	SR	1	435
Scarborough, Thomas	1831	SR	1	527
Scarff, Hannah	1833	TSB	5	80
Scarff, Polley	1838	TSB	5	319
Scarff, Henry	1844	TSB	6	43
Scott, Clemency	1848	TSB	6	202
Scott, Otho	1864	CWB	7	343
Scott, Elizabeth	1864	CWB	7	347
Scarborough, Archibald	1869	BHH	8	128
Scarborough, Edward A.	1869	BHH	8	145
Scarborough, Thomas F.	1872	BHH	8	299
Scarborough, Benjamin	1875	WSR	9	40
Scott, James	1877	WSR	9	147
Scarborough, Hannah	1879	WSR	9	208
Scarborough, Maurice	1881	WSR	9	327
Scarborough, John W.	1882	WSR	9	347
Scarff, Joshua H.	1884	WSR	10	119
Scarborough, Elizabeth F.	1885	WSR	10	156
Scott, Mary Jane	1881	WSR	10	176
Scarborough, Euclidus	1887	WSR	10	201
Scarff, John C.	1876	WSR	10	289
Scott, John	1879	WSR	10	302
Scarborough, Isaac	1887	WSR	10	378
Scott, Ross	1885	WSR	10	415
Scott, Margaret	1888	WSR	10	431
Scarborough, Elizabeth	1883	JMM	11	306
Scott, Ann D.	1886	JMM	11	246
Scarborough, Josiah	1890	JMM	11	356
Scarborough, Rachael A.	1887	JMM	11	364
Scarborough, H. S.	1891	JMM	11	453
Scarborough, Juliann	1888	GSN	12	85
Schlereth, Michael	1898	GSN	12	198
Scarborough, Jacob F.	1900	GSN	12	307
Scott, Daniel	1900	GSN	12	308
Schilling, Henry C.	1902	GSN	12	402

Scott, Eliza	1903	GSN 12	465
Schauck, Rebecca C.	1899	HTB 13	199
Schuster, John	1904	HTB 13	222
Scully, Mary	1906	HTB 13	482
Scarborough, John B.	1905	HTB 13	495
Schlatzer, Ernestine	1903	HTB 14	1
Scarff, Charles T.	1907	HTB 14	88
Scarborough, Mary P.	1901	HTB 14	156
Scarborough, Rachel F.	1905	HTB 14	368
Scott, Robert D.	1912	HTB 14	374
Scarborough, Calvin A.	1916	JA 15	265
Scarff, E. Ellsworth	1894	JA 15	328
Scarff, I. A., Jr.	1917	JA 15	331
Scarff, Isreal A.	1917	JA 15	340
Scarff, Phillip G.	1917	JA 16	38
Schneider, Theodore A.	1900	JA 16	213
Schafer, Margaret K.	1922	JA 16	488
Scarborough, Mary	1924	CSW 17	166
Scott, Mildred I.	1927	CHR 18	69
Scarborough, Nelson	1920	CHR 18	256
Schuck, Catharine A.	1923	CHR 18	310
Scott, Catherine A.	1932	AJG 19	228
Schuster, John P.	1932	AJG 19	336
Schoenhols, William	1891	AJG 19	348
Schultz, Paulina Maliazewska	1934	AJG 19	424
Schilling, Mary R.	1934	AJG 20	16
Schultz, Carrie M.	1931	AJG 20	29
Scarff, J. Howard	1933	AJG 20	161
Schlereth, Catherine		AJG 20	391
Scarff, Amanda J.	1940	AJG 21	10
Schantz, John George	1945	AJG 21	387
Schluderberg, William F.	1957	TLA 24	30
Schelling, Earl H.	1941	RLW 22	45
Schurman, William	1946	RLW 22	79
Schilling, Henry C.	1920	AJG 21	415
Schlusner, Hannah Ries	1932	RLW 22	366
Scott, Rachel A.L.	1951	RLW 22	408
Scarborough, Eva O.	1950	RLW 22	459
Scarborough, Joseph Harvey	1935	RLW 23	320
Sciulli, Dolores	1955	RLW 23	379
Schinault, Bertie	1948	TLA 24	239
Scarborough, Edith A.	1959	TLA 24	315
Scarborough, Bessie E.	1952	TLA 24	478
Schillinger, Henry	1951	TLA 26	243

Schroeder, Charles A.	1960	TLA 26 346
Sewell, John	1805	AJ C 289
Sears, Mary	1831	SR 1 524
Sewell, Clement K.	1843	TSB 6 13
Sewell, Charles S.	1848	TSB 6 197
Sealor, Ellen	1865	CWB 7 377
Seneca, Mary A.	1883	WSR 9 420
Sewell, Maria L.	1901	GSN 12 348
Sewell, Clement K.	1909	HTB 14 40
Seneca, Stephen J.	1918	JA 16 5
Seyfreit, Joseph	1922	JA 16 413
Seneca, Annie E.	1923	JA 16 470
Seagle, Walter T.	1924	CSW 17 270
Segar, J. Clark	1917	CHR 18 294
Sewell, Isaac	1931	AJG 19 277
Selfe, Sallie Ritchie	1935	AJG 19 407
Sewell, Mary M.	1937	AJG 21 344
Seward, Gertie A.	1953	RLW 23 321
Seibert, Herman C.	1957	TLA 24 487
Sentman, Mary Alberta	1958	TLA 25 90
Sheredine, Jeremiah	1775	AJ R 45
Sheredine, Cassandra	1776	AJ R 46
Sheredine, James	1838	TSB 5 367
Shanon, John	1858	CWB 7 162
Shean, Henry W.	1861	CWB 7 243
Shannon, Mary A.	1861	CWB 7 263
Shafer, Jacob	1870	BHH 8 164
Shroff, Joseph W.	1879	WSR 9 229
Shay, Bennett	1880	WSR 9 249
Shields, Timothy	1886	WSR 10 179
Shanahan, Mary	1888	WSR 10 405
Shure, Daniel F.	1889	JMM 11 192
Shanahan, John M.	1884	JMM 11 245
Shanahan, Richard J.	1899	GSN 12 259
Shenk, R. W.	1901	GSN 12 335
Shenk, David B.	1901	(GSN 12 335
		(GSN 12 353
Shea, James	1905	HTB 13 316

Shure, Jane	1901	HTB 13 344
Sheridan, C. J.	1907	HTB 13 371
Shipley, John A.	1909	HTB 14 94
Shure, Georgia Gwinn	1903	HTB 14 115
Shanahan, Patrick J.	1910	HTB 14 145
Shertzer, Mary A.	1906	HTB 14 153
Shure, Grace H.	1911	HTB 14 197
Shanahan, Mary C.	1899	HTB 14 300
Shultz, Jacob	1880	HTB 14 305
Shanahan, Mary L.	1911	JA 15 336
Shanbargar, William	1909	JA 15 472
Shannon, Mary A.	1915	JA 16 230
Shanahan, Dennis J.	1923	CSW 17 33
Shanahan, Hattie B.	1923	CSW 17 308
Sheridan, Ella Emmons	1921	CSW 17 390
Shelton, Laura G.	1915	CHR 18 84
Shaffer, H. G.	1929	CHR 18 178
Shoemaker, Hannah	1929	CHR 18 208
Shure, William	1925	AJG 19 52
Shane, Ellanore	1933	AJG 19 195
Shultz, Jacob	1936	AJG 20 113
Shriver, Harry T.	1937	AJG 20 234
Shriver, Martha M.	1901	AJG 20 365
Sherman, George Theodore	1933	RLW 22 64
Shaw, Fannie B.	1931	RLW 22 85
Shakespeare, Raymond K.	1948	RLW 22 351
Sheppard, Caroline M.	1937	RLW 22 431
Sheridan, Annie E.	1952	RLW 23 265
Shriver, Harriet L. V. B.	1942	RLW 23 480
Shanahan, Margaret E.	1957	TLA 24 220
Shaw, Alexander	1901	TLA 24 302
Shaw, John K.	1904	TLA 24 294
Shafer, Howard Grant	1953	TLA 24 345
Shapiro, Doris	1960	WFNP
Shaw, Otho E.	1949	WFNP 13 735
Sheppard, Jim S.	1950	WFNP 13 965
Shapiro, Ida	1959	TLA 26 258
Schroeder, Caroline	1960	WP& F 14 139
Sims, Alse	1780	AJ R 55
Sims, William	1808	AJ C 413
Silver, Harriet	1816	SR 1 74

Silver, Benjamin	1818	SR 1 167
Silver, William	1837	TSB 5 266
Silver, Elizabeth	1848	TSB 6 171
Silver, David	1854	CWB 7 27
Silver, Charity	1860	CWB 7 228
Silver, Alice H.	1868	BHH 8 59
Silver, Benjamin	1869	BHH 8 111
Singleton, Jacob	1880	WSR 9 248
Silver, Emily M.	1882	WSR 9 355
Silver, Silas P.	1883	WSR 9 424
Sirgable, Augusta	1882	WSR 10 205
Silver, Benjamin Jr.	1888	JMM 11 123
Silver, Mary C.	1893	GSN 12 28
Silver, Mary	1897	GSN 12 79
Simms, Jacob H.	1899	GSN 12 257
Silver, William Z.	1901	GSN 12 360
Silver, George B.	1903	GSN 12 460
Silver, Mary E	1903	GSN 12 490
Sims, Tiney	1908	HTB 13 392
Silver, Sylvester A.	1911	JA 15 284
Silver, Geo. O.	1919	JA 16 193
Silver, Susan	1921	JA 16 357
Simonds, Laura V.	1924	CSW 17 111
Silver, Carrie G.	1924	CSW 17 117
Silver, George E.	1924	CSW 17 176
Siggins, Rev. Francis Xavier	1921	CSW 17 353
Silver, Mary Warnock	1926	CSW 17 428
Sills, John W.	1927	CSW 17 488
Silver, Mary Ellen	1923	CHR 18 120
Silver, Mary Iola	1931	CHR 18 427
Silver, William	1933	AJG 19 208
Silver, W. Scott	1938	AJG 21 112
Silver, Joel W.	1944	AJG 21 360
Simone, Mary	1945	AJG 21 449
Sills, James E.	1947	RLW 22 129
Silver, Edith, W.S.	1948	RLW 22 162
Silver, Eliza Pamela	1942	RLW 22 454
Silver, Francina Hopkins	1949	RLW 23 3
Sillik, George E.	1934	RLW 23 5
Sinclair, Osa S.	1946	RLW 23 109
Sinclair, Gus	1950	TLA 24 133
Singewold, Eleanore	1957	TLA 24 390
Silveira, Gerogia Irene	1958	TLA 27 72

Skeventon, James	1801	AJ C 49
Skillman, Thomas H.	1901	GSN 12 348
Skillman, Joseph F.	1926	CSW 17 408
Skillman, John L.	1927	CHR 18 2
Skillman, William N.	1926	AJG 19 12
Skinner, Katie De Haven	1935	AJG 20 156
Skillman, Blanche L.	1943	RLW 22 336
Skillman, Harry	1950	RLW 23 17
Slack, Elizabeth	1780	AJ R 56
Slade, Ezekiel	1802	AJ C 114
Slade, James W.	1849	TSB 6 222
Slade, Dixson	1851	TSB 6 281
Slade, Ezekiel	1853	TSB 6 344
Slade, John	1855	CWB 7 80
Sleeper, James	1856	CWB 7 103
Slade, Abraham	1860	CWB 7 238
Slade, Washington M.	1867	BHH 8 44
Slade, Rosanna	1873	BHH 8 349
Slade, Ezekiel	1881	WSR 9 308
Slade, Martha	1879	WSR 10 152
Slade, Mary	1882	JMM 11 132
Slade, Caroline	1890	JMM 11 165
Slymer, Sarah H.	1902	GSN 12 451
Slymer, Anthony F.	1903	HTB 13 39
Slade, John S.	1917	CHR 18 30
Slater, John H.	1910	CHR 18 112
Sliver, Rachel Ann	1926	AJG 19 41
Slatherly, Susan Grovenstein	1934	AJG 19 286
Slade, Rose	1928	AJG 19 295
Slade, Asbury	1936	AJG 20 22
Slee, Mattie L.	1932	AJG 21 18
Slavik, Paul J.	1943	RLW 22 230
Slee, John Bay	1946	RLW 22 277
Sliver, Benjamin Harison	1950	RLW 22 289
Slee, Warren Hudson	1950	RLW 22 300
Slade, J. Isaac	1955	TLA 24 84
Slade, Electa M.	1959	TLA 24 470

Smith, Ruth	1774	AJ	R	44
Smith, Samuel	1776	AJ	R	48
Smith, Robert	1776	AJ	R	49
Smith, William	1777	AJ	R	51
Smith, William	1796	AJ	R	73
Smith, Robert	1788	AJ	R	83
Smith, Thomas	1791	AJ	R	90
Smith, Susanna	1795	AJ	R	97
Smithson, Thomas	1795	AJ	R	98
Smith, Patrick	1807	AJ	C	394
Smithson, William	1809	AJ	C	451
Smith, Alice	1810	AJ	C	522
Smith, Hannah	1810	AJ	C	524
Smith, Samuel	1811	AJ	C	546
Smithson, Mary	1812	AJ	C	637
Smith, Josiah	1812	AJ	C	677
Smithson, Nathaniel	1816	SR	1	93
Smith, John	1816	SR	1	100
Smithson, Elizabeth	1818	SR	1	163
Smith, Paca	1830	SR	1	515
Smithson, William	1836	TSB	5	258
Smith, Hugh	1839	TSB	5	253
Smith, Frances	1849	TSB	6	207
Smith, Amos	1849	TSB	6	213
Smith, William R.	1852	TSB	1	284
Smithson, Luther M.	1854	CWB	7	23
Smith, Samuel	1854	CWB	7	38
Smith, Laura I.	1855	CWB	7	56
Smith, Nathaniel	1856	CWB	7	95
Smithson, John	1857	CWB	7	135
Smithson, Thomas	1859	CWB	7	200
Smith, Maria M.	1860	CWB	7	236
Smith, Frenetta F.	1860	CWB	7	237
Smith, Ann	1870	BHH	8	162
Smith, Mary	1871	BHH	8	208
Smith, Elizabeth C.	1871	BHH	8	239
Smith, Christian	1871	BHH	8	249
Smithson, Sally Ann	1876	WSR	9	78
Smithson, William	1877	WSR	9	129
Smith, Mary	1878	WSR	9	187
Smith, Jane	1879	WSR	9	212
Smith, Sarah	1879	WSR	9	218
Smith, Lydia	1879	WSR	9	221
Smithson, George A.	1879	WSR	9	233

Smith, Charlotte R.	1914	CHR 18 348
Smith, H. Edgar	1931	CHR 18 409
Smithson, John F.	1921	AJG 19 56
Smith, Alice Hall	1926	AJG 19 142
Smith, Livingston	1935	AJG 19 354
Smith, Henry M.	1935	AJG 19 380
Smithson, Priscilla F.	1921	AJG 19 440
Smithson, A. Sibella S.	1927	AJG 20 92
Smart, Lottie A.	1942	AJG 21 108
Smith, Ethel Clinton	1945	RLW 22 290
Smith, George W.	1921	RLW 22 471
Smith, Christian P.	1947	RLW 23 328
Smith, Helen T.	1951	RLW 23 483
Smith, John H.	1953	TLA 24 8
Smith, Henrietta Mitchell	1955	TLA 24 182
Smith, Mary Kurtz	1949	TLA 24 228
Smith, Ellen Donnell	1957	TLA 24 231
Smith, F. Nelson	1954	TLA 25 137
Smith, Ed Sinclair	1950	TLA 25 141
Smithson, Emory	1960	WFNP
Smith, Jacob	1960	TLA 25 391
Snodgrass, John I.		JA 16 188
Snodgrass, Hannah	1927	CSW 17 450
Snarely, Jacob	1930	AJG 21 428
Snodgrass, Franklin P.	1960	TLA 26 252
Sommer, Frederick M.	1912	HTB 14 314
Somerville, Laura A.	1908	JA 16 108
Sowden, James D.	1931	AJG 20 455
South, Jerome J.	1938	AJG 21 196
Souter, Robert Kimble	1953	RLW 23 352
Spencer, Zacharias	1783	AJ R 64
Spencer, Enoch	1799	AJ R 105
Sprusebanks, Abraham	1783	AJ 2 61
Spencer, Sarah	1819	SR 1 189
Spencer, James, Sr.	1857	CWB 7 144

St. Clair, Alisanna	1837	TSB 5 310
Stephenson, James	1838	TSB 5 338
Streett, Thomas	1839	TSB 5 410
Stephenson, Eliza	1840	TSB 5 427
Stump, Reuben	1841	TSB 5 517
Stone, John	1846	TSB 6 109
Stone, John	1846	TSB 6 110
Stump, Cassandra	1846	TSB 6 113
St. Clair, Bailey	1847	TSB 6 127
Streett, Roger	1850	TSB 6 245
Steel, James	1851	TSB 6 269
Stokes, David	1852	TSB 6 288
Streett, Martha A.	1853	TSB 6 340
St. Clair, Mary	1853	CWB 7 12
St. Clair, Ann	1854	CWB 7 31
Stamp, Samuel C.	1854	CWB 7 35
Standiford, Lloyd	1855	CWB 7 58
Streett, William, Sr.	1857	CWB 7 147
Stephenson, Susanna	1858	CWB 7 168
Stokes, Harvey	1859	CWB 7 198
Standiford, William R.	1860	CWB 7 211
Stewart, Finley	1860	CWB 7 212
Streett, William	1860	CWB 7 218
Stump, Margaret M.	1861	CWB 7 255
St. Clair, William of Jas.	1861	CWB 7 265
Stritehoof, Peter	1861	CWB 7 270
Stump, John W.	1862	CWB 7 293
St. Clair, Elizabeth	1863	CWB 7 303
Streett, Thomas	1864	CWB 7 348
Streett, St. Clair	1864	CWB 7 363
Stump, Wm. Henry	1865	CWB 7 373
Stump, Mary	1865	CWB 7 374
St. Clair, Elizabeth	1865	CWB 7 388
Stiltz, Robert M.	1866	BHH 8 2
Stump, Ann	1868	BHH 8 99
Stump, Ann	1869	BHH 8 130
Stritehoof, Susanna	1869	BHH 8 105
Stroble, Zachariah	1869	BHH 8 113
Stewart, Robert	1869	BHH 8 141
Stump, Margaret	1870	BHH 8 179
Stump, Margaret	1870	BHH 8 181
Streett, John W.	1871	BHH 8 259
Stump, Hannah	1872	BHH 8 283
Streett, Shadrach, Sr.	1872	BHH 8 292

Streett, Mary Ann	1875	WSR 9	49
Stewart, John	1876	WSR 9	82
Streett, Thomas	1876	WSR 9	123
St. Clair, James M.	1877	WSR 9	130
Stokes, William B.	1877	WSR 9	131
Streett, Corbin G.	1878	WSR 9	167
Stephenson, Mary	1878	WSR 9	188
Standiford, Claudius	1878	WSR 9	193
Stephenson, James	1879	WSR 9	206
Standiford, Isaac	1879	WSR 9	226
Stump, Sarah B.	1868	WFNP.	
Stansbury, James	1880	WSR 9	237
Stillwell, Court	1880	WSR 9	266
Stawbridge, Joseph, Sr.	1881	WSR 9	276
Stump, Herman	1881	WSR 9	299
Stockham, Thomas	1881	WSR 9	326
St. Clair, John V.	1882	WSR 9	363
Stokes, Nathan R.	1882	WSR 9	369
Streett, Margaret	1882	WSR 9	376
Streett, Marryman	1882	WSR 9	386
Stonebraker, John	1883	WSR 9	430
Stephenson, Elizabeth N.	1880	WSR 10	10
Stephenson, William B.	1883	WSR 10	30
Stephenson, Elizabeth	1883	WSR 10	34
Stewart, Luther M.	1884	WSR 10	39
Stockham, George	1880	WSR 10	148
St. Clair, David	1886	WSR 10	169
Streett, John M.	1886	WSR 10	278
St. Clair, Elizabeth	1886	WSR 10	305
Student, James	1887	WSR 10	317
St. Clair, Mary Ann	1869	WSR 10	437
Streett, Anna	1874	WSR 10	451
Stewart, Mary	1878	WSR 10	460
Stewart, Maria E.	1884	WSR 10	462
Stansbury, William	1887	WSR 10	467
Streett, Samuel	1889	JMM 11	32
Stokes, John R.	1889	JMM 11	61
Streett, Elizabeth H.	1886	JMM 11	90
Stockham, John E.	1888	JMM 11	95
Stephenson, Hetty	1883	JMM 11	134
Streett, Thomas H.	1886	JMM 11	166
Standiford, Isaac	1891	JMM 11	193
Stacks, Emmaline	1890	JMM 11	220
St. Clair. Elizabeth R.	1888	JMM 11	250

Stephenson, Ann P.	1888	JMM 11	267
Stilwell, James O.	1880	JMM 11	287
Streett, Hannah	1890	JMM 11	313
Stephenson, Hannah G.	1883	JMM 11	328
Streett, Elizabeth	1881	JMM 11	335
Stine, John	1880	JMM 11	412
Stokes, John H.	1894	JMM 11	487
Stansbury, S. A.	1896	GSN 12	19
Stokes, Henry C.	1897	GSN 12	114
Stokes, Hannah L.	1897	GSN 12	128
Stanfenberger, Apilonia	1898	GSN 12	187
Standiford, Dennis H.	1899	GSN 12	226
Streett, Elizabeth J.	1899	GSN 12	242
Stephenson, Margaret	1900	GSN 12	269
Stonebraker, John C.	1901	GSN 12	334
Strasbaugh, Isabella W.	1901	GSN 12	343
Stewart, Martha E.	1901	GSN 12	350
Stephenson, M. Priscilla	1901	GSN 12	376
Streett, Annie M.	1903	GSN 12	461
Steigler, George	1903	GSN 12	481
Stephenson, Beulah P.	1903	HTB 13	54
Streett, Howard W.	1904	HTB 13	236
Streett, Charles H.	1906	HTB 13	263
Streett, Fanny V.	1905	HTB 13	275
Stone, Joseph T.	1906	HTB 13	315
St. Clair, Bailey, Sr.	1907	HTB 13	366
Stevens, Robert A.	1907	HTB 13	388
Stopple, John Adam	1907	HTB 13	401
Stine, Anna Mary	1899	HTB 13	428
Streett, Susie C.	1910	HTB 14	110
Stearns, John O.	1906	HTB 14	140
Standiford, John E.	1881	HTB 14	269
Stritehoff, Franklin B.	1912	HTB 14	293
Steltz, Laura E.	1911	HTB 14	311
Stansbury, Orilla C.	1912	HTB 14	409
Stewart, Albertine	1913	HTB 14	439
Strawbridge, Nora V.	1915	JA 15	141
Staley, William H.	1915	JA 15	233
Stockham, Charles	1912	JA 15	255
Stoppel, Christiana	1913	JA 15	298
Stump, Herman	1913	JA 15	303
Streett, Mattie C.	1916	JA 15	305
Streett, John Rush	1917	JA 15	324
Stewart, John	1908	JA 15	355

Standiford, Naomi Blanche	1946	AJG	21 457
Strickland, Frank Martin	1933	AJG	21 469
Staniewski, Ignace	1947	RLW	22 11
Steen, John Leslie	1940	AJG	21 416
Stainback, Mary D.V.	1935	RLW	22 274
Streett, Hannah B.	1946	RLW	22 275
Streett, Samuel	1948	RLW	23 130
Stainbach, J. Avery	1955	RLW	23 269
Stilwell, Harold	1942	RLW	23 361
Stansbury, Robert A.	1956	RLW	23 438
Stansbury, Mary J.	1948	RLW	23 481
Stryker, Harriet Daniels	1956	TLA	24 42
Stokes, William Morton	1957	TLA	24 62
Stamper, Bert S.	1957	TLA	24 66
Stevens, Alice	1955	TLA	24 238
Standiford, Edwin F.	1956	TLA	24 280
Stump, Constance Poor	1959	TLA	24 431
Stempel, John Herman	1958	TLA	24 453
Street, Kennedy	1925	TLA	25 111
Stewart, Le Roy	1959	WFNP	13 743
Stump, Carrie T. Riegel	1934	TLA	25 272
Stump, H. Arthur	1928	TLA	25 281
Stamper, Edward D.	1948	TLA	25 338
Sterbak, Marie	1948	TLA	25 373
Steinback, Rozin L.	1927	TLA	26 53
Stolba, Frank J.	1953	TLA	26 83
Stark, Harold E.	1955	TLA	26 193
Steinmetz, Theodore P.	1960	WFNP	14 102
Streett, Thomas Clarence	1947	TLA	26 286
Stewart, Edna L.	1956	TLA	26 419

Sutton, Samuel	1793	AJ	R 95
Sutherland, Alexander	1829	SR	1 485
Sutton, Mary	1852	TSB	6 324
Sutton, I.P.S.	1868	BHH	8 85
Sutton, Samuel	1878	WSR	9 170
Sutton, Jonathan	1882	WSR	9 383
Sutton, Thomas	1878	WSR	10 84
Sutton, William T.	1878	GSN	12 108
Sutton, Susan J.	1898	GSN	12 194

154

T

Taylor, Abraham	1788	AJ R 126
Talbott, Edmund	1794	AJ R 134
Taylor, Jane	1811	AJ C 587
Taylor, Asbury	1811	AJ C 590
Taylor, Jesse	1822	SR 1 252
Tally, Edward	1825	SR 1 340
Tasco, Frank	1828	SR 1 457
Tayson, James A.	1848	TSB 6 192
Taylor, Robert G.	1870	BHH 8 158
Tanguy, Alfred A.	1870	BHH 8 164
Taylor, John	1871	BHH 8 219
Tate, James	1873	BHH 8 323
Taylor, William P.	1879	WSR 9 222
Taylor, Nancy	1879	WSR 9 232
Taylor, Abednego	1879	WSR 9 235
Taylor, William	1883	WSR 10 7
Tate, Martha W.	1883	WSR 10 18
Taylor, Sophrina A.W.	1878	WSR 10 66
Taylor, John	1880	WSR 10 126
Talbot, Benjamin	1875	WSR 10 231
Taylor, Margaret	1885	JMM 11 142
Taylor, Mary A.	1877	JMM 11 293
Tate, David	1893	JMM 11 363
Taylor, James	1896	JMM 11 474
Taylor, Henry L.	1895	GSN 12 102
Taylor, Martha Ann	1903	GSN 12 495
Tasker, Alonzo	1896	HTB 13 28
Taylor, John M.	1899	HTB 13 431
Taylor, Richard M.	1912	HTB 14 389
Taylor, Franklin	1903	JA 15 20
Tallman, Henry	1913	JA 15 112
Taylor, Wm. H.	1921	JA 16 365
Tarring, Henry	1926	CSW 17 484
Taylor, Mary A.	1928	CHR 18 118
Tate, George W.	1919	CHR 18 132
Tagland, Colbin Nicholas	19 ?	CHR 18 179
Taylor, Charles E.	1933	AJG 19 313
Taylor, Anna E.	1928	AJG 19 428
Taylor, Roger	1935	AJG 20 69

Taylor, Richard A. S.	1939	RLW 22 100
Taylor, Florence Grace German	1930	RLW 22 140
Tarring, LeRoy B.	1934	RLW 23 86
Tarquini, Armando	1952	RLW 23 232
Taylor, John Howard	1956	RLW 23 406
Tasker/Tasco, Philip Harry	1952	TLA 24 26
Taylor, Ida V.	1955	TLA 24 184
Taylor, Jesse C.	1954	TLA 24 226
Tarring, Maude A.	1959	
Tennant, John C.	1865	CWB 7 372
Temple, Elizabeth	1877	WSR 9 141
Terry, George W.	1879	WSR 9 334
Terrell, William G.	1893	JMM 11 375
Terrell, Isaac G.	1896	GSN 12 39
Terry, Esther J.	1927	CHR 18 51
Tennant, Annie F.	1927	CHR 18 153
Tennant, Robert	1938	AJG 21 294
Tenakos, John	1952	RLW 23 19
Temple, Leona G.	1948	TLA 24 378
Terrell, Alice G.	1953	TLA 26 212
Thomas, David	1776	AJ R 110
Thomas, Benjamin	1780	AJ R 113
Thorp, Rachel	1781	AJ R 114
Thomas, Henry	1782	AJ R 118
Thomas, Henry	1783	AJ R 119
Thompson, David	1791	AJ R 132
Thomas, John	1797	AJ R 136
Thompson, Sarah	1807	AJ C 97
Thompson, Mary	1805	AJ C 283
Thomas, Mary	1805	AJ C 299
Thomas, Hannah	1814	AJ C 768
Thompson, Aquila	1816	SR 1 70
Thompson, Daniel	1816	SR 1 106
Thompson, James	1821	SR 1 230
Thomas, William	1821	SR 1 238
Thomas, David	1822	SR 1 266
Thomas, William	1830	SR 1 520
Thomas, Abraham I.	1841	TSB 5 551

Thomas, Sarah	1843	TSB 6 6
Thompson, John D.	1843	TSB 6 19
Thompson, Joseph	1848	TSB 6 179
Thomas, William T.	1855	CWB 7 69
Thompson, Daniel	1858	CWB 7 174
Thomas, James	1860	CWB 7 233
Thompson, Charles H.	1862	CWB 7 293
Thomas, Oliver H.	1870	BHH 8 178
Thompson, William	1871	BHH 8 191
Thomas, David E.	1886	JMM 11 38
Thomas, William	1890	JMM 11 155
Thompson, Isaac H.	1889	JMM 11 280
Thompson, Angelina	1892	JMM 11 300
Thompson, Susan G.	1886	JMM 11 371
Thompson, John C.	1892	GSN 12 68
Thompson, James H.	1890	GSN 12 137
Thomas, Nathan W.	1900	GSN 12 279
Thompson, Jno. Wesley	1902	GSN 12 425
Thomas, Daniel P.	1907	HTB 13 398
Thomas, Alfred	1906	HTB 14 21
Thompson, Jas. W.	1913	HTB 14 444
Thompson, J. Crawford	1906	HTB 14 446
Thomas, John D.	1917	JA 15 375
Thompson, Margaret J.	1919	JA 16 99
Thompson, Divis	1921	JA 16 321
Thoene, Wm.	1921	JA 16 494
Thompson, Josiah R.	1923	CSW 17 17
Thompson, Norval R.	1923	CSW 17 43
Thompson, Kate	1925	CSW 17 288
Thompson, Hannah C.	1921	CSW 17 412
Thompson, Isaac Whitaker	1925	CSW 17 458
Thorpy, Margaret	1920	CHR 18 122
Thomas, Elisha E.	1926	CHR 18 200
Thomas, Margaret Ann	1923	CHR 18 424
Thomas, S. Oliver	1931	AJG 19 117
Thorpy, John Salik	1925	AJG 19 213
Thompson, Lida E.	1926	AJG 19 314
Thompson, Edwin R.	1901	AJG 19 341
Thurston, Zachariah	1939	AJG 20 305
Thompson, George Robert	1937	RLW 22 31
Thompson, A. Harold	1947	RLW 22 69
Thomas, Elizabeth Slade	1947	RLW 22 91
Thompson, Harry R.	1945	RLW 22 154
Thompson, John G.	1949	RLW 22 237

Thompson, Anna E.	1939	RLW 22 271
Thigpen, Carrie V.	1935	RLW 22 284
Thompson, Arthur Baker	1950	RLW 22 448
Thompson, Ida F.	1952	RLW 23 154
Thompson, Malvina J.	1940	RLW 23 179
Thompson, Helen W.	1948	RLW 23 317
Thorpe, Benjamin L.	1953	TLA 24 39
Thomas, Hythern	1954	TLA 24 103
Thompson, Charles Alfred	1944	TLA 24 405
Thomas, Gladys Absher	1952	TLA 24 419

Timmons, John	1787	AJ R 121
Timmons, Edward	1827	SR 1 394
Titus, Samuel	1849	TSB 6 225
Tittle, Annie	1859	CWB 7 204
Titus, Lydia I.	1861	CWB 7 253
Timmons, John	1876	WSR 9 113
Tittle, Amos	1875	JMM 11 149
Title, Nelson	1900	GSN 12 270
Tipton, Alfred S.	1911	JA 16 103
Tisdale, Margaret A.	1890	CSW 17 393-4
Tipton, Mina J.	1935	AJG 29 382
Tittle, Carrie Belle	1957	TLA 24 29
Tibbs, Clyde V.	1951	TLA 26 90
Tilley, Elihu H.	1957	TLA 26 247

Toland, Adam	1787	AJ R 124
Totell, Elizabeth	1803	AJ C 150
Tolley, James W.	1812	AJ C 647
Townsley, Jemima	1854	CWB 7 26
Toland, Adam	1860	CWB 7 216
Tobin, James	1866	BHH 8 8
Touchtone, John W.	1884	WSR 10 89
Townsley, Ann Rebecca	1873	JMM 11 392
Tollinger, Hannah E.	1904	HTB 13 42
Tollinger, Alice C.	1890	HTB 13 131
Tobin, Martin	1911	HTB 14 207
Todd, John R.	1909	JA 15 180
Todd, Robert N.	1924	CSW 17 143
Toney, Joseph	1927	CHR 18 25

Todd, G. B.	1926	CHR 18 190
Towner, Jay F.	1935	AJG 19 366
Todd, Lewis A.	1919	AJG 19 489
Tobin, Thomas	1924	AJG 20 72
Townsley, Nora G.	1919	AGG 21 211
Towner, Jay Ferdinand	1945	RLW 22 18
Todd, Lillian K.	1955	RLW 23 289
Townsley, Margaret E.	1947	RLW 23 314
Todd, Ernest Coulson	1950	RLW 23 409
Townsley, Myrtle	1956	TLA 24 171
Thomison, Samuel J., Jr.	1956	TLA 24 213
Townsley, May Anderson	1956	TLA 24 266
Tobin, Emmett D.	1957	filed not prob. 13 388
Tobin, Emmett D.	1957	TLA 24 373
Tontz, John Logan	1954	filed not prob. 13 698
Toney, Hannah E.	1958	TLA 25 168
Tobias, Herbert R.	1957	TLA 26 128

Tredway, Mary	1779	AJ R 111
Tredway, Thomas	1782	AJ R 117
Tredway, Daniel	1810	AJ C 509
Truss, William	1814	AJ C 748
Tracey, Benjamin	1816	SR 1 80
Troutner, George	1825	SR 1 322
Tredway, Sarah	1835	TSB 5 168
Tredway, Thomas	1838	TSB 5 330
Troutner, David	1848	TSB 6 178
Trago, William	1861	CWB 7 241
Trago, Sally	1850	TSB 6 260
Tredway, John E.	1865	CWB 7 396
Trimble, Joseph	1870	BHH 8 160
Troutner, Francis	1881	WSR 10 137
Treadway, Carvil	1887	JMM 11 116
Trimble, Elizabeth R.	1902	GSN 12 435
Treadway, Ellen Barnes	1906	HTB 13 288
Troutman, George M.	1878	HTB 13 452
Trimble, Wm. P.	1908	HTB 14 404
Treadway, John N.	1920	CSW 17 255
Troutner, Mary E.	1932	AJG 19 89
Trago, Wm. Arthur	1916	AJG 19 157
Troyer, Jacob H.	1928	AJG 20 36
Travers, Emma M.	1937	AJG 21 205

Treadway, Oleita V.	1954	RLW 23 448
Trench, Theodosia K.	1958	TLA 24 403
Troyer, F. Melvin	1951	WFNP 14 236
Triplett, Claudia R.	1957	TLA 27 41
Trimmer, Lillian A.	1952	WFNP
Turner, Thomas	1789	AJ R 129
Tucker, Henry	1804	AJ C 235
Turner, Joseph	1832	TSB 5 52
Turner, Andrew	1841	TSB 5 501
Tucker, David	1843	TSB 6 25
Turner, Eli	1863	CWB 7 320
Turner, Mary Elizabeth	1874	WSR 9 16
Turner, John	1880	WSR 9 264
Tucker, David	1881	WSR 9 278
Tuchton, Sampson	1883	WSR 9 418
Turner, Eli	1890	JMM 11 164
Turnbull, John	1891	JMM 11 230
Tucker, Aaron H.	1885	JMM 11 332
Turner, Eli	1892	JMM 11 384
Tucker, Elisha R.	1899	GSN 12 249
Turner, Robert	1875	HTB 13 120
Tucker, Emory	1905	HTB 13 146
Tucker, James F.	1902	HTB 13 149
Turner, Samuel W.	1907	HTB 13 498
Tucker, Eli		HTB 14 225
Tucker, Ellis J.	1891	HTB 14 238
Turner, H. Virginia	1914	JA 15 61
Turner, Thomas	1916	JA 15 278
Tucker, David L.	1916	JA 15 337
Tucker, Sarah E.	1917	JA 15 488
Tucker, Hannah	1901	JA 16 353
Turner, Cornelia Rampley	1923	CSW 17 5
Tucker, Sarah R.	1916	CSW 17 248
Turner, John H.	1916	CSW 17 293
Turner, Henry	1925	CSW 17 421
Turner, Dr. Frank T.	1921	CSW 17 460
Turner, Telitha	1923	CSW 17 463
Turner, Harry F.	1903	CHR 18 340
Tucker, David R.	1925	CHR 18 455
Turner, Zora B.	1931	AJG 20 140
Tucker, Mary Etta	1939	AJG 20 408

Turner, Henry	1940	AJG 20 429
Turner, Williana	1935	AJG 21 2
Turner, James L.	1933	RLW 23 23
Tucker, Lester W.	1944	RLW 23 95
Turner, Mary G.	1946	RLW 23 131
Tubbs, Crickett S.	1951	RLW 23 349
Turner, Robert E.	1955-6	TLA 24 283-7
Turner, John McLeod	1928	TLA 24 425
Turner, Emily N.	1952	TLA 25 132
Tucker, W. Roy	1952	TLA 25 211
Tucker, Minnie E.	1960	TLA 26 125
Twining, Isaac	1882	WSR 9 387
Tweedale, Margaret	1886	WSR 19 286
Twining, Martha E.	1901	GSN 12 331
Tydings, Lloyd	1898	GSN 12 204
Tyrrell, Frank	1958	TLA 25 134
Tydings, Millard E.	1960	TLA 25 202

U

Umbarger, Joseph Newton	1928	AJG 20 78
Umbarger, George Calvin	1952	RLW 23 143
Unland, Frederick W.	1903	HTB 13 26
Unger, Zippora	1895	HTB 13 49
Ushner, Paul	1922	JA 16 379

V

Vance, John	1782	AJ R 140
Vandegrift, George	1812	AJ C 640
Vanhorn, Peter	1801	AJ C 79
Vansicle, Henry	1801	AJ C 81
Vandegrift, George	1817	SR 1 123
Vansickel, Bennett	1818	SR 1 143
Vandegrift, Mary	1819	SR 1 173
Vandiver, Robert R.	1882	WSR 10 122
Vail, Lindley M.	1886	WSR 10 282
Vanhorn, Isaac	1887	WSR 10 323
Vanhorn, David C.	1887	WSR 10 324
Varner, John	1883	JMM 11 80
Varner, Sarah	1890	JMM 11 83
Van Bibber, Geo. L.	1886	HTB 14 257
Vance, Cecelia M.	1905	JA 15 173
Vaughn, Thomas	1921	JA 16 290
Van Bibber, Adele	1913	JA 16 346
Vance, Mary Ellen	1924	CSW 17 76
Vandiver, Annie C.	1938	AJG 20 293
Van Duyne, Charles U.	1947	RLW 23 492
Van Gundy, Charles P.	1947	TLA 24 244
Valero, John (Juan)	1953	WFNP13 962
Vernay, Martha	1894	JMM 11 414
Veseley, John	1923	CSW 17 42
Virden, William W.		GSN 12 82
Virdin, Kate E.L.	1900	HTB 13 449
Vincenti, Giosue	1921	JA 16 331
Viele, Frederick O.	1928	AJG 21 383
Viele, Eunice J.	1947	TLA 24 489
Vogan, James	1784	AJ R 142
Vogel, Fred A.	1927	CHR 18 76
Vogts, Anton H.	1936	AJG 19 408
Voss, Franklin B.	1948	RLW 23 34

W

Watters, John	1774	AJ R 148
Ward, Charles	1776	AJ R 150
Watkins, John	1780	AJ R 183
Wallis, Grace	1781	AJ R 185
Watters, Mary	1790	AJ R 211
Waltham, Elizabeth	1790	AJ R 212
Ward, Edward	1791	AJ R 215
Ward, James	1793	AJ R 225
Waldron, Richard	1797	AJ R 242
Ward, Ann	1802	AJ R 260
Ward, Joseph	1800	AJ C 18
Wallis, Sarah	1802	AJ C 118
Walters, Stephen	1808	AJ C 419
Warner, Joseph	1811	AJ C 584
Watters, Patience	1814	AJ C 732
Watkins, James	1815	SR 1 13
Warner, William	1815	SR 1 65
Watters, Charles	1811	SR 1 115
Waskey, Christian	1817	SR 1 130
Watkins, John	1826	SR 1 361
Watters, Godfrey	1826	SR 1 369
Waskey, Elijah	1827	SR 1 415
Watters, Mary	1830	SR 1 512
Warner, Isaac	1832	TSB 5 36
Ward, Richard	1834	TSB 5 125
Watters, Stephen	1837	TSB 5 316
Walker, Elizabeth	1840	TSB 5 477
Way, Samuel	1844	TSB 6 56
Warner, Joseph	1845	TSB 6 84
Watkins, Abel	1846	TSB 6 98
Warner, Edward	1847	TSB 6 129
Watters, Mary	1847	TSB 6 140
Wadlow, Solomon	1848	TSB 6 165
Wann, John	1849	TSB 6 205
Watson, John	1848	TSB 6 192
Ward, Joseph	1850	TSB 6 264
Wann, Abram or John	1853	TSB 6 345
Warnock, Mary	1853	TSB 6 357
Walker, George	1854	CWB 7 25

Waltham, Hester	1857	CWB	7	136
Watters, Daniel R.	1857	CWB	7	137
Watters, Esther	1860	CWB	7	213
Waltham, Alice Anna	1859	CWB	7	194
Watters, William	1861	CWB	7	254
Walker, Robert	1863	CWB	7	306
Watkins, Rachel	1863	CWB	7	326
Watters, Jane	1865	CWB	7	371
Walker, Catharine	1865	CWB	7	393
Watters, Henry G.	1866	CWB	7	401
Warner, Sarah	1868	BHH	8	64
Waxwood, Benedict	1869	BHH	8	122
Waters, Amos	1869	BHH	8	133
Wareham, John	1870	BHH	8	166
Walker, John	1870	BHH	8	170
Warden, William H.	1873	BHH	8	318
Wareham, Jacob	1874	WSR	9	9
Waterman, Charles S.	1874	WSR	9	24
Walker, Elizabeth	1875	WSR	9	63
Ward, Elizabeth	1876	WSR	9	77
Wallace, Archibald	1876	WSR	9	123
Wareham, John T.	1879	WSR	9	204
Walker, Eliza	1879	WSR	9	215
Watters, J. Wesley	1880	WSR	9	261
Wakeland, James P.	1881	WSR	9	293
Watkins, Susan A.	1881	WSR	9	294
Waters, Abraham	1881	WSR	9	337
Watson, James T.	1882	WSR	9	360
Warfield, Carvil	1882	WSR	9	368
Wallace, Samuel W.	1883	WSR	9	404
Warfield, Isaac	1883	WSR	9	457
Watkins, John	1883	WSR	10	57
Wakeland, William P.	1884	WSR	10	69
Walter, George Wm.	1882	WSR	10	87
Wann, William	1872	WSR	10	90
Waterman, Joseph P.	1883	WSR	10	185
Waters, J. Wm. H.	1887	WSR	10	300
Warner, Silas	1885	WSR	10	308
Watters, Susan J.	1876	WSR	10	412
Waterman, Mary V.	1888	WSR	10	435
Walsh, James	1888	JMM	11	99
Wallis, Joseph W.	1884	JMM	11	120
Wakeland, Alonzo	1891	JMM	11	231
Watters, Walter, Jr.	1876	JMM	11	242

Walter, Charles S.	1915	JA 16 166
Wallis, Ada L.	1919	JA 16 196
Waterman, Sarah Elizabeth	1913	JA 16 349
Watters, Mary E. B.	1924	CSW 17 165
Wallace, Sophronia	1923	CSW 17 179
Walker, Emily J.	1881	CSW 17 259
Wallis, Wilbur F.	1913	CSW 17 300
Ward, Joshua B.	1919	CSW 17 313
Watters, John W., Sr.	1927	CHR 18 26
Wakeland, Sarah Elizabeth	1926	CHR 18 94
Warner, Silas	1928	CHR 18 96
Wallis, William R.	1924	CHR 18 115
Walker, Winfield S.	1922	CHR 18 166
Ward, Tony S.	1929	CHR 18 194
Wagner, Charles J.	1920	CHR 18 223
Way, Laura V.	1930	CHR 18 429
Wallis, Frances A.	1930	AJG 19 63
Wagner, Frederic	1932	AJG 19 97
Walmsley, James W.	1927	AJG 19 188
Watters, William	1932	AJG 19 254
Walker, Catherine	1932	AJG 19 271
Wann, Olivia A.	1933	AJG 19 370
Watkins, David S.	1932	AJG 19 403
Wallis, Sallie S.	1929	AJG 20 19
Waters, Lloyd	1932	AJG 20 52
Walker, Hannah E.	1937	AJG 20 71
Walsh, Mary D.	1936	AJG 20 83
Walker, H. L.	1938	AJG 20 122
Walling, Elbert J.	1929	AJG 20 242
Warner, Mabel V.	1937	AJG 20 283
Wayne, Mary J.	1936	AJG 20 413
Walling, Margaret E.	1929	AJG 20 425
Ward, Mary E.	1932	AJG 20 434
Wallett, Florence M.	1936	AJG 20 468
Walker, Samuel E.	1937	AJG 21 153
Walker, Sr. Wilbur	1946	AJG 21 427
Walter, R. Earl	1946	AJG 21 461
Warfield, S. Davies	1927	RLW 22 241
Walter, Robert L.	1951	RLW 22 350
Watson, S. Martha	1950	RLW 22 370
Walbeck, Cora A.	1950	RLW 22 392
Ward, Samuel W.	1942	RLW 23 61
Walker, May Easterday	1952	RLW 23 141
Wakeland, Harry A.	1953	RLW 23 75

Waream, Annie Elizabeth	1945	RLW 23 190
Walker, William H.	1953	RLW 23 259
Wagner, Rebecca J.	1949	RLW 23 305
Watson, Blanche B.	1944	RLW 23 318
Ward, Eliza B. P.	1953	RLW 23 343
Wann, Bertha L.	1939	RLW 23 467
Watkins, Mary Adelaide	1928	TLA 24 180
Watkins, Charles B.	1915	TLA 24 179
Watters, Grace I.	1954	filed not rec. 13 346
Waskovich, Catherine	1954	TLA 24 292
Watson, Rebecca N.	1955	TLA 24 413
Watters, John B.	1955	TLA 24 486
Waring, Bernard G.	1952	TLA 25 29
Walker, Myrtle	1960	TLA 25 148
Ward, Walter L.	1960	filed not rec. 13 764
Watson, James Oliver	1955	TLA 25 466
Waters, Wm. Henry	1948	TLA 26 27
Watters, John W., Jr.	1929	TLA 26 220
Wagner, Katherine	1951	WFNP 14 109
Wagner, Joseph, Sr.	1951	WFNP 14 110
Ward, John R.	1960	TLA 26 305
Walter, Charles S., Sr.	1960	TLA 26 443
Waream, Walter W.	1959	TLA 26 497
Ward, Dora R.	1952	WFNP 14 347
Wetherall, Henry	1778	AJ R 164
Weram, Abraham	1782	AJ R 187
Wells, Richard	1781	AJ R 189
Wells, Richard	1784	AJ R 191
Webster, Samuel	1786	AJ R 197
Webb, Samuel	1788	AJ R 205
Webster, James	1792	AJ R 221
Webster, Hannah	1795	AJ R 228
Webster, John Lee	1795	AJ R 229
Wetherall, James	1797	AJ R 246
West, Joseph	1798	AJ R 249
Webster, Isaac	1799	AJ R 250
Weeir, Thomas	1800	AJ C 19
West, Jonathan Sr.	1802	AJ C 68
Webster, Margaret	1806	AJ C 153
Weston, Rebecca	1812	AJ C 281
Wetherall, James	1813	AJ C 282

Webster, Richard	1824	SR 1 308
Weeks, John	1825	SR 1 323
West, Nathaniel	1827	SR 1 391
Weaver, Rachel H.	1831	SR 1 530
Wetherall, James	1832	TSB 5 4
West, Thomas	1835	TSB 5 182
Webley, Hannah	1847	TSB 6 150
Webster, George S.	1848	TSB 6 157
West, Enos	1850	TSB 6 243
Webster, Mary	1852	TSB 6 305
Webster, John	1853	CWB 7 9
West, Stacey	1856	CWB 7 104
Wells, Darius W.	1857	CWB 7 143
Webster, Samuel	1862	CWB 7 298
Webster, John W.	1872	BHH 8 294
Webster, Henry	1872	BHH 8 306
Weeks, Benjamin	1873	BHH 8 380
Webster, Noah	1874	WSR 9 25
Webster, John A.	1877	WSR 9 149
Westphal, Edward	1883	WSR 9 447
Weber, C. F.	1886	WSR 10 326
Webster, Edwin H.	1892	JMM 11 315
Wells, George	1893	JMM 11 383
Webster, Susan A.	1895	JMM 11 470
Westphal, Catherena M.	1901	GSN 12 359
Welch, Ann Theresa	1901	GSN 12 361
West, John G.	1901	GSN 12 393
Webster, James	1902	GSN 12 408
Weber, John	1875	HTB 13 72
Weber, Elizabeth	1905	HTB 13 185
Webster, Sophia	1905	HTB 13 262
Webster, Caroline H.	1892	HTB 13 307
West, Wilson D.	1908	HTB 13 486
Webster, M. Elizabeth	1907	HTB 14 5
Webb, Abel J.	1909	HTB 14 148
Webster, Sarah Fletcher	1909	HTB 14 174
Webster, Anna J.	1911	HTB 14 280
Webster, William S.	1902	HTB 14 334
Webster, William	1912	JA 15 33
Webster, John W.	1915	JA 15 222
Wells, William A.	1924	CSW 17 140
Wetherall, J. A.	1899	CSW 17 321
Wells, William J.	1928	CHR 18 59
Webster, Edwin H.	1929	CHR 18 131

Whiteford, Samuel	1833	SR 5 87
Wheeler, John F.	1833	TSP 5 104
Whiteford, Isabella	1839	TSB 5 421
White, Mary Ann	1846	TSB 6 125
Whiteford, William	1849	TSB 6 236
Wheeler, Elizabeth	1852	TSB 6 335
Whiteford, Michael	1853	CWB 7 19
Whitson, Margaret	1854	CWB 7 30
Whiteford, James W.	1854	CWB 7 39
Whiteford, Sarah	1855	CWB 7 75
Whiteford, Sarah Ann	1864	CWB 7 336
Whitson, Joseph	1864	CWB 7 358
Whitelock, Elizabeth	1865	CWB 7 376
Wheeler, Bennet	1866	BHH 8 6
Whann, Isabella	1869	BHH 8 117
Whaland, Harriet H.	1870	BHH 8 159
Whitaker, Samuel	1871	BHH 8 221
Whiteford, Hugh I.	1871	BHH 8 237
Whitaker, Isaac	1875	WSR 9 36
Whitaker, Hannah R.	1875	WSR 9 61
Whiteford, James	1875	WSR 9 67
White, Charlotte	1877	WSR 9 157
Whitaker, Howard	1879	WSR 9 223
Whitelock, William O.	1881	WSR 9 304
Whaland, Robert W.	1882	WSR 9 352
Wheeler, Sylvester	1883	WSR 10 96
Whiteford, Eliza	1879	WSR 10 164
Whiteford, Samuel M.	1887	JMM 11 1
Whalen, Lawrence	1890	JMM 11 183
Why, Sarah	1890	JMM 11 213
Whistler, Samuel F.	1874	JMM 11 244
Whiteford, William E.	1885	JMM 11 424
Wheeler, William L.	1892	JMM 11 432
Whiteford, Rebecca J.	1895	JMM 11 455
Whiteford, Margaret R.	1898	GSN 12 145
Wheeler, Leonard M.	1896	GSN 12 181
Whiteford, Samuel J.	1900	GSN 12 317
Wheeler, Samuel W.	1902	GSN 12 394
White, Alice A.	1902	GSN 12 410
Whitaker, Olivia E.	1896	HTB 13 71
Whitaker, Octavian M.	1890	HTB 13 475
Whiteford, Samuel	1905	HTB 14 172
Whiteford, W. H. H.	1876	HTB 14 218
Whitaker, Annie R.	1896	HTB 14 315

Whitaker, J. Everett	1912	HTB 14 356
White, Rosetta	1894	HTB 14 361
Wheeler, Margaret	1917	JA 15 371
Whiteford, Margaret A.	1913	JA 15 393
Whalen, Mary R.	1913	JA 16 138
Wheeler, Annie E.	1920	JA 16 246
Whitaker, Grace A.	1916	JA 16 338
Whiteford, Annie E.	1921	JA 16 375
Whitaker, Josephine M.	1921	JA 16 381
Whitaker, Aquilla B.	1920	JA 16 168
Whiteford, H. Clay	1924	CSW 17 180
Whiteford, Mary G.	1923	CSW 17 418
Whitaker, Ellen R.	1922	CSW 17 432
White, Eliza	1919	CHR 18 7
Whistler, Harry W.	1927	CHR 18 60
Whitaker, Mary F.	1928	CHR 18 233
Whaland, Jas. Patrick	1924	CHR 18 236
Whiteford, Calvin	1923	CHR 18 314
Whitten, William H.	1914	CHR 18 479
Whitney, Sarah E.	1932	AJG 19 82
White, Thomas M.	1927	AJG 19 217
Whistler, Elijah B.	1906	AJG 19 352
Wheeler, John F.	1932	AJG 19 363
Whiteford, Marian J.	1935	AJG 19 409
White, Margaret A.	1934	AJG 20 5
Whalen, John T.	1937	AJG 20 80
Wheeler, Barnet T.	1935	AJG 20 189
Whiteford, Hugh C.	1927	AJG 20 268
Wheeler, Bennet C.	1923	AJG 20 432
Whittington, John Fielder	1938	AJG 21 100
Whitfield, Harry C.	1927	AJG 21 204
White, William	1932	AJG 21 403
Whiteford, Henry C.	1944	AJG 21 423
Whiteford, Stevenson A.	1925	AJG 21 481
Whitelock, Bella	1942	RLW 22 12
Whitney, William G.	1946	RLW 22 60
Whiteford, Clay P.	1946	RLW 22 135
Whiteford, Alice Scarborough	1947	RLW 22 292
Whitney, Harry C.	1925	RLW 22 437
Whitall, James	1944	RLW 23 161
White, Nancy Allen	1948	RLW 23 253
Whitfield, Alexander	1953	RLW 23 341
Whiteford, William Turner	1951	RLW 23 439
Wheeler, Frank I.	1959	WFNP13 682

Wheeler, Charlotte A.	1959	TLA 25 164
Whisenhunt, Violetta	1954	TLA 26 470
Wilson, John	1777	AJ R 157
Williamson, Robert	1777	AJ R 161
Wilson, James	1778	AJ R 163
Wilson, William	1780	AJ R 180
Wilson, Rachel	1793	AJ R 223
Wineman, John	1795	AJ R 238
Wilmott, Richard	1797	AJ R 244
Wilson, John	1793	AJ R 258
Wilson, John	1800	AJ C 1
Willmer, Lambert	1801	AJ C 52
Wilson, Joseph	1803	AJ C 232
Wilson, Joseph	1803	AJ C 199
Wilson, William	1806	AJ C 330
Willmott, Mary	1807	AJ C 379
Wilmer, William	1810	AJ C 482
Wilmer, James P.	1815	SR 1 57
Wilmot, Ruth	1818	SR 1 165
Williams, Enoch	1819	SR 1 181
Willey, Isaac	1820	SR 1 203
Wilson, Sarah	1823	SR 1 278
Wilson, Eliza L.	1823	SR 1 282
Wilson, John	1824	SR 1 305
Wilson, Martha	1824	SR 1 316
Wilson, Clemency	1824	SR 1 320
Wilson, William	1829	SR 1 482
Wilson, Thomas	1831	SR 1 543
Wiley, Mathew	1840	TSB 5 435
Williams, Charles	1842	TSB 5 597
Wilson, Humphrey	1843	TSB 6 22
Wiley, William	1846	TSB 6 106
William, James	1847	TSB 6 149
Wilson, Cassandra	1847	TSB 6 151
Wilson, Samuel	1848	TSB 6 186
Williams, Elizabeth B.	1850	TSB 6 246
Wilson, Mary	1852	TSB 6 309
Willits, Cassandra	1852	TSB 6 322
Wilson, James	1854	CWB 7 33
Wilson, Samuel E.	1856	CWB 7 113
Wilson, John	1856	CWB 7 116

Wiley, David	1857	CWB 7 150
Wilgis, William	1858	CWB 7 171
Wilson, Mary	1861	CWB 7 240
Wiggers, John H.	1861	CWB 7 248
Williams, Arnold	1863	CWB 7 300
Williamson, Thomas S.	1865	CWB 7 380
Wiley, David N.	1868	BHH 8 93
Wilson, Mary	1868	BHH 8 103
Wilson, Rachel	1873	BHH 8 365
Wilson, Christopher	1876	WSR 9 86
Williams, Martha W.	1876	WSR 9 97
Wiley, M. W. Nelson	1876	WSR 9 109
Williams, Ann	1878	WSR 9 176
Wilson, William	1878	WSR 9 182
Williams, Daniel	1878	WSR 9 185
Williams, James	1878	WSR 9 192
Wilson, Rachel	1883	WSR 9 406
Willis, Julia	1877	WSR 10 28
Wilson, Rachel	1882	WSR 10 35
Wilson, Joshua	1880	WSR 10 101
Wilson, Mary Ann	1882	WSR 10 175
Wiley, Agnes	1886	WSR 10 170
Williams, Lewis J.	1872	WSR 10 401
Wiley, William	1888	JMM 11 170
Wilson, John S.	1888	JMM 11 301
Wilson, John T.	1888	JMM 11 464
Withers, Caroline R.	1880	JMM 11 370
Williams, William M.	1882	JMM 11 389
Williams, Virginia	1891	JMM 11 396
Wiggers, David H.	1895	JMM 11 461
Wilson, Isaac	1896	GSN 12 21
Windolph, John L.	1896	GSN 12 23
Willard, Sarah A.	1897	GSN 12 117
Wilson, Sarah A.	1899	GSN 12 254
Wilkinson, Thomas M.	1900	GSN 12 313
Wilson, David E.	1901	GSN 12 336
Wilson, William H.	1902	GSN 12 406
Williams, Sarah E.	1890	HTB 13 107
Wilkinson, E. L.	1896	HTB 13 117
Wiley, James A.	1904	HTB 13 137
Williams, William E.	1903	HTB 13 141
Wilson, Sarah J.	1900	HTB 13 152
Wiley, Thomas H.	1899	HTB 13 189
Wilson, Humphrey	1892	HTB 13 195

Wilson, Christopher	1906	HTB 13 252
Williams, Richard J.	1906	HTB 13 301
Winchester, Elizabeth S.	1897	HTB 13 417
Wiles, James A.	1908	HTB 13 492
Williams, Mary S.	1908	HTB 14 3
Williams, William J.	1908	HTB 14 107
Wilson, E. E. Hunt	1907	HTB 14 130
Williams, Susan May	1900	HTB 14 132
Windolph, Mrs. A. J.	1907	HTB 14 185
Wilson, R. L.	1909	HTB 14 266
Wilson, Archibald	1902	HTB 14 353
Wilson, Laura M.	1911	JA 15 40
Wilson, Mary A.	1913	JA 15 42
Wilson, Benj. W.	1913	JA 15 63
Wilson, Susanna L.	1914	JA 15 76
Wiley, Ellen D.	1912	JA 15 143
Weikart, Elizabeth	1908	JA 15 154
Wilson, Cassandra	1892	JA 15 191
Wiley, Charles L.	1908	JA 15 374
Wilson, Frances Anna	1904	JA 15 409
Wilson, David	1911	JA 15 458
Williams, James J.	1916	JA 15 499
Williams, Morgan	1914	JA 16 11
Wilson, Elizabeth	1916	JA 16 30
Wilson, Margaret J.	1893	JA 16 31
Wilson, Charles T.	1916	JA 16 269
Williams, Ruth E.	1910	JA 16 295
Williams, Wm. J.	1911	JA 16 393
Wilson, Florence S.	1915	JA 16 480
Wilson, Hannah Jane	1923	CSW 17 77
Wilkinson, Mary B.	1924	CSW 17 123
Wilmore, William P.		CSW 17 212
Wilson, James J.	1924	CSW 17 222
Wilkinson, George A.	1923	CSW 17 227
Wilson, Henry C.	1913	CSW 17 232
Williams, Eliza	1925	CSW 17 272
Williams, Benjamin J.	1925	CSW 17 292
Wirsing, Frederick	1908	CSW 17 375
Wilson, Stephen H.	1921	CSW 17 424
Wilson, David J.	1913	CSW 17 452
Wiley, Bertram Bradford	1928	CHR 18 142
Wiley, Thomas H.	1917	CHR 18 251
Wilson, William J.	1929	CHR 18 263
Wilson, James W.	1927	CHR 18 328

Winterling, Minnie Hare	1954	TLA 25 459
Williams, Lewis J.	1943	TLA 26 270
Wigley, Walter Franklin	1956	WFNP14 207
Wilson, Laura	1957	TLA 26 437
Winterstein, Frederick A.	1959	TLA 27 108
Worthington, Charles	1774	AJ R 146
Wood, Isaac	1777	AJ R 154
Worthington, Samuel	1777	AJ R 159
Wood, Henry	1782	AJ R 188
Wood, John	1784	AJ R 195
Woolsey, Joseph	1800	AJ R 252
Worthington, Charles	1802	AJ R 255
Worthington, John	1803	AJ C 153
Wood, Hudson	1811	AJ C 594
Woolen, Henry	1819	SR 1 196
Wolston, Martha	1828	SR 1 460
Worthington, Elizabeth	1832	TSB 5 16
Wood, John	1850	TSB 6 242
Wood, James	1850	TSB 6 256
Worthington, Anna	1853	TSB 6 347
Worthington, Amelia	1855	CWB 7 61
Worthington, Thomas	1855	CWB 7 82
Worthington, William C.	1857	CWB 7 146
Worthington, William	1859	CWB 7 199
Wood, William D.	1869	BHH 8 121
Wood, James D.	1874	WSR 9 26
Worthington, James C.	1879	WSR 10 53
Worthington, Joshua H.	1880	WSR 10 207
Worthington, Rebecca D.R.	1885	WSR 10 407
Woolsey, William	1888	WSR 10 421
Worthington, Mary W.	1883	WSR 10 438
Woodrow, Frank J.	1893	JMM 11 473
Worden, Tillie	1895	GSN 12 7
Worthington, Blanche H.	1890	GSN 12 64
Woolsey, Rebecca	1901	GSN 12 326
Woodhouse, E.N.	1902	GSN 12 417
Worthington, Rebecca	1898	HTB 13 193
Woodrow, Henrietta T.	1907	HTB 13 334
Wolfe, Laurel	1906	HTB 14 155
Worthington, John D., Sr.	1891	JA 16 432
Wonders, George	1923	CSW 17 54

X

Xenedio, James   1950   TLA 24 372

Y

Yates, John	1855	CWB 7 93
Yarnall, Elizabeth F.	1860	CWB 7 216
Yarrish, Bartholomew	1923	CSW 17 20
Yaskievich, Helen	1949	RLW 23 26
Yellott, Rebecca R.	1853	HTB 14 380
Yellott, Rev. John I., D. D.	1919	AJG 19 344
Young, Robert	1777	AJ R 264
York, Edward	1793	AJ R 266
York, Oliver	1785	AJ R 268
York, John	1783	AJ R 270
Young, George	1801	AJ C 44
Young, Alexander	1805	AJ C 263
Young, Elizabeth	1806	AJ C 309
Young, Benjamin D.	1876	WSR 9 91
Young, Thomas	1883	WSR 9 422
Young, John M.	1900	GSN 12 275
Younger, Bessie K. Frey	1904	HTB 13 60
Young, Barbara A.		HTB 13 340
Young, William R.	1908	HTB 14 8
Yost, Elizabeth	1896	JA 15 471
York, Harriet	1919	JA 16 83
Young, Laura C.	1920	AJG 20 184
Young, John S.	1938	AJG 20 251
Young, Millicent L.	1937	AJG 20 282

Z

Zarges, Marie	1911	HTB 14 264
Zellman, Amelia	1928	CHR 18 337
Zeitler, Susan A.	1932	AJG 20 342
Zellman, Sarah A.	1952	RLW 23 416
Zealor, John S.	1958	TLA 26 267
Zimmerman, Isaac	1864	CWB 7 365
Zimmerman, Mary J.	1890	HTB 14 100
Zullo, Leonard	1953	RLW 23 112

ADDENDA TO HARFORD COUNTY

Amoss, John A.	1852	TSB 6 286
Budd, Charles G.	1899	GSN 12 227
Clayman, Mary	1888	WSR 10 439
Cunningham, Mary	1892	JMM 11 327
Duncan, Joseph W.	1917	AJG 21 376
Elsner, Hulda	1939	AJG 20 292
Ellis, William H.	1933	AJG 20 345
Forwood, Lillian R.	1951	RLW 22 373
Forbes, Theodore Weems	1922	RLW 23 1
Hitrick, Adam	1902	GSN 12 418
Hitchcock, Mary R.	1886	HTB 13 386
Jeffery, John W.	1879	WSR 9 234
Johnson, William	1807	AJ C 480
Keene, Hannah C.	1945	RLW 22 235
Lambright, John H.	1938	AJG 20 323
Lynch, Mary A.	1919	JA 16 82
Maisenholder, Edward C.	1956	TLA 27 44
McKindless, Richard S.	1888	JMM 11 225
Mitchell, Samuel	1867	BHH 8 13
Miller, John W.	1814	AJ C 750
Moore, Catherine Gregory	1953	WFNP 14 349
Mordew, Jacob W.	1913	JA 15 231
Noyes, Victor P.	1942	RLW 23 323
Parker, Mary	1900	HTB 14 11
Poole, James	1915	JA 15 206
Rampley, William	1841	TSB 5 508
Richardson, Samuel P.	1863	CWB 7 319
Riley, Thomas	1864	CWB 7 329
Rutledge, Shadrach	1826	SR 1 386
Sadler, Thomas, Jr.	1916	JA 15 358
Smith, Hugh	1836	TSB 5 404
Smothers, Adaline	1882	WJR 9 379
Spencer, Sallie A.	1908	HTB 13 496
Stokes, Hannah M.	1899	HTB 13 269
Stansbury, John W.	1941	RLW 22 73
Svenson, Alfred	1949	RLW 22 389
Thomas, Elizabeth S.	1945	RLW 22 55
Van Bibber, Hannah C.	1904	HTB 13 302
Van Bibber, Rebecca Michael	1953	RLW 23 263

INDEX TO THE WILLS OF MARYLAND

Wilson, Peter	1811	AJ C 539
Wiley, John	1867	BHH 8 45
Worthington, William	1852	TSB 6 289

INDEX TO THE WILLS OF GARRETT COUNTY

EDITOR'S NOTE ON THE INDEX TO THE WILLS OF GARRETT COUNTY

Garrett County was formed in 1872 from part of Allegany County. Its County Seat is Oakland, and the searcher should write to the Register of Wills at Garrett County courthouse in Oakland regarding the wills referred to here, or to the Hall of Records in Annapolis, where there are microfilm copies.

This index of wills is grouped by first letter of the surname and also by date. Thus, all the decedents whose surnames begin with A and who died between 1873 and 1895 are grouped together, followed by those whose surnames begin with A and who died between 1896 and 1915 and so on. The reference letter is to the liber, or book; the following number is to the folio within the liber.

Although this system is not quite so easy to consult as the more usual system of strict alphabetical order by surnames, it is adequate for the relatively small number of wills recorded in Garrett County to date.

The Hall of Records has microfilmed a typed index compiled by the office of the Register of Wills for the county, and this printed index has been copied from the microfilm. The editor cannot vouch for the correctness of the original index, but where errors have been detected they have been corrected.

INDEX TO THE WILLS OF GARRETT COUNTY,
1872 - 1960

1941	Arthur, Elizabeth Speers	E 264
thru	Ashby, Elsie Wotring	E 430
1950	Arnold, Eva M.	E 435
	Arnold, Eliza E.	E 449
	Arnold, Minnie A.	E 498
	Arnold, Harrison M.	E 539
	Ashby, Sarah Beachy	F 63
	Adams, Bertha Jane	F 129
1951	Ashby, Charles A.	F 172
thru	Ache, George W., Jr.	F 331
1960	Alexander, Susan M.	F 397
	Allen, Jennie Louise McCormick	F 462
	Allan, James Millard	F 469
	Andrews, Charles J.	F 537
	Althouse, Alfred K.	F 554
	Ashby, Dorsey T., Sr.	G 37

B

1873	Beeghley, Joseph	A	10
thru	Barkholder, John A.	A	29
1895	Beaman, George	A	43
	Beachy, Christian J.	A	50
	Beard, John	A	84
	Bird, Eva Jane	A	85
	Brenneman, Jacob	A	137
	Barnard, John Gilford	A	142
	Beckman, John H. E. W.	A	188
	Beachy, Abraham J.	A	240
	Beckman, John	A	282
	Blatter, George	A	329
	Brant, John G.	A	377
	Browning, John L.	A	410
1896	Blamble, John	A	440
thru	Broadwater, Jefferson W.	A	458
1915	Bowman, Melcenia J.	A	470
	Bray, William W.	A	472
	Beachy, Susan	A	516
	Brown, William L.	A	529
	Brenneman, John J.	A	559
	Blamble, Christina	A	610
	Bosely, David J.	B	5
	Broadwater, Araminta M.	B	22
	Bosley, George L.	B	39
	Beeghly, Jonas	B	69
	Boyer, J. W.	B	132
	Barnard, W. H.	B	134
	Ball, M. Ella	B	137
	Bittinger, George A.	B	167
	Broadwater, W. W.	B	180
	Bach, Henry	B	190
	Beachy, Aaron	B	199
	Bradley, Ellen	B	216
	Browning, Stephen	B	224
	Byrne, Mary A.	B	292
	Brenneman, Lydia	B	307
	Bowers, John T.	B	362

1896	Brown, Annie L.	B 366
thru	Broadwater, Sarah A.	B 401
1915	Beeghly, Joseph A.	B 403
continued	Blocher, Matilda	B 422
	Beckman, Henry	B 452
	Bittner, Samuel	B 462
	Burdock, George	B 468
	Broadwater, Amos	B 498
	Beachy, Jonas C.	B 511
	Biddinger, David	B 516
	Bishoff, George E.	B 534
1916	Broadwater, Archibald	B 582
thru	Blackiston, David J.	B 587
1930	Brenneman, Jonas	B 551
	Blocher, James W.	B 557
	Baird, Lucy Hunter	B 597
	Button, Elijah J. M.	C 2
	Browning, Notley B.	C 4
	Bittinger, Jonas	C 15
	Browning, John S.	C 31
	Brown, Austin	C 69
	Baker, Mary E.	C 73
	Browning, John R.	C 80
	Bittner, W. H.	C 90
	Browning, Florence L.	C 113
	Brock, James	C 115
	Bunce, Ida V.	C 152
	Beckwith, E. L.	C 142
	Browning, John F.	C 185
	Broadwater, Mortimer T.	C 195
	Brydon, Susan V.	C 201
	Bailie, William	C 234
	Beeghly, George W.	C 255
	Bolden, D. E.	C 266
	Beckman, Sarah	C 270
	Bray, George W.	C 278
	Beeghly, Jacob	C 295
	Black, James H.	C 298
	Brown, Margaret	C 300
	Browning, Ralph T.	C 329
	Blocher, Etta	C 333
	Barnard, Fannie L.	C 352
	Black, Alice E.	C 375

1916	Beachy, Leo J.	C 377
thru	Beachy, Christian S.	C 398
1930	Bray, Sarah A.	C 416
continued	Bush, Louis	C 427
	Broadwater, William D.	C 435
	Blocher, George W.	C 451
	Best, Marmaduke C.	C 457
	Brown, Miles M.	C 458
	Blackburn, Mary E.	C 484
	Beachy, Jonas J.	C 567
	Bevans, Ambrose J.	C 536
1931	Bowser, Jacob E.	C 594
thru	Baker, Jacob	C 595
1940	Beevers, Sarah L.	D 1
	Britton, Edward R.	D 3
	Broadwater, William E.	D 26
	Blocher, Savina B.	D 27
	Bevans, Ella	D 35
	Brown, James H.	D 37
	Burkhard, Fred	D 47
	Baker, Daniel	D 51
	Bowman, John W.	D 78
	Baker, Mary J.	D 100
	Brenneman, William	D 106
	Boyd, James Graham	D 119
	Bray, Abe	D 130
	Beachy, Elmer J.	D 145
	Beachy, Jacob	D 148
	Browning, Meshech A.	D 163
	Bradley, Thomas	D 171
	Burke, Mary	D 185
	Beckman, Herman Henry	D 205
	Billmeyer, Ella	D 248
	Browning, Edward A.	D 322
	Brenneman, Lydia J.	D 323
	Broadwater, Perry B.	D 353
	Brown, William McCulloh	D 366
	Bonig, Henry C.	D 457
	Beckman, John H.	D 479
	Broadwater, Alice Sines	D 483
	Bosley, Hattie A.	D 487
	Bowman, Lewis	D 494
	Browning, Carter B.	D 522

1941 thru 1950 continued	Bray, Richard B.	E 572
	Burgess, E. Grant	F 86
	Bach, Henry	F 99
	Bowser, Frederick W.	F 134
1951 thru 1960	Bloch, Jesse A.	F 145
	Bowers, Garfield L.	F 161
	Browning, William R.	F 185
	Beachy, Leah	F 189
	Beitzel, John	F 215
	Brobst, Hattie M.	F 244
	Brenneman, Mahlon S.	F 248
	Bolden, Edith N.	F 328
	Bardall, John C.	F 345
	Barach, Joseph H.	F 370
	Bittinger, Sadie E.	F 366
	Burrell, Irma G.	F 376
	Burch, Simon A.	F 386
	Browning, Anna M.	F 410
	Brenneman, Thomas H.	F 411
	Broadwater, George L.	F 413
	Broadwater, Wade H.	F 431
	Boggs, Katie O.	F 433
	Broadwater, Ethel	F 437
	Bender, Mary Stanton	F 511
	Barton, Glenn	F 514
	Bolden, Emroy D.	F 527
	Brown, Prema	F 534
	Bell, James B., Sr.	F 544
	Bishoff, Thomas E.	F 563
	Brown, Adanda Hochman	F 573
	Bender, Samuel Stanley	F 574
	Broadwater, Effie F.	F 587
	Black, Harry James	G 16
	Beachy, Fannie	G 23
	Brandt, Joseph Larry	G 50
	Butler, Edward G.	G 112
	Beckman, May	G 117
	Blamble, Charles L.	G 136
	Bitzer, William O.	G 150
	Broadwater, Gratten V.	G 157

C

1916 thru 1930 continued	Creutzberg, Herman	C 92
	Cleveland, Mary C.	C 176
	Cassell, Elizabeth	C 248
	Cover, George W.	C 289
	Crane, W. E.	C 320
	Connell, Ellen	C 343
	Caton, Katherine	C 356
	Collier, Mary Weller	C 357
	Crawford, George H.	C 372
	Craig, Albert D.	C 410
	Casteel, Sharlotte F.	C 423
	Carr, Thomas	C 467
	Custer, Maria	C 470
	Custer, Emanuel	C 485
	Canty, William	C 498
1931 thru 1940	Coddington, Melville	D 9
	Crittenden, Thomas B.	D 60
	Callis, William	D 144
	Carder, Martha J.	D 160
	Carr, Larney P.	D 190
	Carroll, Patrick J.	D 215
	Carney, John A.	D 251
	Crane, Mary E.	D 270
	Clayton, Mary E.	D 280
	Carroll, Howard B.	D 297
	Craver, Frank A.	D 304
	Cornwell, Lucretia J.	D 314
	Conner, Julia	D 325
	Campbell, Thomas D.	D 374
	Casteel, Truman W.	D 376
	Clayton, John H.	D 469
	Crowe, John L.	D 470
	Cochrane, Susan E.	D 572
	Carroll, John	E 4
	Calhoun, Annie E.	E 23
1941 thru 1950	Coddington, Eldridge M.	E 128
	Canty, Matthew P.	E 137
	Conneway, William Jackson	E 159
	Crowe, Ada J.	E 178
	Carr, Lloyd Logan	E 271
	Chadderton, Jesse G. Wheeler	E 285
	Canty, Bridget Cecelia	E 297

D

1873	Dorn, Yost	A 91
thru	Davis, Lucinda	A 108
1895	Daily, Ann Rebecca	A 152
	Dailey, John	A 165
	Durst, Michael S.	A 205
	Durst, John S.	A 301
	Davis, Joseph B.	A 319
	Deakins, Maria L.	A 342
1896	Davis, Maria E.	A 424
thru	Deitrich, John	A 487
1915	DeWitt, William of Joseph	A 497
	Dick, John Craig	A 533
	Dorsey, Patrick	A 623
	Dashiell, Nicholas L.	B 1
	Deal, Edward	B 96
	Duckworth, Aden C.	B 156
	Durst, Hanson B.	B 162
	Duckworth, Zephaniah	B 205
	Durst, Asa	B 242
	Duty, Andrew W.	B 347
	DeWitt, Hannah E.	B 391
	Davis, Thomas E.	B 419
	DeWitt, Arch. C.	B 460
	Duckworth, Floyd	B 548
1916	Davis, John M.	B 565
thru	Delawder, May I.	C 55
1930	DeBerry, Clark	C 66
	Delawder, Titus	C 79
	Durst, Mary A.	C 93
	Durst, Sarah	C 102
	Dunham, Jane R.	C 194
	Droege, Emily P. E.	C 202
	Dorsey, Carrie	C 221
	Davis, Charles S.	C 334
	Deveny, Thomas A.	C 349
	Delawder, James A. (King)	C 355
	Davis, David B.	C 365

1951	DeWitt, Hiram Colfax	F 143
thru	Dorsey, Daniel W.	F 156
1960	Dawson, George Z.	F 181
	Duckworth, Roland S.	F 184
	Doerr, Joseph A.	F 209
	Davis, Robert Y.	F 214
	DeVelbiss, Larry Rizer	F 222
	DeWitt, J. Arthur	F 250
	Dunham, Laura B.	F 351
	Dugan, James V.	F 352
	Durst, Martha	F 365
	Deal, Emma May Durst	F 388
	Dawson, Margaret Y.	F 394
	Davis, Bertha Ellen	F 475
	DeBerry, William Pinkney	G 108
	Davis, Wilbur L.	G 122
	DeWitt, Benjamin H.	G 120

E

1873	Engle, Samuel	A 254
thru	Ensign, Howard B.	A 358
1895	Ensign, Maria C.	A 362
	Eggers, Henry	A 370
	Edwards, Julia A.	A 385
	Elwood, Winneford	A 413
1896	Echard, Peter H.	A 594
thru	Edgar, John A.	B 411
1915	Echard, Levi	B 430
	Elliott, Isaac	B 469
1916	Elkins, Stephen B.	C 34
thru	Eger, Theodore A.	C 46
1930	Ely, John Calvin	C 111
	Englehart, Elizabeth	C 171
	Enlow, Adolphus P.	C 207
	Enlow, David T.	C 269
	Eggers, Charles	C 271
	Engle, Ralph	C 360
	Eisler, John A.	C 421
1931	Echard, Jacob L.	D 72
thru	Echard, Elizabeth	D 127
1940	Ebert, Katie	D 247
	Edgar, William H.	D 473
	Enlow, Dora C.	D 503
1941	Elliott, Mary Alice	E 109
thru	Engle, Etta V.	E 248
1950	Eggers, Clara Mary	E 250
	Ellithorp, Chauncey E.	E 305
	Elliott, Carroll A.	E 391
	Edwards, Charles U.	E 504
	Englehardt, Lena	F 121
1951	Evans, E. S.	F 140
thru	Eggers, Henry J.	F 223
1960	Edgar, Adeline M.	F 262

F

1873	Fike, Christian of John	A 1
thru	Fike, William	A 13
1895	Friend, Andrew	A 64
	Frantz, John of Jos.	A 122
	Frey, Samuel K.	A 145
	Fuller, Henry	A 160
	Faherty, Mathias	A 174
	Farrell, John	A 176
	Fazenbaker, Marcus	A 223
	Foley, Thomas	A 296
	Friend, Lucinda	A 306
	Friend, Joseph of John	A 381
	Friend, Stephen W.	A 399
1896	Fickey, Andrew J.	A 493
thru	Frazee, Matthias	A 502
1915	Freeland, Mana S.	A 553
	Feik, Henry	A 557
	Friend, Joab	A 571
	Fazenbaker, George W.	A 578
	Frazee, W. W.	A 591
	Fike, Ami M.	A 604
	Friend, Hanson B.	A 606
	Felsing, Henry	B 20
	Finzel, John S.	B 37
	Frost, Thomas W.	B 71
	Faucett, Eliza Jane	B 102
	Fearer, John H.	B 147
	Fresh, Jacob	B 177
	Freeland, Abraham	B 197
	Faherty, Michael	B 336
	Friend, Joseph F.	B 358
	Frazee, Jefferson	B 381
	Friend, Taylor	B 396
	Fresh, Martin L.	B 436
	Friend, Amos W.	B 438
	Fresh, Leah	B 472

1896	Friend, Elijah M.	B 492
thru	Frazee, Richard T.	B 500
1915	Friend, Clara B.	B 541
continued	Frazee, Judson	B 543
1916	Fox, Adam	B 558
thru	Finzell, Edward	B 561
1930	Frazee, Isabelle	B 563
	Filsinger, Otto	B 575
	Fisher, John M.	B 581
	Frick, Elise Dana	B 592
	Failinger, George	C 7
	Frazee, Isaac N.	C 19
	Friend, Phoebe M.	C 54
	Fazenbaker, Jesse F.	C 56
	Filsinger, Martin	C 65
	Fazenbaker, Margaret Jane	C 88
	Franklin, Mary Mitchell	C 89
	Frazee, Elvira	C 95
	Frazee, Jefferson	C 101
	Fulk, Mary E.	C 137
	Ferguson, Louisa R.	C 143
	Fazenbaker, Otho H.	C 158
	Filsinger, Catherine	C 192
	Friend, B. F.	C 291
	Foley, John, Sr.	C 294
	Fallon, Maggie S.	C 301
	Folk, Jonas J.	C 317
	Fike, Levi J.	C 321
	Frazee, Matthias	C 335
	Fleming, Rosalie	C 370
	Fike, Rebecca J.	C 382
	Fowler, Henry C.	C 389
	Fallinger, John	C 394
	Friend, Kate M.	C 411
	Feeney, Peter	C 415
	Friend, David H.	C 421
	Fichtner, Daniel F.	C 428
	Falkenstine, Clamensa	C 465
	Friend, Richard	C 466
	Friend, Cornelius W.	C 475
	Frazee, Lott W.	C 519
	Frazee, Lafayette	C 532

1951	Friend, Arch C.	F 374
thru	Friend, Willie S.	F 390
1960	Fouch, Edwin O.	F 391
continued	Frazee, Lydia C.	F 417
	Fazenbaker, Stella F.	F 440
	Fike, Ervin T.	F 448
	Frazee, James	F 490
	Friend, Inez M.	F 503
	Friend, Earl C.	F 552
	Friend, Manilla B.	F 567
	Friend, Claude F.	F 568
	Fansler, Stark Andrew	F 589
	Fitzwater, Ada B.	G 13
	Friend, Alice	G 22
	Feld, Ray	G 51
	Fluke, Blanche	G 140
	Falkenstein, John McClellan	G 153

G

1873	Groeumiller, Michael	A	56
thru	Groer, Michael	A	61
1895	Grimes, Thomas	A	66
	Gorr, Phillip	A	133
	Groer, Barbary	A	237
	Gipson, Handy	A	297
	Graham, Francis B.	A	299
1896	Grant, Rebecca M.	A	445
thru	Griffith, Phebe Ann	B	59
1915	Graham, Mary N.	B	101
	Galloway, Emily Ann	B	111
	Good, Mary E. F.	B	125
	Glover, Nancy	B	151
	Gauer, Jacob P.	B	153
	Gilbert, W. H.	B	169
	Grove, Dennis	B	173
	Georg, Catharine	B	290
	Gnagey, Eliza	B	317
	Gordon, Robert H.	B	345
	Gauer, John N.	B	395
	Glotfelty, Nimrod	B	496
1916	Goehringer, John G.	B	594
thru	Garthright, Sarah E.	C	9
1930	Georg, William	C	13
	Groer, Joseph	C	21
	Gephart, George F.	C	25
	Grove, Sarah E.	C	45
	Grubb, Elizabeth A.	C	125
	Gnegy, Daniel	C	155
	Grove, Lee	C	160
	Griffin, Josephine	C	162
	George, Henry	C	163
	Glover, Milton	C	166
	Griffith, Hiram	C	170
	Gonder, Mary Martha	C	179
	Garthright, P. T.	C	182
	Grant, John Alexander	C	218

1916	Grusendorf, Christian J.	C 280
thru	Garlitz, Susan C.	G 287
1930	Gauer, George H.	C 325
continued	Green, Benjamin F.	C 342
	Glover, Charles M.	C 400
	Gortner, Frederick	C 429
	Graham, Francis C.	C 437
	Gnegy, Clara V.	C 448
	Gates, Joseph P.	C 505
	Glover, Martha	C 535
1931	Goehringer, Matilda	C 579
thru	Gies, William	D 7
1940	Gortner, Lewis	D 11
	Guard, M. Ella	D 33
	Garlitz, Freeman F.	D 113
	Guthrie, Charles A.	D 114
	Griffin, William B.	D 115
	Georg, Savilla	D 217
	Gill, M. Gillett	D 263
	Gortner, Peter, P.	D 274
	Garlitz, Charles R.	D 351
	Glotfelty, Jacob J.	D 359
	Greene, Annie	D 520
	Green, Horace Joseph	E 9
	Glotfelty, Albert A.	E 44
	Goucher, John F.	E 88
1941	Glotfelty, William	E 182
thru	Garrett, Mary Elizabeth	E 201
1950	Gage, Jennie W.	E 219
	Gilpin, David W.	E 319
	Gilpin, Mary Jane	E 320
	Gonder, Thomas A.	E 376
	Gnegy, John S.	E 409
	Gnegy, Mary	E 410
	Garrett, James	E 413
	Glass, Solomon	E 428
	Glotfelty, Amelia S.	E 477
	Gonder, William A.	E 541
	Groves, Waltman W.	F 20
	Garlitz, John A.	F 57
	Gretton, Frederick Thomas	F 80
	Garlitz, William B.	F 98

INDEX TO THE WILLS OF MARYLAND

H

1873 thru 1895	Hagans, George M.	A 22
	Hook, John L.	A 80
	Humberston, Azariah	A 82
	Harden, William	A 99
	Hays, Elizabeth	A 110
	Hauser, Elizabeth	A 124
	Hamill, Henry	A 134
	Hileman, David L.	A 156
	Harvey, William	A 192
	Hair, Henry M.	A 217
	Healy, Patrick	A 368
	Hamill, Patrick	A 401
1896 thru 1915	Hetrick, John C.	A 433, 447
	Hornbrook, Rachel	A 466
	Harvey, Meshack	A 449
	Hall, William H.	A 482
	Hoye, Daniel J.	A 500
	Hubbard, John P.	A 518
	Horwitz, Theophilus B.	A 616
	Huston, Henry Clay	B 74
	Hartman, Mary A.	B 88
	Haymond, Madisonia	B 142
	Hensey, August	B 255
	Hetrick, Victoria	B 270
	Hughes, Ellen	B 285
	Hoye, William H.	B 330
	Hansel, William P.	B 354
	Hilleary, Charles E. M.	B 388
	Hardesty, Thomas Bushrod	B 439
	Humberton, Noah	B 444
	Hanft, Charles C.	B 449
	Hank, Mary E. V.	B 506
1916 thru 1930	Harvey, Mary	B 590
	Haenftling, Alexander	C 11
	Hershberger, Mary	C 50
	Hawk, Amandus	C 77
	Hayes, John W.	C 83

1931	Hardesty, Bushrod L.	D 327
thru	Hamill, Rose Cornelius	D 339
1940	Hoffman, Christina	D 342
continued	Harrison, Willoughby	D 486
	Hardy, Katharine	D 511
	Hughes, John A.	D 551
	Harvey, Clarissa C.	D 597
	Hone, Gertrude	E 24
	Humberston, Hiram	E 37
	Hartman, John A.	E 43
	Hoover, George	E 76
	Hart, Annie M.	E 80
1941	Hauger, Gilbert Clinton	E 135
thru	Hoye, Francis Patrick	E 168
1950	Howard, Charles McHenry	E 191
	Harvey, Josephus	E 231
	Harvey, Harriet E.	E 252
	Hardesty, Eva Trader	E 263
	Hawk, Alice B.	E 296
	Hauser, David Ezra	E 295
	Harvey, Hester A.	E 338
	Hazlett, Robert	E 339
	Hank, Arminius S.	E 374
	Hinebaugh, Mahlon C.	E 416
	Hetrick, Elizabeth	E 432
	Harvey, Scott	E 433
	Hershberger, Noah E.	E 467
	Helbig, Andrew W.	E 500
	Helbig, Cecelia Ellen	E 503
	Holtschneider, John	E 509
	Hamill, Margaret C.	E 557
	Hetz, Paul L.	E 558
	Hamill, Moses R.	E 576
	Harvey, Virginia May	E 579
	Hoye, Joseph Michael	E 586
	Harton, Theodore M.	F 1
	Harton, George M.	F 7
	Hogue, Lucretia F.	F 23
	Hauser, William Albert	F 53
	Hall, Lawrence Lee	F 65

INDEX TO THE WILLS OF MARYLAND

I

1873	Ingman, Polly	A 116
thru	Ison, Rev. Benjamin	A 569
1950	Isenberg, Milton W.	C 412
	Irwin, John D.	C 440

J

1873	Johnson, Reverdy	A 45
thru	Jankey, Mary	A 316
1895	Joyce, James W.	A 353
1896	Jones, James	B 106
thru	Johnson, Samuel	B 130
1915	Jarboe, Zilphie	B 332
	Jarboe, John M.	B 426
	Jennings, Ervin E.	B 473
	Johnson, Baker	B 550
1916	Jones, Scott T.	B 586
thru	Jones, Anne	B 595
1930	Jennings, Cortez H.	C 126
	Johnson, Levi Hilleary	C 395
1931	Jones, Daniel S.	C 561
thru	Jones, S. F.	C 568
1940	Joseph, Louise R.	D 54
	Jefferys, Joseph	D 75

1931	Jamison, Richard S.	D 103
thru	Jacobs, Mary F.	D 445
1940	Joseph, Corydon S.	D 496
continued	Jinkins, Charles H.	D 576
	Jennings, Samuel D.	D 585
	Jennings, Juliet McAboy	D 589
	Jones, Anna P.	E 93
1941	Jennings, Mary P.	E 368
thru	Jackson, Samuel Harold	E 414
1950	Jarvis, Mary H.	E 478
	Jefferys, Matilda	E 578
	Jones, Harland L.	F 43
	Johnson, William Amos	F 67
1951	Jones, Alvah K.	F 190
thru	Jones, Carrie Mayer	F 196
1960	Jefferys, Gertrude C.	F 286
	James, Laura B.	F 383
	Johnson, Eva Long	G 30

K

1873 thru 1895	Kerling, John	A 24
	Kent, David	A 151
	Kenedy, William	A 181
	Klipstine, Catharine	A 182
	King, Augustus	A 190
	Kearney, Michael	A 225
	Kerrigan, Roger	A 292
	Kelley, B. F.	A 331
	King, Abraham B.	A 404
1896 thru 1915	Kolb, Frederick N.	A 514
	Kitzmiller, Emily	A 555
	Kelley, Alfred	B 128
	Kilbourn, Elbridge G.	B 144
	Kepner, Margaret J.	B 240
	Kitsmiller, John	B 263
	Kerfoot, John R.	B 316
	Kimmell, Chauncey F.	B 356
	Kelley, Mary Clare	B 374
	Krause, Ferdinand	B 409
	Kolb, John	B 431
	Knauer, John G.	B 503
	Knauer, Fredericka H.	B 513
1916 thru 1930	Kitzmiller, Alexander	C 12
	Kemp, Dr. H. M.	C 117
	Kurtz, Dennis H. & Leonard B.	C 140
	Kinsinger, Levi	C 149
	Krug, Henry	C 149
	Kelley, William M.	C 261
	King, Emanuel B.	C 390
	Kamp, Fred	C 446
	Knepp, William H.	C 517
	Kaese, Henry A.	C 523
1931 thru 1940	Klipstein, Sarah E.	C 558
	Kunkel, Elizabeth Jackson	D 31
	Koch, Sophia	D 137
	Kamp, Henry	D 147

L

1873	Loftus, Mary	A 37
thru	Lawton, Samuel	A 186
1895	Long, Forney L. G.	A 336
	Lowdermilk, Samuel P.	A 407
1896	Livengood, David	A 455
thru	Laffey, Mary	A 481
1915	Loar, D. H.	A 489
	Lohr, Alexander	A 582
	Lashorn, Joseph	B 118
	Lowdermilk, Thomas J.	B 261
	Lowdermilk, James H.	B 300
	Lowdermilk, John M.	B 434
	Lohr, P. P.	B 457
1916	Laffey, Patrick	B 569
thru	Layman, Thomas H.	B 573
1930	Lawton, Margaret	C 1
	Lashorn, Henrietta R.	C 43
	Lauer, Margaret K.	C 279
	Liller, Henry R.	C 308
	Loar, Mary C.	C 339
	Legge, George W., Sr.	C 461
	Lichty, Christian	C 462
1931	Loar, Thomas J.	C 557
thru	Lynch, P. C.	D 5
1940	Lichty, Simon J.	D 41
	Legeer, Michael	D 46
	Littman, Louis	D 50
	Lantz, Alex	D 109
	Lohr, Wade H.	D 121
	Lowdermilk, J. Milton	D 131
	Littman, Julius	D 154
	Lee, Salem	D 363
	Loechel, Samuel C.	D 459
	Loechel, William C.	D 476
	Laughlin, Rachel E.	D 584
	Livengood, Wilson	E 52
	Long, John A.	E 85
	Lohm, Ella R.	E 100

M

1873	Miller, Harriet	A 131
thru	Miller, John P.	A 169
1895	Miller, Timothy	A 270
	Matthews, George	A 311
	Michael, David	A 313
	Mehan, Mary M.	A 387
	Mosser, Jonas	A 389
1896	Murphy, William B.	A 418
thru	Moxey, David A.	A 464
1915	Michael, Jesse	A 491
	Murray, H. M.	A 506
	Markley, Elizabeth	A 511
	Martin, Francis	B 64
	Magruder, James	B 94
	Moody, Mary E.	B 112
	Male, George W.	B 140
	Miller, George O.	B 146
	Mosser, George L.	B 155
	Mosser, Jacob	B 175
	Miller, Samuel J.	B 213
	Myers, Caroline E.	B 227
	Murphy, Richard N., Sr.	B 259
	Mosser, Annie F.	B 296
	Maulsby, Thomas A.	B 297
	Minnick, George	B 341
	Mullen, Andrew	B 351
	Miller, Philip M.	B 379
	Mitchell, Almira L.	B 407
	Mattingly, Meshach	B 425
	Minnick, Julius	B 466
	Michael, George Thomas	B 509
	Miller, Jacob S.	B 523
	Miller, John P.	B 526
	Michael, Andrew J.	B 539
1916	Moody, Charles C.	B 562
thru	Miller, Susan M.	C 5
1930	Martin, Thomas	C 8

1931	Martin, John L.	D 225
thru	Maust, Fearson	D 233
1940	Moon, Penelope C.	D 239
continued	Michael, Nathan T.	D 241
	Miller, Henry P.	D 252
	Magruder, George W.	D 288
	Miller, Anna J.	D 301
	Meyers, Charles	D 321
	Moon, John Thomas	D 504
	Moore, Archibald	D 508
	Meadows, Enoch L.	D 525
	Mellon, Andrew W.	D 541
	Miller, Wilson E.	D 595
	Moon, Lucinda S.	E 16
	Matlick, Samantha H.	E 21
	Morris, William H.	E 26
	Murphy, Henry P.	E 33
	Murray, William	E 34
	Mellon, Andrew W. et al	E 54-63
	Mellon, Paul et al	E 54-63
1941	Marley, George	E 124
thru	Miller, Frederick P.	E 138
1950	Maust, Frank A.	E 154
	Maust, Aaron C.	E 156
	Metcalfe, Adelia Catharine L.	E 185
	Miller, Harry L.	E 188
	Maroney, Richard K.	E 198
	Miller, George A.	E 232
	Maffett, Ellen (Nellie) Maria	E 302
	Minnick, Lillie	E 324
	Meadows, Roxilla V.	E 325
	Mersing, Pierce Lenus	E 347
	Morgart, William A.	E 352
	Mosser, Minerva A.	E 356
	Miller, William	E 358
	Miller, Susan	E 364
	Miller, Catherine	E 366
	Miller, Mrs. E. S.	E 366
	Michael, Peter F.	E 398
	Mersing, Garnetta S.	E 475
	Miller, John M.	E 521

Mc

1873	McKimmy, James	A	3
thru	McRobie, Elisha D.	A	6
1895	McGoffin, James	A	26
	McInnes, Alexander	A	98
	McRobie, Delilah	A	221
	McKinzie, Francis	A	372
1896	McCleery, Peter	A	428
thru	McGoffin, Polly	A	438
1915	McCleery, Catharine E.	A	442
	McKinzie, Leo	A	453
	McRobie, Mary E.	A	478
	McRobie, Samuel A.	A	484
	McKenzie, Ambrose	B	193
	McKenzie, Isabelle	B	225
	McKenzie, Kletus	B	308
1916	McRobie, Hulda	C	91
thru	McGraw, Mary B.	C	156
1930	McLeary, Sarah Jane	C	165
	McKenzie, Urias	C	198
	McLean, Dougald	C	404
	McAndrews, Bridget C.	C	487
1931	McKenzie, Henry	D	86
thru	McCullough, Mary E.	D	168
1940	McClintock, Carl E.	D	286
	McLean, Barbara Ellen	D	365
	McAndrews, Philip P.	D	378
	McComas, Henry W.	E	1
	McIntire, Charles N.	E	65
	McQuilkin, Lola Asenath Holman	E	103
1941	McComas, Sarh Ann	E	380
thru	McCaslin, Charles A.	E	516
1950	McGettigan, Catharine A.	E	548

N

1873 thru 1895	Nethken, Sarah C.	A 20
	Niner, Christian	A 303
1896 thru 1915	Newman, Henry	A 431
	Newman, Harvey B.	B 274
	Nine, William	B 527
1916 thru 1930	Nathan, Peter	B 571
	Nally, Delia C.	C 222
	Nine, Peter F.	C 354
	Nicholson, R. J.	C 453
	Nathan, Michael	C 522
1931 thru 1940	Nesbitt, Mary V.	D 43
	Nine, Ervin	D 104
	Nydegger, John F.	D 161
	Newman, Richard	D 298
	Nicola, Franklin Felix	D 554
1941 thru 1950	Nedrow, Willey C.	E 184
	Nine, Minnie A.	E 351
	Nine, Luther C.	E 456
	Nordeck, George Ray	E 550
	Nogle, Prudence Jane	E 588
	Nethkin, Bartlett B.	F 79
1951 thru 1960	Niner, Mary E.	F 279
	Nine, Charles Washington	G 25
	Nethken, Charles Ervin	G 55
	Naylor, Arthur Ellsworth	G 147
	Nethken, Warder Reese	G 161

O

P

1873	Pennington, Josias	A 31
thru	Poleman, Frederick	A 239
1895	Platter, Jacob	A 321
	Platter, George	A 329
1896	Phillips, Elizabeth	A 426
thru	Pysell, Jacob	A 509
1915	Palmer, Innis N.	B 50
	Perry, E. Tayloe	B 119
	Perry, Robert M.	B 195
	Phoebus, Annie J.	B 210
	Powell, W. E.	B 245
	Peisen, Andrew	B 302
	Pysell, Andrew	B 318
	Paugh, Jahu	B 320
	Prichard, Amos N.	B 328
	Perry, Emily S.	B 334
	Peisen, Emilie	B 337
	Peddicord, Thomas J.	B 353
1916	Porter, George T.	B 553
thru	Peddicord, Mary E.	C 20
1930	Pipes, Felix Hugh	C 23
	Pool, William H.	C 107
	Popp, George	C 147
	Phillips, Florence E.	C 338
	Pew, Susan A. R.	C 405
	Pleasants, Anna Maria	C 424
	Popp, Lewis	C 433
	Patton, Mary Elizabeth	C 480
	Pope, J. R.	C 514
1931	Pope, W. T.	C 554
thru	Patton, Elizabeth	C 591
1940	Perine, Elias Glenn	D 254
	Perine, Ann C.	D 276
	Patton, Henry A.	D 335
	Pendergast, Martin	E 17
	Pysell, Mary E.	E 29
	Paugh, Perry	E 82

Q

R

1873	Ryland, Sylvester	A 36
thru	Ross, James	A 41
1895	Ridder, John	A 195
	Rinhart, John G.	A 215
	Ross, William of H.	A 227
	Roth, George	A 229
	Royer, John	A 284
	Rosenberger, John, Sr.	A 307
	Ringer, Conrad	A 351
	Rosenberger, Mary M.	A 415
1896	Richter, Henry	A 460
thru	Rolf, William	A 474
1915	Rowan, John W.	A 549
	Riley, Catharine	A 612
	Reichelt, Henry A.	B 8
	Russell, Robert	B 14
	Ritchie, Louis W.	B 44
	Robeson, William A.	B 182
	Ryland, James J.	B 218
	Rathbun, Erastus	B 335
	Ringler, Jacob W.	B 360
	Ries, Frederick	B 400
	Rosenberger, Adam	B 428
	Rosenberger, Elizabeth Catharine	B 433
	Reichenbecher, Peter	B 450
	Roth, John H.	B 461
	Richardson, Mary	B 476
	Rosenberger, Martha E.	B 491
	Rolf, Catharine	B 518
	Ridder, Henry W.	B 529
	Rathbun, Mary	B 537
1916	Rider, George W.	B 566
thru	Rush, Playford	C 49
1930	Roth, Aris C.	C 57
	Rodeheaver, Mary Ann	C 72
	Rosenberger, Margaret	C 122
	Rosenheim, Sigmond	C 216

1951	Ridder, Oscar S.	F 203
thru	Roland, William	F 220
1960	Rinn, Samuel A.	F 229
	Rathbun, Fellice A.	F 288
	Richwine, Alva M.	F 316
	Rolf, John W.	F 364
	Rosenberger, Annie E.	F 450
	Ryland, E. C. W.	F 480
	Rush, Resley C.	F 499
	Russell, Archibald G.	F 501
	Ruhl, Julia W.	F 506
	Ridder, Gary Lee	F 526

S

1896	Sweet, Maria R.	B	114
thru	Savage, Ur Thomas	B	149
1915	Steyer, John George	B	163
continued	Spiker, Joseph A.	B	166
	Stake, Edward	B	186
	Spiker, Abraham J.	B	188
	Stahl, Lottie	B	191
	Sausman, Louis	B	220
	Stark, Henry	B	221
	Shellebarger, Samuel	B	234
	Stanton, Ann Isabella	B	275
	Smouse, Catharine A.	B	277
	Shaffer, Maria	B	321
	Stanton, Eli	B	343
	Smouse, Edward	B	405
	Shaffer, Joseph	B	406
	Smith, Samuel	B	413
	Smithman, Joseph H.	B	423
	Sines, William Taylor	B	445
	Sebold, Andrew	B	447
	Snider, John	B	455
	Sawyer, Sarah O.	B	465
	Specht, S. P.	B	514
	Schlossnagle, John J.	B	520
	Steiding, Amanda	B	524
	Speicher, Conrad M.	B	531
	Shaffer, William L.	B	532
1916	Speicher, Jonas A.	B	568
thru	Smith, Minnie	B	570
1930	Sheets, William H. H.	B	603
	Smith, Elizabeth	C	3
	Shaw, Fannie E.	C	18
	Shartzer, Leonard	C	29
	Shirer, Elizabeth	C	30
	Shartzer, George	C	39
	Sines, William	C	118
	Smearman, Josiah J.	C	124
	Stanton, Mary E.	C	138
	Shaffer, Henry A.	C	151
	Sincell, Edward H.	C	178
	Slabach, Catherine	C	183
	Stanton, Ruth T.	C	187
	Shaw, Sarah Jane	C	190

233

1931	Schrock, Jonas M.	D 308
thru	Steiding, Herman	D 329
1940	Snyder, Anna Beachy	D 330
continued	Sanders, John H.	D 356
	Shaffer, Lloyd C.	D 373
	Shevel, George	D 461
	Sharpless, William S.	D 462
	Sisler, Horace R.	D 471
	Shank, Catherine E.	D 489
	Speicher, Arthur Lee	D 491
	Stahl, George D.	D 506
	Savage, Isaac	D 509
	Spahr, Chester O.	D 512
	Stump, Jacob	D 552
	Smith, William A.	E 3
	Sereno, John S.	E 19
	Sangston, Charles L.	E 41
	Sines, John	E 49
	Spiker, George	E 51
	Shepard, Donald D. et al	E 54
	Shank, Horace R.	E 75
	Smith, Phil F.	E 99
	Smith, Anastasia Elizabeth	E 106
1941	Sines, Elijah	E 116
thru	Speicher, William H.	E 118
1950	Schaefer, Christena	E 129
	Sembower, Charles	E 142
	Stanton, William E.	E 172
	Schmale, Conrad	E 221
	Shaffer, Mary E.	E 227
	Sanner, Emma K.	E 242
	Steyer, Charles A.	E 255
	Stanton, Edgar V.	E 270
	Stahl, Luther L.	E 275
	Smith, C. Ney	E 293
	Steyer, Sarah E.	E 299
	Savedge, Charles R.	E 334
	Shaw, John K.	E 381
	Schmidt, Nancy	E 383
	Swauger, Clark Marvin	E 443
	Swauger, Albert	E 459
	Sisler, Lidia Anna	E 460
	Sincell, Benjamin H.	E 464

1951	Schmidt, Henry A.	F 461
thru	Specht, Emma F.	F 464
1960	Snyder, Albert C.	F 465
continued	Stern, George	F 474
	Stevenson, John Haddock	F 500
	Stuck, Clara Alvernon	F 505
	Sharpless, William H.	F 508
	Sanders, Joseph H.	F 546
	Smith, William Cecil	F 569
	Shaffer, John Adam	F 575
	Saucer, Enzie	G 7
	Sisler, Grover C.	G 18
	Steiding, Sue Elizabeth	G 32
	Sharps, Clarence E.	G 36
	Snyder, Rex	G 47
	Shaffer, Harry C.	G 81
	Sincell, Sallie B.	G 127
	Sears, Howard Jackson	G 132
	Silbaugh, Albert	G 135
	Snyder, William	G 154
	Shillingburg, Jennie May	G 177

T

1873	Turney, Hannah R.	A 4
thru	Thompson, Israel	A 58
1895	Totten, Ezekiel	A 158
	Tice, John	A 161
	Travers, Harriet	A 207
	Totten, William P.	A 235
	Titchnell, William	A 294
	Townsend, William P.	A 326
	Tower, Rebecca P.	A 334
	Tillson, Edward C.	A 344
	Taggart, Louisa	A 347
	Turney, Abraham	A 374
	Tichnell, John M.	A 395
	Tasker, Mary	A 397
1896	Townshend, Singleton L.	A 476
thru	Thompson, Israel O.	A 521
1915	Thompson, Rev. John	A 525
	Thompson, James P.	A 580
	Thompson, Henry	A 608
	Tasker, Alice C.	B 67
	Turney, Eliza M.	B 184
	Thomas, John W.	B 268
	Townshend, Elizabeth R.	B 287
	Talson, George W.	B 372
	Thompson, Isaac I.	B 442
	Totten, Delia I.	B 521
1916	Thistle, J. L.	C 61
thru	Thompson, H. S.	C 173
1930	Thomasson, Nanniene M.	C 177
	Turney, Joseph F.	C 228
	Thrasher, Lorenzo D.	C 330
	Taylor, Eleanor	C 208
	Thayer, John O.	C 495
	Teets. George W.	C 525

GARRETT COUNTY, 1872-1960

1931	Tower, E. Z.	D 53
thru	Thorn, Sarah R.	D 133
1940	Thayer, Alice	D 159
	Truesdell, George	D 176
	Tibbetts, Fred H.	D 317
	Tibbetts, Nettie B.	D 319
	Teets, Eugene	D 336
	Thomas, M. Carey	D 380
	Talson, Elizabeth T.	D 528
	Thayer, Fannie B.	D 538
	Thrasher, Franklin H.	E 31
	Thayer, William M.	E 83
1941	Turner, Joshua H.	E 195
thru	Thayer, Fred A.	E 200
1950	Turner, Maud E.	E 234
	Taylor, Laura C.	E 256
	Thrush, Hubert O.	E 337
	Teats, Noah L.	E 589
	Titshnell (Tichnell), William C.	F 70
1951	Treacy, James P.	F 167
thru	Trotter, Mary Ellen	F 173
1960	Thayer, Frederick A., Jr.	F 240
	Thrasher, Harry U.	F 245
	Tasker, Mary Almira	F 256
	Teets, Charles G.	F 260
	Tressler, John W.	F 402
	Tichnell, Frederick J.	F 423
	Turner, William L.	F 458
	Tressler, Jennie E.	F 471
	Tasker, Nellie	F 477
	Tasker, Daniel W.	F 478
	Teats, Catharine	F 488
	Teets, Earl F.	F 564
	Thompson, Charles Sylvan, Sr.	G 14
	Tasker, Scott B.	G 33
	Tasker, Minnie S.	G 34
	Throp, Gertrude G.	G 94
	Taylor, Charles R.	G 111
	Thrasher, Nettie L.	G 156

U

1873	Umbel, Elisha	A 125
thru	Umbel, Isaac M.	B 272
1950	Upole, Margaret	C 281
	Umbel, Lloyd	C 518

V

1873	Vance, Amelia H.	B 544
thru	Vansickle, George H.	C 38
1960	Vandersall, Louisa M.	C 454
	Vodopivec, Frank	E 161
	VanSickle, Louetta	G 243

W

1873	Ward, Ulysses	A	17
thru	Webster, Louisa I.	A	28
1895	Ward, William	A	68
	Warnick, Kesiah	A	78
	Wilson, Thomas	A	87
	West, Truman	A	89
	Wolf, Charles	A	101
	Walter, George Jacob	A	120
	Wilson, Hester A.	A	138
	Wass, William	A	289
	Wilson, Jonathan H.	A	340
	Wagner, Henry S.	A	349
1896	Walter, Martha E.	A	435
thru	Wonderly, Julia A.	A	468
1915	Walsh, Edward	A	535
	Wright, Sarah	A	538
	Ward, Annie M.	A	561
	Walter, Hanson	A	584
	Warnick, Mary Elizabeth	A	596
	Wilson, Jeremiah M.	A	598
	Wagner, John A.	A	614
	Winters, John L.	B	98
	Wilhelm, Benjamin	B	99
	Walker, Mary F.	B	207
	Whitmer, William	B	231
	Wilson, Jacob	B	264
	Weir, James	B	266
	Wilson, Jeremiah M.	B	281
	Warren, Martha	B	288
	Wilson, Genus G.	B	305
	Wilt, Peter M.	B	309
	Welch, Brison	B	314
	Wilderson, Mary C.	B	324
	Willison, Andrew J.	B	369
	Weems, Rachel A. D.	B	383
	Welch, Thomas B.	B	386
	Wiley, Thomas B.	B	410

1931	Weems, Rachel	D 516
thru	Walsh, Theresa	D 540
1940	Wilson, Mary M.	D 578
continued	Wilson, Calvin	E 7
	Westlake, B. Frank	E 15
	Walker, Albert J.	E 46
	Welch, Margaret M.	E 102
1941	Willt, George W.	E 110
thru	Walls, Jacob Edward	E 121
1950	Wolfe, Laura	E 123
	Wiley, Lydia	E 133
	White, Albert T.	E 141
	Winebrenner, Enoch	E 186
	Winner, Mary Hoye	E 235
	Warnick, Anna J.	E 239
	Wiltrout, Ida V.	E 240
	Williams, Elizabeth J.	E 247
	Wittig, Margaret M.	E 270
	Winters, Silas Camden	E 346
	White, Bertha	E 408
	Warnick, George	E 441
	White, Nathan Floyd	E 551
	Winters, Roy O.	F 19
	Wilt, Rosanna Matilda	F 45
	Wotherspoon, David B.	F 69
	Whittaker, J. W.	F 84
	Wallace, Edward J.	F 91
	Wright, A. R.	F 93
	Winebrenner, Laura	F 103
	White, Clarence O.	F 130
1951	Wilson, Elmer C.	F 139
thru	Wildesen, Fannie B.	F 206
1960	Winters, Nellie L.	F 219
	Whorton, Edna A.	F 243
	Watson, Martin L.	F 291
	Walsh, Annie	F 305
	Wilson, Frank M.	F 306
	Warnick, C. Blanche	F 330
	Weaver, Maurice H.	F 334
	Walls, Olive P.	F 355
	Wolf, Mary M.	F 443
	Wenige, Estella	F 452

243

INDEX TO THE WILLS OF MARYLAND

Y

1873	Yutzy, Jacob	A 8
thru	Yoder, Rudolph	B 116
1940	Yommer, George	B 244
	Yoder, Barbara	B 258
	Yommer, John	B 340
	Yoder, Urias D.	B 427
	Yuhas, John	B 499
	Younkin, Charles H.	C 219
	Yoder, Elsie W.	C 358
	Yoder, John U.	D 84
	Yelloly, John	D 204
	Yoder, Ezra M.	E 69
	Yoder, Simon M.	E 70
1941	Yoder, Benjamin H.	E 112
thru	Younkin, Lillie B.	E 259
1950	Yommer, Henry	E 396
	Yoder, Edward M.	E 592
	Younkin, Richard F.	F 46
1951	Yutzy, Lester C.	F 320
thru	Yoder, Henry E.	F 382
1960	Yoder, Monroe D.	F 442
	Yutzy, Della Crane	G 119

Z

1873	Zehner, Henry	B 393
thru	Zehner, Charles E.	D 94
1960	Zeck, Alexander	D 196
	Zehner, Roy H.	F 513

ADDENDA

1951	McLain, John G.	F 590
thru	Prevost, Louis Claude	F 466
1960